A Year in the Life of a Field

Michael Allaby

A YEAR IN
THE LIFE OF
A FIELD

David & Charles
Newton Abbot   London   North Pomfret (Vt)

British Library Cataloguing in Publication Data

Allaby, Michael
A year in the life of a field.
  1. Meadow ecology – England – North Cornwall
(District) – Case studies
  I. Title
  574.5'264   QH138.N8/

  ISBN 0–7153–7889–9

Library of Congress Catalog Card Number: 80–68681

Set by Typesetters (Birmingham) Limited,
and printed in Great Britain
by Butler & Tanner Limited, Frome and London
for David & Charles (Publishers) Limited
Brunel House   Newton Abbot   Devon

Published in the United States of America
by David & Charles Inc
North Pomfret   Vermont 05053   USA

Contents

Introduction

On a crisp, blue morning in January, 1979, I visited Cross Park for the first time. I walked around it slowly, spent some time gazing over the gate at the Moor to the north, looked south across the valley and to the china clay pits in the far distance, and I made up my mind. I had been looking for a field that I might observe through the course of a year. Cross Park is the field I chose.

It is a perfectly ordinary eight-and-a-half acre field. If you were to glance at it you might judge it to contain little that could be of interest to anyone. Each time you visit the countryside you see thousands of fields just like it. If aerial photographs suggest to you that the landscape of Britain resembles a patchwork of fields, hedges and roads, then Cross Park field is one small, unimpressive patch in the overall pattern. It is a field in a million and exactly like all the others. That is why I chose it.

I could have hunted for a field that has been permanent pasture for centuries, that is so rich in wildlife and so untouched by humans as to be almost a nature reserve: the kind of field on which preservation orders might be placed. Such a field can be found, although there are not many of them. It would not have suited me, though. I appreciate the need to retain areas in which natural events may proceed undisturbed and where they can be studied, but I am deeply suspicious of 'living museums'. For me, the countryside is inhabited by humans as well as other species, and the 'untouched' field is as much a human artefact as the field of waving wheat. Farmers created our countryside and continue to create it; while small abandoned areas are not without interest, a study of the countryside that omits human beings is contrived. I needed to examine an area in which the fashioning of the landscape continues through the efforts of men and women to wrest a living from the land. I wanted a field with humans, a field that is on a farm and is part of that farm.

I live in North Cornwall, where mixed farming is practised. Most farms raise cattle for beef or dairying or both, have some sheep, and grow such arable crops as are needed to augment the staple diet of ruminant animals, which is grass. Cross Park is part of such a farm. For several years it grew barley, in the autumn of 1978 it was sown to a mixture of perennial ryegrass and clover, and throughout 1979 it grew grass. It was cut for hay once and for much of the year it was grazed by sheep.

I studied and commented on the wildlife of the field, but as I did so I also explored its history and the history of the small area in which it is located, and I watched and commented on the farming. The enterprise was gentle and unspectacular, but very rewarding. My year in Cross Park was a year of discovery. No one should expect a field that is farmed to support so rich a flora and fauna as one that is not, but even so the population of species that shares the field with the grass, clover and sheep is large and even the most apparently insignificant of creatures is adapted to the circumstances in which it lives in ways I find fascinating. I hope I have communicated the wonder and delight with which I learned to appreciate the communities of molluscs, insects, spiders and small mammals that live on and with the many plants.

The history of the field and the area is no less fascinating. Inevitably, my account contains some speculation but so far as I have been able to verify it, it is broadly accurate. We worry, and rightly, about the rate at which modern farming is changing the countryside, but in Cross Park I found at least one area that has remained almost unchanged, perhaps for well over a thousand years. There is a peace in that field, born of the wind that sighs over the Moor and the inevitability of change from season to season. Human affairs count for little there, and our arbitrary marking of the passage of time means nothing where the cycle of life repeats itself endlessly, In human terms great events have taken place nearby, some of them within sight of the field, yet the field has changed little. Its boundaries were established long ago and, when it has been farmed, the farming has been much the same as the farming it sustains today. At other times it has run wild and been covered with furze. For a while it was a football pitch. Through all this it has remained, remains, and will remain.

The people have changed rather more, but even then I suspect the changes are rather superficial. The farm of which Cross Park is part has been in the same family for two centuries and the cycle of tasks that comprise farming is dictated by the land, the seasons, and the weather from one day to the next. These do not change. All that changes is fashion. It is only where the farming pattern is broken completely, as in the purely arable regions from which most cattle and sheep have disappeared, that the way of life changes radically.

I visited the field frequently throughout the year and at the end of each month I wrote a chapter based on the notes I made on the spot and on my remembered impressions. I did not look back over these chapters until I had reached the end and the final chapter had been written. I wished each month to be described as I experienced it, so that the book might have some feeling of spontaneity. This technique brought with it an additional benefit, and a risk; the benefit is that my discovery of the field is shared with you, naturally, as it happened. If you embark on a similar enterprise you will probably have similar adventures. At the same time, however, impressions and 'facts' recorded early in the year may turn out to have been false. The book may then contain internal contradictions and my comments, especially those made in the first winter and spring, may appear foolish later. If I seem naïve or even silly, it is the price I must pay, for apart from being a journal of events in the field the story is also of my own experience of the field, and if it is to tell of my education and development it must be honest. In the end, after I had written the last chapter, I looked back over the earlier chapters, but I altered very little.

Obviously, the field is real, and its real name is Cross Park. I have not revealed the name of the farm, nor that of the village in the valley below it, and I have changed the names of such local people as enter my story. This minor subterfuge is intended to protect the farmer and the field from visitors. Inevitably, the text contains many clues to the location of the field and I have no doubt that, armed with the appropriate Ordnance Survey sheet, you could find it. I hope you will not do so or, if you do so, that you will not visit it. The point, after all, is that Cross Park is very ordinary, yet it is unique. That is true of every field, and your 'Cross Park' should be one of the many fields you see next time you visit the farmed countryside that is nearest to your home. It is there that you will find and experience for yourself the underlying texture of history, both human and natural.

Of course, I did not simply visit Cross Park and record what I saw and heard. A certain amount of background reading was necessary and at the end of the book I have added a list of the research material I used. I have included in the list the field guides that I found most helpful.

The idea for a book of this kind came first from David & Charles, and I must thank them for launching me on an enterprise that I believe may have changed me and that most certainly has enriched my life. I must thank, too, George and Audrey Best, Dr Paul Chanin, Barbara

Garratt, Dr Gillian Matthews, Cecil Sleep, Piers Smerdon, Stella Turk, Dr Frank Smith and V. A. Wheatley. Each of them has helped me and without any one of them the book would have been more difficult to write and less informed than I hope it is. Many of them visited the field with me and I will remember with pleasure the walks and conversations I enjoyed with them. Not least of the benefits that have accrued to me during this happy year has been the opportunity I have had to make new friends.

Michael Allaby
Wadebridge, Cornwall
14 January 1980

January

A common gull swooped low over the centre of the field, where a small flock of sparrows and chaffinches were feeding, then banked steeply as it climbed away. It did not land. A crow uttered a cry somewhere in the distance, out of sight. A thrush, perpetually in a panic, hurried from one part of the hedge to another part of the same hedge. It was a quiet time, except now and then when the north wind moaned across the Downs from the high moor.

The year began dramatically, with snow on New Year's Eve blocking the steep lane from the village up to the field. The lane remained blocked for four days and was still banked by snow a fortnight later, when the thaw had freed all roads. By the end of the month there were still a few patches of dirty, wet snow in sheltered spots by the roadside. The snow returned once during the month, but settled for only a few hours.

The weather had been bad generally in the south-west of England. Conditions were not so harsh as during the Great Freeze of February, 1978, when heavy, drifting snow buried moorland farmhouses up to their bedroom windows, but it was enough to block the A30 a couple of times and to reduce the M5 in Somerset and Devon to a single lane in each direction. It was bad enough to summon out the television crews and to set the helicopters flying, and farmers like to think they are remembered when such conditions prevail. The southern edge of Bodmin Moor—or Fowey Moor, as it used to be called—is far enough west and far enough south to avoid the worst of the hard winters, at least as these are known in other parts of the country.

All the same, the Downs and the high moor were bleak and threatening, and the field itself, tamed by centuries of farming, was empty and cold. The 600ft contour runs across the field, which slopes gently up to the moor to the north. To the south it overlooks the valley and the village dominated by its fifteenth-century church, but in winter the cosiness of the village, nestling in the shelter below, serves only to emphasise the remoteness of the field, its distance from human affairs, its position on the outer edge of civilisation, for today, and perhaps for a very long time, it marks the upper boundary of cultivation.

The ground was hard and frozen. Splinters of thin ice twinkled in the sunshine and vanished when the heavy clouds rolled ponderously across the sky from the west with a load of snow destined for someone else. Snow was forecast far more often than snow fell.

The field was not so bare as it looked. It was ploughed and cultivated in the autumn, as soon as its crop of barley had been harvested, and then it was sown to grass, a mixture of perennial ryegrass and clover helped on with a dressing of lime and straight potash fertiliser. It had grown barley, using compound fertilisers, in 1977 as well as in 1978. Now it was entering the first year of a three-to-five-year ley. It was to become meadow, and by the time winter set in the young grass was established securely, its leaves standing an inch or so above the surface.

The field is called Cross Park. The name itself is ancient. The lane up from the village past the main entrance to the farm, the lane that was blocked by snow, joins another small road which runs along the southern edge of the field so there is a road junction by the gate into the field. Such junctions are often called 'crossroads', even when in fact the roads do not cross, but the cross in Cross Park is something different. At one time it may have borne its Cornish name, *Park-an-Grouse*, which means 'field of the cross'. At one time there was a cross. It vanished years ago. Local people believe it was taken down the hill to the neighbouring farm and placed in an orchard. Cornish crosses were for ever being moved and used for other purposes. The Cornish people may not have invented recycling, but their recycling of crosses was very common.

There are two crosses in the village churchyard. The finer of them is one of the best preserved of all Cornish crosses, and it was this habit of recycling that saved it. The old Norman building was demolished and rebuilt in the fifteenth century by masons who used the cross as though it were any other piece of stone, building it into the east wall of the chancel, from whence it was removed in modern times to its present position outside the church. Since those early Tudor builders seem to have had little regard for the sanctity of the cross, probably it was already so ancient that they took it for granted. In fact it has been dated approximately as ninth century, which means it must have been made during the time of Alfred the Great, or perhaps even earlier, in the reign of one of his brothers or even of their father, Ethelwulf. The cross is decorated with fine knotwork, scrolls and plaitwork.

Most of the original Cornish crosses are very ancient. Their manufacture developed into a major growth industry during the eighth and ninth centuries, but many are still older. Almost invariably they are made from granite, a stone which went out of fashion during the twelfth century and was not used again to any extent until the fifteenth century. It seems likely that the Cornish crosses are debased forms of the Irish crosses, with inferior carving due to the difficulty of working the Cornish moor-stone, or surface granite.

The Dartmoor granite is about 275 million years old, and the Cornish granites were probably introduced at about the same time. At one time the south-west peninsula was formed as part of a series of folds in the rocks that ran east-north-east to west-south-west. Then, during the Armorican orogeny, in the Upper Palaeozoic, new folding occurred on an east-west line. The rocks that were folded were sedimentary rocks, probably of great thickness, slates and phyllites that miners call

The top of the finer of the two parish crosses (*left*) is more elaborate than most, the cross itself being cut right through the stone; even the cross is alive with its own layer of lichen. The less elaborate cross (*right*) is topped with a cross within a cross; it stands above the road

'killas'. Magma intruded beneath the folds and cooled slowly. As the overlying rocks were eroded away, the domes in what had been folds remained as granite bosses to form the bases of the present day moors from Dartmoor west.

The Cornish granites are mainly coarse-grained and have been more or less decomposed by the intrusion of water, which dissolves the feldspars, and by chemical action that began as the magma cooled and produced other minerals along with the granites. These provided the lodes of metalliferous ores that have dominated the entire history of Cornwall and, as an extreme end product of decomposition, the kaolin that supplies the industry that dominates much of the landscape and provides even more employment than tourism. There is china clay beneath the moor, too, but it is sited a long and inconvenient way from the sea for transport and the moor itself has a degree of legislative protection, being designated an Area of Outstanding Natural Beauty. The curious weathering of the Cornish granites also produced bizarre and weirdly beautiful shapes, such as that of the Cheesewring.

Later mountain building raised high platforms on parts of the moors, and at one time the tors may have stood as granitic islands towering above a sea that covered the lower land. The land was flooded again at the end of the most recent ice age as melting floodwaters from the receding ice sheet to the north poured south, but as the floods began to abate and more temperate conditions established themselves, the dwindling rivers deposited rich alluvium over wide expanses of the moors. In places the blanket hill peat is up to 18ft thick.

The badly decomposed state of most of the granites and their coarse-grained structure makes them poor building material, but the fact that they cleave in straight lines to form boulders that lie about the surface has always made them easily available. So the old crosses were of granite.

Cornish people have always had a liking for crosses. Most of them were used to mark sacred sites, such as churches or chapels, or formed gravestones or memorials to individuals. These were the largest and most handsome crosses: crosses marking the ways to churches were like them, but smaller. Lych-stone crosses were also popular, but from medieval times these were Gothic in style. Crosses were also used to mark the boundaries of church property and parishes. The glebe that includes Cross Park was marked out by crosses at one time, a cross at each corner like a miner's claim might be staked out. Those crosses have vanished. In 1925 the Truro Diocese published *The Cornish Church Guide* by the Rev C. Henderson, who quoted a charming anecdote: 'In 1427 Dr Reginald Mertherderwa by his Will directed new stone crosses

Across the galvanised five-bar gate on the north side of the field, great boulders of moor-stone, covered in lichens and mosses, lie there for the taking. Beyond this wild ground stands the small mountain of quarried granite beside the abandoned and semi-derelict quarry hut

to be put up of the usual kind in those parts of Cornwall from Kayar Beslasek to Camborne Church where dead bodies were rested on their way to burial, that prayers might be made and the bearers take some rest.' Some of these crosses can still be found, although there are none at Camborne.

Everything seems to be made from moor-stone. It is hardly surprising, for across the galvanised five-bar gate that divides Cross Park from the wild Downs great granite boulders covered in lichens and mosses still lie about, there for the taking by any would-be builder with a block and tackle and strong shoulders. A little way beyond the boulders there is a granite quarry with its own small mountain of blocks. That has been there at least since the Ordnance Survey of 1880-81: it is shown on the 1888 edition of the map though not, for some reason, on the 1906 edition. There is a derelict hut beside the mountain, one more of the countless abandoned mine buildings that give the Cornish uplands their peculiar air of desolation. It looks forbidding, haunted even, in the pale, cold, January light. There is nothing new in this ancient place. We can expect no surprises. In 1584, John Norden wrote *A Topographicall and Historical description of Cornwall* as part of *Speculi Britanniae*, his mammoth survey of the whole country.

His Cornish survey was not published until 1728, but it had not dated except, perhaps, in its spelling. The landscape had changed little and his descriptions are often apt, even now. He wrote:

> Ther is a Stone called a *Moar-stone*, which lyeth despersed upon the face of the mountaynes and on the confused rockes; Stones verie profitable for manie purposes, in buylding most firme and lastinge; weather nor time can hardly penetrate them. Notwithstandinge their naturall obduritie, the Country people haue a deuice to cleaue them with wedges like loggs of wood, of verie great length, and of what quantitie of bodye they liste; so that they make of them, in steed of timber, mayne postes for their howses, Dorepostes, Chimnye and wyndow peeces, and aboue all subporters for their out-howses of greateste receyte. And this kinde of stone hath a glittering hew, as if it were sett with the sparkes of Diamondes.

Old Norden had an eye for beauty if beauty there were, and perhaps he was a bit of a sentimentalist. All the same, the gate-posts on the four gates of Cross Park are of his Moar-stone. Were they there in his day, 'sett with the sparkes of Diamondes'? They may well have been. The farm certainly was.

The moor-stone was used by the old ones, the early peoples who lived on the high moors, and it is because they built their walls from a material of such 'naturall obduritie' that we can know of them. The area above Cross Park was inhabited in prehistoric times and it was the descendants of these Mesolithic, Neolithic, Megalithic and Beaker peoples who flourished in the Bronze Age, which began about 2000BC. They farmed, and some of their fields are still in use today, older than those of the Cornish Celts, for the first of the three Celtic invasions that made Cornwall a Celtic province was not until about 550BC, when the Bronze Age was giving way to the new-fangled Iron Age.

The Bronze Age was a boom period for the moor people. You cannot have a Bronze Age without bronze, and you cannot have bronze without copper and tin. The moor had both. Even when iron became more fashionable for making tools and weapons, the bronze workers remained in business, supplying ornamental bronzes to wealthy chieftains and their wives, and, of course, there was the almost legendary Mediterranean trade. That depended on the state of things in Spain, for Spanish tin was much more conveniently located for traders living on the shores of the Mediterranean. In the fifth century BC, however, the Carthaginians conquered Tartessos, so shutting off the tin supplies to Greece and to the Greek colony at Marseilles. The Greeks looked northward and their interest in Cornish tin was inherited by their successors, the Romans, who periodically had difficulty with Spain. In the third century AD the Spanish mines were

16

lost for good and the Romans established camps in Cornwall. Some of the rubbish they left behind them—the buckles and coins they lost and the weapons they threw away—are still found. Rome even paid for a few roads to be built in Cornwall, but by then time was running out for the Empire and by the early part of the fifth century Roman support had been withdrawn. Still, they did build one or two roads, and Cornwall has always needed better roads but lacked the wherewithal to pay for them.

The Bronze Age and Iron Age farms were oases in oceans of moorland wilderness, a patchwork of small fields protected then, as now, by stone hedges. There were two kinds of field, the in-field and the out-field. The in-fields surrounded the buildings in which humans and animals lived, and they were farmed all the time. The out-fields formed circles around the settlement outside the in-fields, and they were cultivated in rotation, being returned to fallow when they became exhausted. Eventually, of course, the out-fields from one settlement merged with those of neighbours, but in some places the old pattern remains. Wherever the field boundaries form long, continuous curves that may once have formed a complete circle, enclosing small fields of irregular shape and size but with a proportion of fields that are almost square, the landscape may date back to the Bronze Age, especially if there is an ancient site more or less at the centre of the circle. Was Cross Park a Bronze Age out-field? It could have been. The building of modern lanes has disrupted the patterns to some extent, but on the hillside below Cross Park the outer boundaries of the fields form three concentric curves, and the farm contains a site of great antiquity.

The farm is mentioned in Domesday. The Domesday records for south-west England are more detailed than for any other region except East Anglia. The survey itself was completed in just a few months, in 1086, by inquisitors who worked circuits and who took down sworn statements, partly to establish who owned which land and partly to determine taxes. This information was summarised in one book, nicknamed Great Domesday even during the lifetime of those who compiled it, for, like the Biblical Domesday, it represented the great reckoning against which there could be no appeal. The East Anglian records were published in full in a separate work, called Little Domesday, and the full data collected by the Exeter circuit were also published separately. Sometimes there are discrepancies between the Great (Exchequer) Domesday and the Exeter Domesday. The farm that includes Cross Park, for example, is assessed in one place at one hide and elsewhere at two hides. In Cornwall, which was rather different from the rest of the country, a hide was equal to twelve geld-acres, the unit of area that was used in making tax, or geld, assessments. The farm also included three leagues by two leagues of pasture, but there is no way we can calculate what area this represented. Certainly an eleventh-century league was not the three-mile league of more recent times. Pasture was grazing land, distinguished from meadow which was grassland from which stock were excluded to allow the grass to be cut for hay. There was not much meadow in Cornwall then, possibly because in those days grass intended for conservation would have been cultivated only on lowland alluvial plains, of which Cornwall has very few. It is also possible that the eleventh-century farmers did not need hay. The climate was much warmer then than it is now and the long growing season would have allowed beasts to be outwintered. Cross Park is to be meadow, temporarily, so that is a change. It is not much of a change, though, over nearly nine hundred years. In the field next to Cross Park there were Devon Closewool sheep grazing by the end of January. It is a stock farm, now as then, and Cross Park's eight-and-a-half acres of grass will be grazed by sheep after the hay or silage has been made.

It is a productive area and always has been. The Domesday inquisitors observed the division of the county into hundreds, the system invented more than a century earlier by the Saxon king Edmund I, and Norden used the same system. Cross Park lies in the hundred of West:

> The hundred of *Weste*, so called in regarde of the Hundred of *Easte*, called also *East Wiuelshire*: It lyeth betwene the hundred of *Easte* easte, and the hundred of *Powder* weste; the *British Sea* sowthe, and the hundred of *Trigg* north, and is a uery frutefull hundred.

So said John Norden. The Exeter Domesday records that in 1086 Cornwall contained 12 mares (*equae*), 58 forest mares (*equae silvestres*), 352 unbroken mares (*equae indomitae*), 21 rounceys (*roncini* or *runcini*) which probably were pack horses, 55 cows (*vaccae*) and, so the great book says, one bull (*taurus*) who must have spent much of his time travelling, 1,063 assorted non-ploughing animals (*animalia*), 906 nanny goats (*caprae*), 505 swine (*porci*), 240 wethers (*berbices*) and 13,003 sheep (*oves*). Obviously, sheep farming was the main enterprise and some of the flocks were large, running to several hundred ewes.

The animals would have been sold at Bodmin market. This was the only regular market in Cornwall that remained the property of the church by 1086. It was administered by the canons of St Petrock, but all the other markets had been seized or taken over by the Count of Mortain, who seems to have had an eye for business.

Trees do not grow well above the 600ft contour, where they are exposed to the salt-laden, dehydrating Atlantic gales. In the Cross Park hedges there are just a few specimens that stand bare, defiant, but not high, out of the banks

The forest mares, assuming that they lived in or near forest as their name suggests, would not have ventured as far as Cross Park. The record may be incomplete, but it records an area of woodland two leagues by one league on the Camel estuary, but no more woodland on the north side of Cornwall anywhere west of Bude.

Upland Cornwall is still no place to grow trees. On the granite bosses the soil is usually too shallow. Cross Park lies on the very edge of the granite, where the underlying rock may be slate, but even where there is sufficient depth of soil for rooting, trees are dehydrated by the salt-laden Atlantic gales. One or two rather scrubby trees stand bare, defiant, but not high, out of the hedges that surround Cross Park on all its four sides. These are Cornish hedges, of course, made as earth banks with a stone wall core, and overgrown by a tangle of woody vegetation.

If it existed in the eleventh century, Cross Park would have been at the very edge of the moor, as it is now, for by then the prosperous moorland settlements had long vanished. Hardly anyone lived in the uplands, above the 400ft contour. Elsewhere there were substantial villages, many hamlets, and scattered farmsteads, but it was wild, unpopulated country. The population of the whole county was probably no more than 24,000 to 30,000 people and around Cross Park the density of population is estimated to have been about 4.1 persons per square mile. Nowhere did the population density exceed 5 persons per square mile, except along the border with Devon. That lay more or less where it lies today. It was established in 928 by King Athelstan, one of whose predecessors, King Egbert, had defeated the Cornish, or West Welsh, at the battle of Hengestesdun (Hingston Down) in 838 and declared himself king of Wessex and All England. Athelstan completed the job by banishing the West Welsh from Exeter and drawing the line on the map. The Cornish freedom fighters had been assisted in their attempt to drive off the English by Danish pirates who just happened to drop by at a convenient moment and were conscripted. They lost the war all the same, but it may have initiated the traditional Cornish pastime of piracy which later became almost a cottage-industry. The Saxon kings put an end to Cornish independence, but not to Cornish rebellion. That is alive and well and based upon a nationalist movement and a revival of interest in the old Cornish language, which belongs to the Cymric or Brythonic dialect of Celtic, as do Welsh and Breton. You can sit examinations in Cornish but, so far as I know, only in Cornwall.

The moorland was not cultivated in the eleventh century but almost certainly it would have been used for rough grazing by sheep and cattle, as it is today, and the peat may have been cut for fuel. A small amount is still cut. The Domesday inquisitors would have had no interest in such homely matters nor, indeed, in the extent to which earlier English conquerors had taken over the more important settlements and imposed their mark on the pattern of place names. In his essay on Cornwall in *The Domesday Geography of South-West England*, edited by H. C. Darby and R. Welldon Finn, Dr W. L. D. Ravenhill comments:

> The landscape of Cornwall, in its human aspect, was made up not only of nucleated villages but also of hamlets and isolated farmsteads. While we may not associate English names exclusively with the former and Celtic names with the latter, there is a degree of correspondence. The presence of so many small settlements accounts for the fact that so few Cornish Domesday place names have become the names of modern parishes. These small settlements, with the Celtic names, gave to the human geography of Domesday Cornwall a character quite unlike that of the rest of southern England.

The hedges around Cross Park had been cropped level earlier in the winter, like caricatured Prussian haircuts, all flat along the top except where the occasional plant had been allowed to grow taller, like an unruly tuft that had escaped the clippers. It is almost impossible to retain hedgerow trees where the principal form of management is mechanical cutting, because the machine does not discriminate between tall shrubs and saplings. If the trees are allowed to grow to maturity there is a further danger that they will shade nearby shrubs so that gaps appear in the hedge which will no longer be stockproof. In most cases hedgerow trees are incompatible not only with mechanical cutting, but also with stock management. In Cornwall, however, the hedges are stockproof to a height of six feet or more because they are built of stone and earth, a dense barrier that would deter even a goat, and vegetation growing luxuriantly in them is a bonus. Trimmed, the Cross Park hedges stand eight or nine feet high, except along the lower edge, where the field borders the road and stands about eight feet above it, as is common in Cornwall.

A hedge that has been clipped looks slightly absurd and if a flail cutter has been used it looks demolished, a ruin of tattered, bare wood. It suffers no damage, however, and the effect disappears as soon as a new year's growth appears to heal the wounds. Apart from the fright they may receive from the noise and smell of the cutter, the wildlife suffers little, although the high-nesting birds must find new quarters. Even they are not disturbed, of course, because most farmers do not

The hedges were trimmed flat in the autumn, the tops all level except where the occasional plant has been allowed to grow on. The hedges are stone walls covered by earth banks, in which a mass of woody vegetation is established

trim hedges while birds are nesting. Hedges are more than important for wildlife. Over most of Britain they are vital, and it is surprising how much habitat they offer. The hedges around Cross Park are more than eight hundred yards in total length—almost half a mile—and in the corners where the plough cannot reach they extend forward into triangular patches of uncultivated ground.

The machines were silent now. A few implements lay about the headlands, masses of rusting ironmongery abandoned after the last time they were used. A disc harrow was in one corner; a zig-zag harrow with rigid tines rested against the vegetation at the foot of the hedgebank to one side of the gate. They would have been unsightly had it not been for the fact that their colour blended precisely with that of the remains of the autumn umbellifers, making them nearly invisible. At the top end of the field there was a rack from which stock could be fed hay, equipped with wheels and a corrugated roof to keep the hay dry.

It was the month when all is still, or seems to be. Small animals were hidden, hibernating or at least sleeping for much of the time to conserve energy. The migrant birds had left long ago and it would be many more months before they returned. The invertebrates were dead or dormant. The place looked vacant.

It was not empty, though. The bare wood of the hedgerow displayed the oak galls, hanging like late fruit. They are not fruit, of course; these solid galls are made by insects, gall wasps of the superfamily Cynipoidea of the order Hymenoptera. The female wasp pierces the plant tissue and lays her eggs in the wound. The eggs hatch and each larva secretes a chemical irritant that induces the plant to grow excessively until the gall is completed and then to continue to renew it as the growing grub eats away at its store of nutrients. The grub is completely enclosed in its central chamber where it is surrounded by a 'pith' of thin-walled, succulent cells which regenerate as fast as they are eaten. The pith is surrounded by harder cells that form a protective layer for the grub, and the whole gall is cased in a skin or bark. The real cunning this parasite displays lies in its ability to compel the plant to produce nutrients during the winter, when the plant is dormant, so that the adult insect can emerge into a world full of growing vegetation where, of course, it must mate and the female must find a new host to feed its own brood. Plant galls of this kind seldom cause any serious injury to their host unless, as sometimes happens, they are formed on the growing tips of young shoots, when they can be fatal to the plant. The shape of the gall is very specific to particular insects, and the chemical composition of the gall is specific to the host plant. They used

The gall wasps that are clever enough to induce plants to feed them in the depths of winter, are highly vulnerable to hungry birds that can chip away at the hard galls in search of their succulent occupants

to encourage oak galls in the west of England because at one time the tannin they contained was an important raw material for making ink. Tannins may amount to 45 to 65 per cent of the weight of an oak gall. It is rumoured that the decline in the oak population in Cornwall is due to the success and then the abandonment of the old gall-ink industry. This seems a little improbable, but the galls are certainly very common.

If the parasite is clever enough to compel a plant to feed it at a time when the plant feeds nothing else, it has overlooked one potential enemy cleverer than itself. Hungry insectivorous birds have discovered its secret and although it is a tedious business for a bird to chisel away at a tough gall to reach its juicy occupant, those that take the trouble can have no difficulty in finding the galls, which are not hidden, and there is not a thing the grub can do about it because it lacks the equipment that enables the adults of its kind to bore a small hole through the imprisoning walls and escape. You can tell whether or not an intact gall is occupied by looking for this borehole, whose existence indicates the departure of the wasp.

The over-wintering birds were present. This year they were behaving strangely. December had been unusually mild and robins had been seen going about in pairs, which can only mean they had been deceived into believing it was time to start nest building. Rooks had been seen carrying twigs. When the cold weather came both species reverted to more seasonal behaviour. The starlings left the higher ground and people said there were far fewer than are generally seen in mid-winter. In the valleys they were, if anything, more numerous than usual, so perhaps the upland residents had migrated to more sheltered conditions where food was more plentiful? On the other hand, the chaffinches were more numerous than in most years.

Early in the month the hedgerow banks revealed little. They house many rabbits, but the entrances to the burrows looked undisturbed. During the short time snow lay on the ground in the middle of the month a few daytime rabbits ventured forth to travel a few yards down the hedge and disappear again, but these were the adventurers. By the end of the month they were out in greater numbers to find what nourishment they could from the young grass. Their droppings were everywhere, but never more than a couple of yards from the shelter of the hedge.

The rabbits, too, had changed their habits. In recent years they had been breeding right through the autumn and winter. Is this an adaptation to myxomatosis? Traditionally, the breeding season for wild rabbits runs from January to June and although there have always been exceptions, with some individuals breeding out of season, most does are supposed to be in anoestrus during the second half of the year. Copulation continues, but no pregnancies result. During the last few years, however, does have been found in oestrus throughout the year.

The foxes may have been active, too, for there were signs of disturbed earth at the entrance to other large burrows and, a few feet from the hedge, were the unidentifiable remains of what was once a small, furry animal, possibly a rabbit.

The rabbits are recent arrivals. They were not here at the time of Domesday, although those Norman statisticians may have brought a few with them and the local baron, Richard Fitz Turold, may have introduced a colony to supply tasty morsels for the baronial table. It was the planting of hedges up-country, in the lush farmlands of East Anglia and the Midlands, that really caused the spread of the rabbit, by providing it with shelter and burrowing facilities right in the middle of its food store. The rabbit did not become a serious pest until the eighteenth and nineteenth centuries.

Today farmers hate it, for the damage it does to vegetables of all kinds. They form local societies to try to destroy it, but their victories are ephemeral. The rabbit is one of nature's survivors. Apart from farmers with guns and traps its most serious enemy is the fox, and the fox has few enemies if any. It is another survivor. People hunt foxes, but they rarely catch them because the purpose of the hunt is to dress up in funny clothes and ride about on horses rather than to kill animals. Those who defend fox-hunting on the ground that it is a necessary form of vermin control are out of touch with reality. The control has no effect on the foxes, and foxes are not vermin anyway, and have never been classed as such: they are useful predators whose disappearance from the landscape would leave the countryside with some really serious problems—mainly from rabbits.

It is not only farmers who hate rabbits. So do the arachnologists, the students of spiders and their relatives. They dislike sheep, too, and for the same reason. Both sheep and rabbits are nibblers, animals that graze the herbage closely, and as they graze they consume vast numbers of arachnids. Indeed, the spiders they consume inadvertently contribute a significant amount of protein to the diet of these hypocritical herbivores.

It may be, though, that the most serious pest of grassland is not the rabbit, but a minute animal that lives among the roots, secure and invisible. Nematodes are thread-like creatures, usually transparent, and the largest of them is not much more than a millimetre long. Unlike most soil animals, they have not the slightest interest in dead organic matter. There may be up to one million nematodes in the soil beneath ten square feet of grassland, most of them in the top four inches, and they belong to any of about a thousand species. The other nine thousand species of nematodes live in water. According to their species, they have various dietary preferences. Many subsist only on living plant tissue. Some, like the potato eelworm, extract sap from plant roots. Others eat single-celled organisms and there are others again that prey on other nematodes or on creatures smaller than themselves. The charge against them—that they reduce the productivity of grassland very substantially—is based on circumstantial evidence. Studies were made of the theoretical dry-matter production of particular grasses under simulated farm conditions. When the results were compared with measurements of actual yields of dry matter, there was a huge discrepancy. It was not a matter of a pound or two here or there but of tons. Now, no one has actually observed the nematodes munching their way across the pastures and meadows of England, but they have been counted, the preference many of them have for eating the roots of plants is known, and a quick multiplication sum to relate the number of individuals and their daily food intake to the total consumption of the entire population in a particular area produced an answer conveniently close to the missing grass that should have been there but was not. It was the equivalent of a smoking gun and the nematodes were found guilty. A few years ago sentence would have been passed on them and carried out with dedication by armies of pesticide salesmen and sprayers, but today people are more cautious. The nematodes have a right of appeal. Like all creatures, they surely have a role in the living world. They may play no direct part in the decomposition of organic matter, but perhaps even those that are obviously harmful to crops form an important part of the food supply of animals we would rather retain than lose. By eliminating one pest, might we create another? It has happened before. Might the predatory nematodes not serve a useful function by regulating the population not only of other nematodes but of animals that could become pests if they were given a chance?

Perhaps, though, the real reason why little has been done about nematodes on grassland is that grass is something of a poor relation to other plant crops. It will grow on land that is of little use for anything else, humans cannot eat it, so why spend money on it? If they wished to do so, farmers could control nematodes fairly successfully by using nematicides.

Now, though, even these most numerous of all soil animals were inactive. Everything was waiting for the spring population explosion. Here and there in the banks isolated primroses hugged the earth, green and prominent, almost ready to flower.

February

Spring arrived abruptly, at precisely seven o'clock on the morning of Tuesday, 20 February. The day dawned with a blue sky flecked with puffs of fracto-cumulus cloud tinged with pink, and a sudden din of birdsong as each species staked out territories. Three swans whirred low overhead in their loose V formation, heading for the estuarine feeding grounds. It is not particularly unusual to see swans in flight, but ever since I can remember the sight and even more the sound of their flight have thrilled me. I think these birds would continue to thrill me no matter how often I saw them. In my youth, when the RAF taught me to fly aeroplanes, we student pilots were shown films of swans and similar large birds in flight, landing and taking off, and there were photographs of them on the walls of our classrooms. These were the masters of the air we were to emulate in our heavy, noisy, crude, clumsy machines. These were our real teachers. I dare say all is different now and that student pilots are taught to admire other models. If so, the change is a sad one.

Spring had arrived. The valley primroses had been in flower for weeks, some of them since before Christmas, and now they were joined by the first snowdrops. By the end of the month the daffodils were above ground and pushing upward, and crocuses and violets were flowering. On the evening of the 27th the peace was broken by the croaking of frogs on the postage stamp of a pond at the back of the house, and a few days later there was a mass of spawn, larger than I had seen in previous years. This unusually prolific breeding by the frogs was not confined to our area this year: I heard of similar rates of breeding elsewhere.

All of this took place close to sea level, but Cross Park is higher and those few hundred feet make a great deal of difference. The sun shines there, too, of course, and for the first time there was a hint of warmth in it early in the month, but the plants were very late, just as they were late in the lanes, where even the dog's mercury, usually early, had not appeared by the end of the month.

There were still cold days to endure and frosty nights from which to hide, but the 20th marked the turning point and these minor stings in the tail of winter were not to be taken seriously. The hold had been broken. By the end of the month there was the first hint of the wet, blustery weather traditionally associated with March.

Before that, though, the weather had been bitter and fierce. The 11th was very cold and windy and some snow fell during the night. By early morning it was reduced to slush, but in Devon and Somerset falls were much heavier. On the following day, the 13th, there was severe flooding on several parts of the south coast of England, but most seriously at Portland, where the coastal defences were overwhelmed.

A combination of gales and high spring tides caused the freak conditions that led to the damage. Storms in mid-Atlantic created a large swell and this led to waves 20 to 25ft high in the Channel. The waves moved north with the wind and when the tidal movement was added to them they grew to heights of 40 to 50ft. These were the waves that struck Portland and, although there was criticism of delays in the construction of new and better coastal defences, no sea wall would have been capable of holding back waves of that size with a gale driving them. Portland suffered severe damage, but similar waves occurred elsewhere. At Plymouth, vessels were moved out of Millbay Docks for safety and even so some of them were damaged.

The gales and freak waves were followed, on the 15th and 16th, by a high-pressure system that brought easterly winds from north-central Europe, and heavy snow fell in many places. By the afternoon of the 16th the wind had dropped and by the 18th the weather was much milder, with mist and moderate rain, but no snow or ice.

The grass in Cross Park was established well enough to feed a small flock of about fifty-five Devon Longwool sheep for a few days early in the month. They were there on the 11th, but stayed for no more than four or five days. The sheep huddled together in a flock that was tight enough to confuse any would-be predator but loose enough to allow room for each animal to graze. They were not to be approached, these sheep, and when the leaders of the flock moved, the congregation followed. Now and then an individual would graze her way out of the group, then realise her vulnerability. The slightest disturbance would send her hurrying back. Sheep do not like to be alone.

It was an archaic sight for a cold, bleak day. A time traveller leaping forwards from the New Stone Age might span the 5,000 years that have elapsed since his day and observe little change. He would find the metal implements left in odd corners curious and he might wonder at the sheep themselves. He would be familiar with sheep, as well as with cattle and dogs, for his people were farmers and quite civilised. They made pottery, had efficient stone axes they used for clearing forest, and they hunted and fought with stone-headed maces and arrows. Their maces must have been much admired, for they remained in use well into the Early Bronze Age, perhaps as weapons, perhaps as symbols of high office, perhaps as both. He may not have visited Cross Park before, for the region was not densely populated in those days. Neolithic remains have been found at Carn Brea but there is no firm evidence that they lived anywhere else in Cornwall. Yet they may have done, for these were the henge builders. They built Stonehenge, for reasons that are far from clear to us. Perhaps people came there from a wide surrounding area to worship or to celebrate the wonders of science and technology? We have employed the priests of our advertising agencies and tourist boards to widen the circle of influence and people still visit, in larger numbers than ever, to celebrate the wonders of the modern science of transport, and to worship gold. The Neolithic masons are also believed to have built the Stripple Stones henge and this monument, on the southern slopes of Hawk's Tor, is about 3½ miles from Cross Park as the crow flies. Maybe our visitor passed the field on his way to or from the henge?

The sheep, though, would have startled him, for they are quite unlike the sheep he may have tended. His sheep are likely to have been descended from the urial, a wild sheep that came originally from the region between what are now the Punjab and Baluchistan. The European mouflon was crossed with these early sheep much later, and this crossing altered their appearance. The urial sheep is brown, with large horns that curve back over the head in a wide spiral, and like all wild sheep and the first domesticated breeds, it has no woolly fleece. Wild sheep have double coats consisting of dense, short woolly hairs that lie next to the skin and longer guard hairs that form a complete outer coat over them. For reasons no one understands, after sheep were domesticated they lost their outer coats and their inner coats grew longer and thicker, as though to compensate, until the animals had fleeces. Even then, the wool was shed each year by moulting, as it still is in primitive domesticated breeds such as the Soay and St Kilda.

So our sheep would seem startling to someone from the distant past. They have no horns, they are white, and they have fleeces. What is more, the fleeces are cut from them every year: that would have been difficult, perhaps impossible, with stone implements. The white colour is a recent development and a product of deliberate breeding to produce wool that is convenient to process. The older Soay and St Kilda fleeces are varying shades of brown.

Modern sheep still retain their ancestral habits, however. By and large they prefer higher ground—although many breeds have been adapted artificially to conditions in the lowlands—and they live together in family groups or flocks, generally with the older males apart from the ewes, lambs and younger males. They were domesticated first for their meat and milk, with hides, horns and bones as useful by-products. Our Neolithic visitor would know nothing of spun and woven wool. That came later.

Was Cross Park in existence as a field in Neolithic times? It is unlikely. Settled farming was still new then, heralding a period of great expansion. Before that, during the Mesolithic period (which began in Cornwall around 6000BC) there were a very few settlements, some of them on the Moor, and if there had been earlier Palaeolithic hunters and gatherers they left no traces that we can identify. The Mesolithic people used implements or weapons called 'pygmies', or 'microliths', with small flint blades about an inch long and very sharp on both edges and at the point, and apart from Cornwall they have been found in western France and Britanny. They left no pottery that has been found and probably they made none. The Neolithic period began here around 3000BC, and these New Stone Age people did make pottery, as we have seen, but a kind of semi-nomadic pastoralism may have been more familiar to them than settled farming—until, that is, the invasion of the Beaker Folk, about 2000BC, who came from Spain and were ugly as sin. Small men and women they were, but powerfully built. They had round heads and prominent brow ridges. They used to bury their dead trussed in the foetal position along with a small beaker, 6 to 8in high, which is how they earned their name. Three of these beakers have been found in Cornwall. They were advanced, though, despite their unlikely appearance. They had more efficient stone tools and their knives were made from copper. It was their knowledge of metal working that was developed much further in the Bronze Age that followed.

The climate was better in those days. It was drier and warmer than it is now. The Moor would have been less exposed, although it possessed few trees. It was because it was open, in contrast to the densely wooded valleys, that it was attractive to settlers, and very attractive it must have been, for the Cornish uplands are rich in the remains of henges, standing stones and chambered tombs. The standing stones are called 'megaliths', or 'menhirs', which is a translation of the Celtic *mên*, meaning stone, and *hîr*, meaning long. It was the Neolithic farmers and henge builders who buried their dead—at any rate the important ones—in chambered tombs built from stone and covered with earth to make barrows and tumuli. Over the years the wind and rain have washed away the earth from some of these tombs to leave the stonework exposed. The Cornish people call them 'quoits' and there is one about half a mile from Cross Park.

The Bronze Age people also favoured spectacular burials and many of their barrows have remained undisturbed, even by archaeologists, to the present day. About a mile and a half from Cross Park, on Treslea Downs, there is one of their barrows complete with a 'peristalith'—a circle of upright stones—to retain the structure.

The Bronze Age people brought a more important innovation: they ploughed their fields. They continued to do so for a long time, and the effects can still be seen in some places. They ploughed along the contours and each time they did so a little soil moved down the slope. Eventually the upper edge of the field was lowered and a bank was formed at the lower edge, to give a kind of terraced effect, although this was not the result of deliberate terracing.

The Iron Age began about 550BC, with the first Celtic invasions by people who still preferred to live on the higher ground, usually above the 500ft contour. Cross Park might have suited them very well, and it may be that they inherited the field from earlier times, or enclosed it themselves. They were a quarrelsome lot. At least, they built many castles and forts and so presumably a good deal of their time was spent in fighting. On the Moor, a little over half a mile from Cross Park, there is a site labelled on the map as 'Bury Castle'. 'Bury' means 'fortification', and this could be an Iron Age site. The people grew corn, cultivated first in the Near East, and they raised sheep on an in-field, out-field farming pattern. They lived in small, round huts made from stone and covered with earth, grouped together in villages. The nearest circle of huts from that period is less than three miles from Cross Park. Their most important site, though, was a little further away, at Trevelgue Head, near Newquay, where they had a cliff castle that was occupied from about 200BC. The people there smelted iron and made bronze. Something like half a ton of metal and slag was found when the site was excavated. They ate cattle, sheep, goats, pigs, birds and shellfish, and they used the antlers of deer to make implements. They also spun, and left behind many spindle whorls. Presumably they were spinning wool, so the sheep must have had fleeces by that time.

Cross Park today lies precisely on the upper edge of farmed land, with only the hedge and a gate separating it from unreclaimed moorland. The Bronze and Iron Age peoples preferred to live at higher altitudes, and for them Cross Park may have been rather low-lying. The idea that it may have been farmed so long ago is based on the pattern of outlying fields, the use of the name 'Park', and the proximity of a site of whose antiquity there can be no doubt.

In January I noticed the shape of the field boundaries to the west of Cross Park and, interestingly, to the west of them again it is possible that the curve reverses, as though to enclose an adjacent farm. This is less certain because there the curve of a stream and its valley, and the contours of the land, may well have determined the location of the field boundaries, so that their resemblance to older patterns may be coincidental. Those immediately to the west of Cross Park, however, run at right angles to the contours, in a pattern that would seem inconvenient today and that is unlikely to have been achieved simply by accident.

All of this, though, was based on a map made after a survey conducted in 1880-81 and it needed to be checked, You can see the windsock belonging to the Cornwall Flying Club from the field, and I explained my problem to the chief flying instructor. On the 25th I flew over the area and could see that the 1880 boundaries were still there and, if anything, more pronounced on the ground than on the map. When the photographs were developed, they revealed curious markings on the field next to Cross Park and on the field three fields away from it to the north-west (to the right in the photograph), and marks on the moorland above Cross Park that look as though they might be traces of earlier fields that have since been abandoned.

The name 'Park' is an Anglicisation of the Cornish 'Parc', which means 'field' or 'enclosure'. In the old in-field, out-field system, the field closest to the human dwelling was called the 'gew', which means 'hedged-in place'. Beyond the gew lay the parc, a slightly more distant enclosure, and beyond that again was the 'gweal', a much larger field carved out of an out-field. If the fields to the west of Cross Park, with their broadly concentric pattern, are gweals, then we might expect to

Cross Park seen from the air. In the lower right corner of the field can be seen the opening on to open moorland. Next to the moorland is a small field that is mostly overgrown, with a small stand of trees. This land is not part of the farm, nor is the field below it with the cottage and buildings. The farm itself is in the top left of the picture. The houses beside Cross Park are council houses and nothing to do with the farm

The farm, looking like any farm, lies below Cross Park. This picture was taken from the field

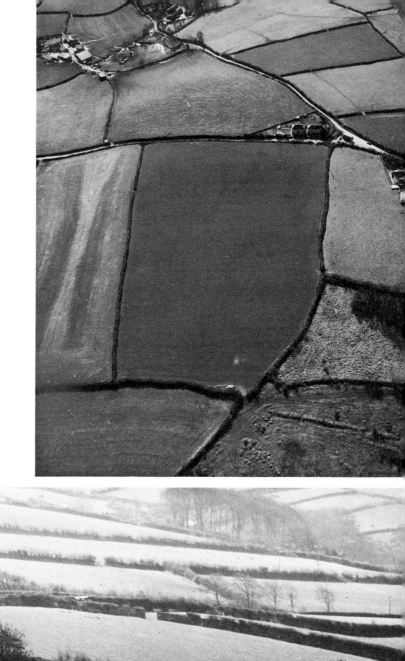

find gews to the east of the parcs. The pattern could date from the Iron Age or possibly from the Bronze Age, for Late Bronze Age farmers, from about 900BC, used the same arrangement of fields.

If the pattern of fields encloses an ancient farmstead, then it would be a help to locate the farmstead, especially since the fields concerned lie a little low for such early settlements. Drawing a kind of 'best fit' curve along the boundaries of three layers of fields shows that the arcs they describe are very nearly parallel to one another, the fields in the outer layer being much larger than those closer to the centre of the circle. The circle that would complete the arcs would be very large indeed, but enclosed by the triple arc, and not far from its centre even today—at one time the arc may have stretched further—lies the modern farmstead, which is known to have existed at least for 900 years, and its well.

The well is important, and most assuredly ancient. Strictly speaking, it is not a well at all today, but a natural spring bubbling up at the surface. Tradition holds that there used to be a chapel above it, so that the water would have filled a chamber with access through the floor of the building, making it a true well. Springs and wells were always mysterious and magical to our remote ancestors and most of them acquired a god, or at the very least a demigod, to care for them and those who used them. Later these divinities were absorbed into Christianity along with the legends and shrines associated with them and, in Cornwall, most of them were given the name of a saint. This well, or spring, has no saint of its own, although it is more than likely that some old god lurks nearby. It is called, simply, a 'Holy Well'. It missed acquiring a saint. The great age of the Cornish saints was from 450 to 550AD, when evangelising holy men and women arrived from Ireland and Wales, established themselves in spots where they could achieve some measure of self-sufficiency, and devoted their lives to religious observances, contemplation, and preaching. The seeker after self-sufficiency is likely to favour a location close to a dependable supply of potable water and so it is reasonable to suppose that these holy persons settled themselves close to springs. This is how many of their names came to linger on, for the local Celts acclaimed them as saints. These Cornish saints were not made in Rome, but on the spot, and hundreds of them are immortalized in peculiarly Cornish place names, like St Jidgey, St Kew, St Eval, St Mawgan (who was obviously Welsh), St Just, St Blazey, St Buryan and all the rest, including the more famous St Austell and St Ives. If a well has no saint associated with it, this may be because the well did not exist during the fifth and sixth centuries, which is unlikely, or because it was already a very holy place. In fact, this holy well may be one of the oldest Christian sites in Cornwall, and already ancient when it became Christianised.

The Cornish historian, the Rev Richard Polwhele (1760–1838), described it as 'sacred before the saints' and the Misses M. and L. Quiller-Couch, who visited it in the late nineteenth century, confirmed this opinion. Their book (*Ancient Holy Wells of Cornwall*, published by Charles J. Clark) appeared in 1894 and in it they reported that about thirty-five years earlier, say around 1859, there was a corner still standing of what had been the chapel. By the mid-1870s it had fallen and the site looked like a graveyard because of the stones that lay everywhere, all covered in lichens and mosses. Until about 1855 the water from the well was used locally for baptisms. According to the Misses Quiller-Couch, one by one the stones were removed and used in buildings on the farm, but with their carved faces turned against other stones to disguise them, as though the farmer felt a little uneasy at committing what might be sacrilege. Today the spring is situated in a depression, below the level of the surrounding ground. The Rev A. Lane-Davies, in *Holy Wells of Cornwall*, published by the Federation of Old Cornwall Societies in 1970, quotes Mr T. Quiller-Couch, who reported that 'a plot of ground 80 feet long and 42 feet broad is walled up to the height of the top of the well on which according to tradition there was a church or chapel', and he also quotes an earlier historian as saying that 'this venerable well is walled in and arched over with moor-stone, exhibiting some ruins which according to tradition belonged to an ancient chapel'. Today the site is overgrown and wet. No stones are visible at the surface, but the well itself still flows inside its chamber of moor-stone, which is just high enough for me to stand in with head suitably bowed. Its walls support a community of plants that like wet, dark places.

There is no reason to suppose that the chapel did not exist and the present farmhouse incorporates some stones that may have come from it. If the chapel did exist, it must have been the first of the churches in or near the village. Today there are two churches, the Church of England parish church and a Methodist chapel, but there was an earlier church on the site of what later became a castle, and the chapel above the holy well was older than any of them.

During Roman times the area may have been relatively peaceful. The Roman army built a camp about six miles from Cross Park, at Nanstallon, and occupied it for 20 to 25 years. Probably they wished to supervise the many native hill forts in the area, and their departure after what was, for them, a fairly short stay, suggests that the natives may have been friendly.

The first visitor from the Mediterranean to Cornish shores was not Roman, though, but Greek. Pytheas of Massalia (Marseilles) lived about 300BC and became a famous explorer and geographer. He may have been the first traveller to notice that the length of day, and the ratio of the length of the hand of a sundial and its shadow, change as you move north or south. Later navigators used this observation to calculate latitude. He noticed that the Pole Star does not mark the true North Pole, and that the Moon affects tides. In other things, though, he was absurdly gullible, believing far too readily whatever he was told, and his estimates of distances were often wildly inaccurate. He was a keen, and probably accurate, observer of local customs, and he described the people of Cornwall. His principal work, called *On the Oceans*, was lost and although later authors quote from it and cite it, it is difficult to imagine what it may have been like, except that it described his travels in the north. All that remains of his own writing is a fragment of a second book, apparently written as a sequel to the earlier one, in which he described the coasts of the Mediterranean. He is quoted by later authors as saying of Cornwall: 'A stormy strait separates the shores of Britain, which the Dumnonii hold, from the Silurian island. This people still retain their ancient customs; they refuse to accept coin and insist on barter, preferring to exchange necessities rather than fix prices'. The Silures were a tribe living in the eastern part of South Wales. This account was probably written about 330BC and it shows that the Cornish were trading, but that they were less advanced than the peoples of southern Europe, who were using money by that time. It also shows that the Dumnonii were occupying south-west Britain, just as they continued to do during Roman times.

In the first century AD, Diodorus Siculus, a Roman, described the inhabitants of Land's End (Belerion) as being 'very fond of strangers, and from their intercourse with foreign merchants, are civilised in their manner of life'. These people were tinners, streaming tin, smelting it, and making it into ingots, called 'astragali', shaped so they could be carried conveniently by pack animals. The astragali were taken to Ictis, which we call St Michael's Mount, from where they were exported.

Of course, it is a long way from Cross Park to Belerion, but metal working was practised closer to home and it continued, off and on, throughout history, subject to the vagaries of the market. As recently as the seventeenth century tin was being smelted not far away. According to a survey conducted in 1650, a man called Peter Hawke, who lived at Saltash, was the supervisor of four blowing houses. One of them was at St Nyott (modern St Neot) and not far from it there was a blowing house in the same parish as Cross Park, at Nuland Praze, which should have come under Mr Hawke's jurisdiction. A survey showed it to be in operation in 1659, but there is no entry for it in the coinage books for 1660, so it may have ceased to function in that year. Blowing houses were buildings in which tin was melted from the natural black ore to the white metal.

If you stand in the field, quite still, and wait, a sense of its age comes over you. Look to the north and the unreclaimed moorland rises bleak and forbidding. Look south and you see the deep valley, the patches of woodland, the fields on the other side, and it seems as though nothing has changed for many centuries, or could change. No doubt the field was once covered by moor-stone, just as the moorland next to it is now. The stones must have been shifted by men and their draught animals —more likely oxen than horses—and used to build the enclosing wall that became the hedge. Today the soil is deep and tan coloured, suggesting that the field lies precisely on the edge of the granite boss. The moor soil on the other side of the gate is wet and black, a mixture of stone peat and water that supports heathland vegetation dominated by the gorse that is called 'furze' in Cornwall and that grows everywhere. The gorse, though, is an immigrant, like the people.

Three species of gorse are found in Britain. *Ulex europaeus europaeus* is the familiar furze of the west that flowers in winter and spring, but that

Beyond Cross Park lies the unreclaimed moor, its surface still dotted with the moor-stone described by John Norden and, in the background, a disused quarry

often displays a few of its cheerful, bright yellow flowers throughout the year. *U. gallii*, the dwarf furze of north-west Britain, and *U. minor*, another dwarf species found mainly in the south-east, are much less common. Was the European gorse introduced with the Normans, along with the rabbit, or by the Romans, or did those invading Celts bring it with them much longer ago? After all this time, who knows?

It is a plant that has its uses. I have seen horses eating it when nothing else was available, and cattle and sheep will dine on its tender young shoots when the grass is poor. Farmers used to harvest it to make great furze ricks, storing the dry gorse for use as fuel and bedding for animals, and you can even harrow with it if it is suitably weighted before being dragged over the land. It is pollinated by insects, especially the bumble bee. There are one or two gorse flowers in the hedge, stragglers from last year, still ready to attract the first of the flying insects.

It is a place where legend blends into myth. The Cornish version of the King Arthur myths are based on this region. It is a little more than five miles from Cross Park to Dozmary Pool, the moorland tarn that mystified our ancestors by maintaining a constant water level through the most severe drought without the help of any inflowing surface streams, although there is one small stream that flows away from it. This, so they say, is the lake into which the magical sword Excalibur was thrown, and it is believed to be bottomless. In fact it is shallow, like most tarns, nowhere exceeding a few feet in depth. Camelot is supposed to have been located in the valley of the nearby River Camel. That is myth and if King Arthur existed at all as an historical personage there are several other parts of Britain with a more substantial claim to him. It may be that the Arthurian stories are medieval embellishments of tales of the wars that lasted for many years in places where Celt and Saxon found themselves in confrontation and stalemated. This was such a place and there must have been many skirmishes and battles, countless atrocities, and many incidents of heroism and generosity that might have inspired those who heard of them with fear or admiration. The old tales would have been told and re-told on dark winter nights, morals drawn from them for the edification of the young, and people must have marvelled and, perhaps, pined for the lost days when heroes were heroes, villains were villains, and life was simple.

King Mark certainly existed. Mark is a corruption of his Latin name, Marcus, but he was also known as Cunomorus. It was his child bride, Iseult, who was brought to Cornwall from Ireland by Tristram, who was, according to the story, the nephew of Mark. While on the boat both the bride and her escort drank accidentally of the love potion prepared for King Mark and Iseult by her mother. They fell in love, fled from the king but were recaptured. Eventually peace was restored but the price of peace was the departure of Tristram for Britanny, where he married another Iseult, whom he did not love. He was wounded by a poisoned weapon and lay dying, the original Iseult being the only person who could save his life. He sent a message to her, instructing those who brought the reply to raise a white sail on their ship if they were returning with Iseult, and a black sail if they travelled without her. Iseult made the journey, but Tristram's jealous wife told him that the ship bore a black sail, and Tristram gave up the struggle, dying before Iseult could reach him. Finding him dead, Iseult threw herself upon his body, embraced him, and died. They were buried side by side, in two graves, and from the graves there grew two trees whose limbs became so intertwined that they could not be separated. It is one of the most famous of all stories of tragic love.

Rather less than ten miles to the south of Cross Park there is the site of an Iron Age camp, called Castle Dore. It was deserted throughout the Roman period, but in the sixth century AD it was rebuilt as a wooden palace within the older defences. It is possible that this was the palace of King Mark, who is known to have ruled this part of Cornwall at about that time. An inscribed stone was found there, dated as mid-sixth century. The inscription reads: '*Drustaus* [or possibly Drustanus] *hic iacit Cunomori filius*', 'Here lies Drustaus [or Drustanus] son of Cunomorus'. Cunomorus is believed to be Marcus, or Mark, and Drustaus is believed to be Tristram, so that the final reading of the inscription is: 'Here lies Tristram son of Mark'. The legend holds that Tristram was the nephew of Mark, not his son, but the stone is intriguing, to say the least. It is called the Castle Dore, or Tristram, stone, and predictably it was moved. Today it stands at a road junction about 1½ miles from its original site.

Mark was not the only Cornish king who ruled from near Cross Park. About five miles to the east, at St Cleer, there is another inscribed stone. This one reads: *Doniert Rogavit pro Anima*, 'Doniert ordered this for his soul'. Doniert was Dumgarth, a chieftain or king of the Cornish who died in a drowning accident in 878AD. He was probably the last Cornish king of these parts. The Saxons had already conquered the kings of East Cornwall, in 838AD, so Dumgarth must have had a Saxon successor. It is likely that Cornish kings continued to rule further west, where the Saxon penetration had not reached. King Ricatus is believed to have been one western king who ruled later than Dumgarth. Even so, the conquest was completed, more or less, by about 940, and it was during the reign of Athelstan that the county was given its modern name, originally 'Cornewalas', from the Saxon word 'wealos', which means 'strangers'. The 'Corn' may come from the Latin *cornu*, meaning horn referring to the shape of the peninsula. That was when the region was divided into hundreds and parishes were formed. The first diocese, with Bishop Conan seated at St Germans, was instituted in 931, and the Cornish, who had been Christian for centuries, were brought from their Celtic church into the expanding Catholic church, unified and governed from Rome.

I located the Cross Park cross, and unravelled a little of its history. Some years ago, men from the neighbouring farm were laying new drainage pipes by the crossroads in the village when they found the cross, which had been laid over a small stream to enable travellers to pass. It had become buried below the surface of the road, but the installation of piped drainage meant it was no longer needed and so it was removed, not to its original field, but to the farm of the workers who found it, where today it stands in an orchard, just visible from the road if you know where to look. It is inscribed 'I.B.', the 'I' in this case being the antique form of 'J', which means that the inscription must have been made not later than the seventeenth century, for by that time 'J' was becoming fully established as a letter of the alphabet in its own right.

The hedges were a tangle of woody plants through which the smaller plants had not yet appeared. There was oak, holly, thorn and bramble as well as gorse, and dense mats of ivy. The foxgloves were green but had not yet produced new stems: they looked like large primrose plants. The polypody was there, too, a fern that is common in damp places throughout the northern hemisphere. It is an insignificant plant that you might pass by a thousand times with never a thought for it. The species deserves more respect, for of all the things here, except the rocks themselves, it is one of the most ancient. Its direct ancestors flourished long before the appearance of flowering plants. Lacking the ability to produce flowers, it developed a most complicated method of reproduction involving two generations, only one of which is sexual.

The familiar fern plant is recognised by its fronds, which are true leaves growing from a stem that in most species, including the polypody, lies below ground. The fronds begin as croziers, tightly coiled and hairy, which open as fully formed leaves. Late in the year the undersides of the leaves bear what at first look like pimples and then like dark spots. These are the 'sori', or fruiting spots, and each one consists of many individual structures, called 'sporangia', more or less fused together. These dry in the summer sunshine and as they do

A frond of polypody, its 'sori' arranged in neat patterns. Different ferns use different patterns, but all of them are very regular

so their cells first contract, then suddenly and violently expand to their original size. This tears apart each sporangium and ejects from it the spores it contains.

The spores are carried by the wind and those fortunate enough to land in a warm, moist place begin to grow. They grow into gametophytes, small plants that lie on the surface and are eventually just about large enough to see with the naked eye. They are complete, and while there are some primitive ferns that produce large gametophytes that cannot feed themselves without the assistance of a myccorhizal fungus, which extracts nutrients from decaying matter for the benefit of its host, most gametophytes are independent. They have chlorophyll so they can synthesise sugars, and they obtain mineral nutrients from the soil by means of fine, hair-like cells called 'rhizoids'. On its underside the gametophyte bears male and female sexual organs, the antheridia which produce sperms and the archegonia which produce eggs. When these are mature, just a little water from the soil is enough to make the antheridia discharge their sperms, which swim toward the eggs in the archegonia, which open to form tubes to receive them. Where sperm and egg fuse a new, asexual plant begins to grow. This becomes the sporophyte, the familiar fern plant which produces the spores, and the gametophyte shrivels and dies, its contribution to the continuation of the species complete.

Because the sperms must swim to the eggs, ferns can never move very far from water. You will not find them in dry deserts, but a moist soil is enough for them. Our coal seams are made from the remains of plants very like the humble polypody, and they were old even in the days of the Carboniferous swamps they liked so well.

Like all Cornish hedges, Cross Park's are very wide because of the thickness of their stone core, and they offer shelter to many species. Later they would provide nesting sites for many songbirds, but there was little bird life so early in the year. On 11 February I saw a flock of lapwings in the next field to the south; lapwings are not a common sight in this part of the country. I saw a magpie resting on top of the hedge on the south-eastern side of the field, and its relatives, the rooks, were never far away, but the small migratory birds had not yet arrived and the native birds had retired wisely to the greater comfort of lower altitudes. There were a few great tits at the top end of the field, next to the Moor: I saw four of them, but I saw them only once. Not even they were nesting yet.

As I walked the field looking for signs of life, I found signs of death. In the top centre of the field I came across the remains of what had been a skull. It was small, and had once belonged to an undersized rabbit, probably a young one. There were no other bones near it and it may have lain on the ground for some time, although I had not seen it on earlier visits. A more interesting skeleton lay close to the gate on the lower edge of the field, partly hidden among the long grass. It appeared to be complete, and was of an animal two to three feet long. Since no part of it had been removed or displaced, the animal must have died from natural causes. The skeleton fell to pieces as soon as it was touched. The skull and jawbones, which I retrieved along with several teeth, belonged to a carnivore that had large forward-looking eyes, most probably a very large domestic or feral cat.

There were signs of life, though, and plenty of them. I counted the burrows in the hedgebanks before the vegetation grew to hide them. In the long hedge that forms the north-western boundary of the field I counted twenty burrows, and four scrapes where burrowing had been commenced and then abandoned. Some of the burrows were large and still in use, others older and possibly deserted.

Beside the hedge, close in, there is a much used track where the grass does not grow. A similar track runs beside the hedge on the opposite, south-eastern, side of the field. Along the top north-eastern hedge I counted nine burrow entrances, and on the south-eastern hedge seventeen more. There were none along the lower edge of the field, where the hedge is low and there is a wide belt of uncultivated ground full of long grass.

There were many droppings, some of them quite fresh. The sheep left some, of course, and the rabbits contributed more, moving further into the field as the month progressed, but there were other droppings that were too large for rabbits, too small for sheep, and were probably left by hares. There were others, too, left repeatedly during the month on or close to the hedge-side tracks, that were too large even for hares.

The hedges are used as highways and they carry considerable traffic. The stone core makes a Cornish hedge impenetrable. Rabbits and other small burrowers cannot tunnel through it, so if they wish to cross into the next field they must go round and through the gate, or over the top. Many go over the top, sometimes travelling along the relatively flat top of the bank so that a small path is formed with many slides down the bank.

The very small animals were stirring. There were a few tiny burrows at ground level, and tunnels behind mats of long grass where bank voles and other small creatures ran. The first of the invertebrates put in an appearance, too. In one or two places there were quick scurryings from creatures that escaped before I could see them clearly, and beside the south-eastern hedge the remains of a snailshell had been left, probably by a song thrush.

There was not much human activity, though. On the lower ground and in the valleys farmers were manuring their grassland by the end of the month, but up at Cross Park manuring is done a little later. For the moment the field was left, waiting for the ground to warm and dry. while the wild things had it to themselves.

It makes a lot of difference, these 600ft, and conditions are harder than at lower levels. Not that life has ever been easy, though it is easier now than at any time in the past and the people are healthier. A little more than a century ago, but at this time of year, there was a severe outbreak of smallpox not far away in Bodmin. A report in the *West Briton* of 11 February 1853 complained that money spent to vaccinate the children of Bodmin had not been used properly and that half of those at risk had not been treated. 'The small pox is now raging,' said the reporter, 'the corpses of four children were in one and the same funeral procession here on Saturday last'.

Life has never been easy for the poor, but they have remained in continuous occupation here as empires have risen and fallen, as the centuries have come and gone. They were here about 5,000 years ago and I dare say they will still be here 5,000 years from now. And spring has come.

March

If you stand in Cross Park with your back to the Moor and look down over the deep valley, to the right of the church but just to the left of the little airfield where the flying club members can just be picked out as they move to and from their small monoplanes, you will see some high ground. It is about a mile away, rather bare and treeless. According to one version of the story, if you had stood in the field and looked across that way on a day in early March, 1646, you would have seen played out on that piece of downland one of the last dramas of the Civil War. At least, it marked the end of the war in these parts. The other version of the story holds that the drama took place further to the south, over behind the village church. In either case it may well have been visible from Cross Park.

The Cornish were staunchly Royalist throughout the war, even when it must have been obvious that the King was in a hopeless position. There were three important Royalist centres, at Launceston, Truro and Bodmin. The Cornish formed military committees to co-ordinate the war effort in 1642 and they did not disband them until the Restoration, in 1660. They fought with everything they had, and especially with the geography of the peninsula, which was difficult to invade in those days.

The King appreciated the loyalty of the Cornish, although there was little he could do for them. He sent a letter that he directed should be read in every church and chapel. It is a rather touching document. He thanked the people for their support of his cause at a time when there was little he could do for them. He could promise them no reward, he said, and he appreciated that their support for him brought them into great danger. The letter was written at his camp at Sudeley Castle on 10 September, 1643. Six years later he was dead. The letter survives. It was painted on a board and is displayed above the north door in the village church where, presumably, it has hung since the Restoration.

There was a good deal of fighting around Bodmin but it fell eventually, early in 1646. General Fairfax and his Parliamentary troops had closed the passes over the River Camel at Wadebridge and held the bridge, and he placed guards near Lostwithiel to prevent the escape of the Royalist horse to the west. On 25 February he advanced into Launceston and by 2 March he was very close to Bodmin. That was when the Royalist leaders and notables left, travelling down to Land's End. At ten o'clock that night they embarked for Scilly, with such wealth and possessions as they could carry with them. Piracy was a well established local industry by that time, and, despite their fervent Royalist sympathies, the seamen robbed their passengers, rather like the scorpion who stung the frog that was conveying him across an otherwise impassable river.

General Fairfax's troops were also advancing from the north. They crossed the Tamar and reached Stratton, a more important town in those days than its neighbour Bude. That was on 24 February, following a battle in which the Royalist Major-General Webb was defeated. When the news of this defeat reached the Royalist

This aerial photograph shows clearly the way the field boundaries to the west of Cross Park form three concentric arcs. The dark lines on the moorland above the field look as though they may be the boundaries of old and now abandoned fields

commander-in-chief, Sir Ralph Hopton, who was at Camelford to the south, he sent Sir Thomas Bassett from Launceston to Lostwithiel with 500 horse and the two regiments of Cornish Trained Bands that remained to him, led by Sir Charles Trevanion and Colonel Edgcumbe. Then he occupied Bodmin himself with some of the horse and some broken regiments of foot. That was when he placed 400 horse on the downs near Cross Park to watch the road for General Fairfax's advance.

There was no battle. The people had endured years of war and were heartily sick of it. Perhaps they could have been induced to fight had they feared the consequences of defeat, but General Fairfax was gaining a reputation for leniency, not to say generosity toward his foes. When he captured Launceston he released the prisoners from the castle, gave each of them a shilling and a pass to take him home, and so made sure that stories of his treatment of prisoners advanced before him. He gave orders that the Cornish were to be treated kindly, and they were. His popularity grew and so did that of his well-behaved troops, until at last the Cornish people turned against the defeated and bankrupt Royalists and welcomed the Parliamentarians. That was the end of the war so far as the Bodmin area was concerned. It all happened just 333 years ago, almost to the day, and much of it almost within sight of the field.

Cornwall was a wild, remote place in those days, Then as now there were only three main roads into the county, and the minor roads were few and poorly maintained. In the seventeenth century you could enter Cornwall by crossing the Tamar at Polston Bridge, then climb the hill into Launceston and continue across Bodmin Moor to Camelford and from there to Padstow and Truro. The second road entered at Newbridge, passed through Liskeard, Lostwithiel and Grampound, whose name is a corruption of the Norman French *grand pont* meaning 'large bridge', and joined the northern road at Truro. The third route followed the south coast, crossing the Tamar at Plymouth, by ferry, and going through Looe to Fowey, St Austell and Tregony and from there to Penzance and Land's End. These roads were linked to one another by unmade tracks and many journeys must have involved travelling cross-country.

Much more of the high ground was being farmed at the time of the Civil War than had been farmed during the Middle Ages, and some of it was growing cereals. Cornwall exported cereals in the early seventeenth century, most of it rye. No one grows rye here these days, except occasionally to feed cattle. It is a good crop that thrives on land too poor for wheat or even barley. It can be grazed green and then allowed to grow on for its grain and straw. It will tolerate acid soils and it positively dislikes very fertile conditions and wet, heavy land. It has extensive roots that help it survive droughts and its roots help to stabilise light soils that might otherwise erode, so that sometimes it is grown for that reason. It is generally grown on sandy soils. Its grain has as much protein as barley or wheat, but it lacks gluten and so rye bread is heavy but highly nutritious. Sometimes rye is grown just for its straw: it yields about two-and-a-half times more straw than grain by weight and the straw is long and tough, with virtually no nutritional value, so it can be used as bedding for animals without any fear that they will eat it. The straw also makes good thatch. If you do not care for rye bread, the grain can be made into rye whisky or gin, and rye starch makes a useful glue. Maybe it will come back into favour again one day and we will grow more than the 15,000 acres that is all the rye we grow today in the whole of Britain.

Rye is said to be the most recent cereal to be cultivated. In Roman times it was a novelty crop, but very likely it began life as a weed in wheat that became so persistent that farmers gave up the wheat and took to harvesting the rye instead. At all events it was fashionable enough in Cornwall in the days when local farmers sent their grain to make dark, heavy bread for up-country folk.

It was not love of farming that led to the cultivation of the uplands, but the failure of mining. Today there is a tradition that Cornish workers devote part of their time to mining, part to farming and part to fishing. The tradition may have originated in Tudor times, when incomes from mining declined badly and many tinners took to agriculture in order to survive. They were forced to work the uplands because only there could they find vacant land of any kind. Hard work it was, too. The stones had to be cleared from the surface and made into walls, the existing moorland vegetation had to be removed, and the soil had to be made fertile. Some carted up tons of sea sand and spread it on their fields. Others burned off the vegetation. Some enthusiasts did both. It worked, and the miners survived. John Norden saw it all in the late sixteenth century:

> . . . yet is the soyle of the Countrye for the moste parte but meane, especially in the middle parte, a greate parte wherof mountanous, moarish, and craggie, which beyng yet husbanded, as the Countrye lately hath taken Course, by burning their grounde and by soyling it with sea sande it becometh verie profitable, especially for Rye . . .

Some of it seemed even prosperous. Norden described the parish bordering the one that contains Cross Park:

. . . a parishe standinge nere the Moares and craggie hills, yet are there pastures within the parishe that will keepe fatt oxen all the wynter, and in as good case as in some places they can be kepte with haye; and the soyle beareth as good corne: As *Dauid* sayth, *A handfull of Corne shalbe sowne in the earthe, euen in the tops of the mountaynes, and the frute therof shall shake like the mountaynes of Libanon:* So doth God blesse the earth, not for their merite that dwell therin, but that his name mighte be glorified therin.

There were some quite practical advantages, too, for he continues:

This parishe is a libertye, wher the Shirifes Baylye can not areste, or otherwise entermedle without the lisence of the Lorde of the Mannor or his officer.
These days the Shirife and his doughty Baylyes entermedle at will and nary a lisence is to be seen. Oh for the good old days! The pastures still keep cattle through the winter, but it is difficult to reconcile the frute shaking like those alarming mountaynes of Libanon with the picture of modern farmers chewing their nails over the monthly milk cheque and the green pound. Perhaps they are different people. Perhaps it is a different world. Perhaps the farmers are terrified of the visit from the Baylye. It is quite likely.

The mining has always had its ups and downs. Most of the good ores are worked out now, but when world prices rise poorer grades become practicable mining propositions and there is talk of mines opening again. Usually world prices fall again either just before the mines reopen, or just after, and bankrupt someone. The battle to keep Wheal Jane and Mount Wellington working was fought hard and long. In the end Mount Wellington closed but they managed to keep its pumps working so that water from the flooded galleries did not seep through to flood Wheal Jane. Today the campaign is directed toward saving Wheal Jane, and the jobs of the miners who work in it. The story is an old one, as old as the mines are deep and their galleries long. Not so long ago, before they invented lifts, the miners used to climb all the way down, hand over hand, and at the end of twelve hours spent beating the solid rock with picks and hammers they climbed all the way back up again. While elsewhere the coal miners complained of their working conditions, the Cornish mineral workers soldiered on stolidly under far worse conditions. It makes you wonder why it meant so much to them, and why it still does. Many emigrated to become tin and other mineral workers in far corners of the world, yet in those days a miner who was still alive past his thirty-fifth birthday was a freak.

These days it is china clay. You can see the kaolin lunar landscape from Cross Park, away to the south around St Austell, a place of grey and white mountains and gleaming plains, and of deep turquoise lakes. There are not many places in the world where you find china clay and still fewer where you find it as a primary deposit, to be mined where it forms. In America, for example, the china clay was moved by geological processes to form secondary deposits that can be scooped up by strip mining. The Cornish china clay is not like that. It increases in quantity and often in quality the deeper you go, because it is formed by the chemical decay of feldspar in the granite, working from below. It is a recent industry. There was not the slightest risk of General Fairfax leading his troops into a china claypit ambush because the material and its potential usefulness were not discovered until a century later. It was used to make porcelain, of course, in imitation of that made in, and called, China. That is why the material is called 'china' clay, or by its Chinese name, 'kaolin'. These days, though, most china clay is used in making paper. It is the gloss on the glossies and it is also a filler, filling up the tiny spaces between the cellulose fibres and making the paper whiter, more opaque, and generally better for printing. It is also used in making plastics and paints, and in medicines. Apart from the kaolin and morphine that has calmed many a queasy stomach, it is the inert material to which minute amounts of drugs are added to make pills. We swallow immense amounts of china clay. It does us no harm, which is sometimes more than can be said for the drugs it carries with it.

The landscape is original. They call it the Cornish Alps, which is something of an overstatement. There is a reason for its appearance. If you want to obtain china clay, the first thing to do is to remove all the topsoil and dump it somewhere. Then you dig a hole to expose the clay. You remove the clay with a jet of water from a thing like a water cannon that washes it out, then you pump the slurry away to a series of settling lagoons, where first the large grained sand settles and then, in later lagoons, the clay itself in finer and finer grades composed of smaller and smaller particles.

The trouble starts when your hole reaches more than a certain depth, because suddenly it becomes very expensive indeed to pump all that liquid up and down and to remove all the rocks and debris that stand between you and your fortune. When the customer starts to react to your rising prices by swallowing fewer pills it is time to up stakes, move a few hundred yards away, and start all over again. This means you must be rather careful where you dump all the rubbish, because there is a real risk you may have to move it all again later to get at the china clay that lies beneath. Nor can you put it back into the hole you just left, because there is high quality clay down there and you know perfectly well that next week or next year someone will invent a splendid new machine that will make it possible for you to open that pit again. So the china clay landscape covers a large area with its holes and

49

hills, and some of the holes are used to store the water that is used in such copious amounts.

The enterprise booms and there is a constant need to find new sites for tipping the waste. Early in March it was announced that the industry was looking for a further 1,000 acres by 1984, most of it for tipping, and most of it, probably, on land adjoining the existing workings. In years to come, the horizon you see from Cross Park may change a little. The days of the old conical tips have gone, though. Since the Aberfan disaster all waste tips have to be made in large steps, or lifts, each one levelled before the next is built in top of it, so that the mountains are giving way to ziggurats, stepped pyramids, each with three steps. They have to separate the wastes, too, so that sand and earth cannot be mixed, and they are reclaiming the sides of the tips. They seed them with grass, which is then grazed by Soay sheep. It is not very likely that the entire china clay landscape will become green —at least not in the foreseeable future—but little by little the landscape is changing. It is all very sensible, of course, and there is a whole long string of beneficial side effects; yet the old wastelands had a drama of their own. It would be sad to lose them.

Much closer than that, not quite two miles from Cross Park, this bit of Cornwall is rehearsing for the twenty-first century, with new uses for old rocks. They are planning to drill an exploratory hole through the overlying strata and into the granite that lies beneath in a search for a source of geothermal energy. It is only one of several test drillings that are being made in various parts of south-west Britain. There is no guarantee that it will succeed, but if it does Cross Park could find itself close to a power station, or even on the edge of an industrial estate, perhaps a century from now.

There are places in the world where water lies in great reservoirs not far beneath the surface, at very high temperatures and under great pressure. Sometimes it reaches the surface to spurt from the ground as geysers, or to seep out as hot springs and pools, or boiling mud. Elsewhere, and probably much more commonly, there is dry rock that is much hotter than the surrounding material. If you can find a reservoir of this hot rock and if you can shatter it to fragments so that water can percolate through it, then theoretically it should be possible to pump cold water down one hole and catch it when it spurts hot from another hole as a man-made geyser. It will not last forever, of course, because over the years the water will cool the rock, but it may be possible to go on obtaining hot water for a generation or so. The test drillings are paid for jointly by the Department of Energy and the Common Market, both of which are seeking alternatives to oil. This

50

new drilling will test a theory that hot rock contained beneath rock of a quite different kind may be hotter than hot rock that is part of a continuous mass whose upper levels are cold.

If hot water is obtained from this source, it will have to be used on the spot or it will go cold. It can be used as pre-heated water for a steam turbine generating station, or to heat buildings. There are some tricky problems to overcome, not the least of which is the probability that the emerging water will contain all sorts of dissolved salts acquired as it passes through the rocks, which will make it highly corrosive to most metals and, if it escapes, more than a little poisonous.

It was a wild month. There was a thaw at the end of February that seemed to me like the beginning of spring, but over most of the country to the north there were hard frosts almost every night, intermittent heavy snow, and cold winds. Farming came to a standstill. Spring sowing was impossible and in most places it was not possible even to cultivate. The crops sown in the autumn were suffering from the frost, yellowing as their leaves were killed. The oilseed rape, a crop that has become highly fashionable with farmers and popular with the government over the last few years, suffered not from the frost directly but from the pigeons that ate it as their other sources of food vanished beneath the snow. The grass on Cross Park grew hardly at all, but even so it fared better than many newly sown leys, which would have to be seeded again.

Lambing must have been affected. Many ewes were housed under cover and apparently the fall of early lambs was about average in the lowland flocks, but conditions were much harder in the uplands. There were not many lambs to be seen for most of the month, but by the end of it they were there, in the field across the road from Cross Park, suckling energetically and waggling their behinds in ecstasy as they did so.

There were gales, especially early in the month. On the night of the 8th and 9th it blew hard and rained, and it was still very windy on the 9th, a day of sunshine and showers, a March day. On the night of the 15th and 16th there was a slight frost and the 16th started cold, with sleet and the soft hail that meteorologists call 'graupel', a delightfully vague word that actually means 'sleet', although, depending on the context, the verb *graupeln*, in German, can mean to sleet, to hail, or to drizzle. Graupel looks like hail but splatters when it strikes the ground. Later on the 16th there was persistent, wet snow. It did not settle so far west as Cross Park, but in other parts of the country it did. The A30 was almost blocked near Exeter. The 17th was much warmer, and fine and sunny. The wintry weather returned, though, a few days later.

51

There was more graupel and sleet on the 21st and a moderate frost on the night of the 22nd and 23rd. On the 29th the gales returned to scour the ground beneath a sky the colour of Cornish slate.

By the end of the month people were saying that this was the worst winter since 1947, at least in the north of England and in parts of Scotland. By an odd coincidence, really bad winters always seem to begin in an even numbered year: 1940–41, 1946–47, 1962–63, and now 1978–79. In the north-east, the deep snow melted just as, on the 29th, the worst rainstorms for twenty years, driven by strong winds, added more water to cause floods up to 5ft deep in some places. In Newcastle, where they expect to receive about 1.9in of rain in the whole of March, they had 1.6in in one day. In County Durham they had 2in of rain in 24 hours, Chester-le-Street was under 4ft of water, and at Tynemouth the wind speed gusted to 70mph. This is number 11 on the Beaufort scale, a gale gusting to storm force, and very rarely experienced in Britain or even in British coastal waters. Elsewhere in the region the Newcastle Weather Centre reported gusts of 50 to 60mph, 9 to 10 on the Beaufort scale, and, technically, 'strong gale' to 'whole gale'. In North Wales waves were driven across sea fronts when a 32ft tide was backed by a gale. The winds and rainstorms were abating by the end of the day, and they did not return.

The plants began to identify themselves in Cross Park in the course of the month. There were daisies flowering in the field, although they were few and far between, and the chickweed was established firmly over most of the field. Perhaps it was taking advantage of the poor growth of grass and probably it was there all the time, but I noticed its tiny, delicate white flowers for the first time on the 13th. The sheep will appreciate it when and if they are allowed to graze it, and chickens enjoy eating it, which I suppose is how it got its name. People can eat it, too, or so they say. According to Richard Mabey, who is an authority on such matters, it used to be sold in the streets by itinerant vegetable sellers, to be eaten raw or, more usually, cooked like any other green vegetable. It is very small, though, and you would need to collect a great deal of it to make the harvest worthwhile.

The first gorse bush flowered at about that time, bringing a little gaiety to a cold, moderately windy morning. The north wind had cleared the mist that hung over the high ground at dawn and there was drizzle and rain, but the gorse added some colour. They say you can make a wine with gorse flowers if you can collect enough of them, but I have not tried it.

Buds were starting to appear, and where rabbits had disturbed the soil on the hedgebanks opportunist plants had produced cotyledons

The first gorse bush flowered during March

from seeds germinated in the first hint of warmth. Birds were beginning to sing and across the entrance to one burrow there was a brand new spider's web. There was one entirely new rabbit burrow and many small burrows. The small mammals were becoming very active.

Heavy snow is more help than hindrance to the small mammals of the hedgerows. It lies on top of the bracken, grass and brambles, leaving room beneath it for mice, voles and shrews to scurry back and forth unimpeded. It shelters the soil, too, so there is protection from all but the most severe frosts, and the food that lies on or near the ground is hidden from larger creatures. Pigeons, squirrels, and larger animals have to scratch or dig for food through the snow. The small mammals have been found breeding under such conditions. Bank voles and wood mice have been caught beneath the snow in mid-February and were in full breeding condition, although litters born during winter are smaller, so it seems that winter conditions affect the secretion of gonadotrophins.

There have been countless scientific studies of British small mammals, but there are still mysteries to be unravelled. No one is quite certain why they should breed in the middle of winter at all. Probably they will breed if they have plenty of food, but there is more to it than that. Lemmings will breed in winter, but they do not do so if their numbers are high or declining, and it is more than possible that bank voles and wood mice, too, breed only when some condition of their population is satisfied.

In March, when the new plant growth is appearing, the wood-mouse population is almost at its lowest, and continues to decline until late summer. That is something else that has puzzled scientists for a long time. Wood-mouse populations reach their peak in late autumn and early winter. They decline rapidly during mid- and late winter and more slowly through the spring, becoming more or less stable during summer, then start to increase again from July. During the spring, the animals no longer depend for food on the materials, principally acorns, left from the previous year. They eat insects and the young growing shoots of plants. They are breeding, too, so their numbers should be increasing.

What seems to happen is that the coming and going of migrants alters the numbers. In summer, wood mice live in colonies and they occupy a territory. Each colony is dominated by one or two males who can be kept happy by shows of submissiveness from their subordinates. These males keep out quite a lot of would-be immigrants to the territory. When adult males were removed from an experimental area, the number of immigrants increased, young mice and other subordinates survived better, and the autumn increase in numbers began much earlier than usual. Some immigrants arrive and stay, however, and during the late winter and early spring they begin to depart. They have never been accepted as members of the colony, and never can be, because like most animal societies those of mice are held together by very strong family bonds. All the members share genetic material and it is the genes that must survive rather than any individual. As the young are born, the males, and perhaps some of the females, too, behave aggressively toward them, treating them as though they were unwelcome immigrants. This aggression would reduce their rate of growth if they were to stay and most of them leave to find new territories and mates, and to found new colonies. Their departure and the high mortality among those that stay reduce the population, in which old adults are also dying, and the hostility that the males continue to show to intruders during the summer prevents the population from increasing again. By autumn, though, many of the old and most aggressive males have died, there is more food so that those young that have survived thus far are safe, and the new males are not yet sexually active, so they are not aggressive. Transient mice can enter the territory and so the population increases. A great deal depends on the number of active adults. If there are too few during the summer the entire social structure may break down and the territory be lost. Where there are many adults, the new generation is able to take over a firmly established territory.

The food supply in the late autumn is also important. The more food there is, the more mice there will be; but the more mice that survive the winter, the steeper will be the population decline later, and the longer it will be before the numbers start rising again. The result of all this is that the size of a population can vary widely in early spring but in most years it will be about the same in any given area by autumn.

The aggression has been observed in the laboratory, and it was found there that it can be quite severe but that not all adults are aggressive and some will tolerate young mice which then grow normally.

There is another curious fact, and one not confined to mice. When the food supply is low there are few animals. This sounds reasonable and you would expect the cause to be the starvation of many individuals. The animals that are found, however, are perfectly well fed and healthy. This makes it look as though the biggest and strongest animals take as much food as they need, leaving insufficient for the others, but the surviving, healthy animals are not especially large, even for mice. Probably what happens is that the large animals may be aggressive and strong, but they need relatively large amounts of food if they are to remain in good condition. If they cannot obtain enough food they will deteriorate, despite their strength and vigour. There are other animals, though, that are smaller and so need less food. They, too, are in good condition and as their large rivals become weaker they flourish, because they find it easier to obtain as much food as they need. Eventually it is the small, healthy individuals that outlive the big ones. The same phenomenon is seen in wood pigeons and in foxes. Small may or may not be beautiful, but it can be successful!

You could tell the small animals were active, because the hunters were at work. As I came down from the field back towards the village there were two buzzards floating on the air over a nearby field and a little way down the road from them I saw a third buzzard and a bird of which I caught only a silhouetted glimpse but that looked to me like a harrier. Seen so briefly against the light I could not tell which harrier, but any harrier is an unusual sight in this part of the world. Buzzards are common and I have seen them near Cross Park several times since that first encounter. They are protected by law, like all birds of prey, but they take enough poultry for them to be regarded as a nuisance.

They are spectacular birds, the largest birds of prey we see in regions where the eagles do not penetrate.

The rabbits were becoming very active and now and then you might see the back of a vole or mouse as it scampered away from you into the cover of the long grass. Badgers may well visit the field. On the 13th I saw a few footprints on the track beside the hedge on the south-east side of the field. It was difficult to find footprints at any time because frequent and often heavy showers throughout the month washed them out as soon as they were made, but those on the 13th were fairly definite, and made by large paws with three distinct toes pointing forward.

Badgers have a complex social life and each of their family groups, or 'clans', has a home range, sometimes quite a large one, in which members move around on their own. Hans Kruuk, a zoologist from Oxford University, spent many hours and recorded hundreds of observations of badgers foraging for food. The only ones he ever saw in groups were cubs less than six months old, sometimes with an adult female and sometimes without, and he never saw adults competing for food directly. They are very well organised. When two badgers meet inside the range of one of them, they seem to recognise one another as individuals or at least as members of the same clan, but if a badger meets a stranger from another sett in its range it attacks it at once. Recognition is mainly by scent. Like many nocturnal animals, eyesight is not very important to them and they do not see at all well. Every member of a clan bears a common scent and this is achieved by individuals within the clan pressing their anal region against the side or rump of one another whenever they meet. Presumably this leaves secretions from the scent glands around the anus or below the tail.

Badgers live together peaceably enough. Adults can take precedence over cubs and occasionally a large boar seems to dominate others, but this kind of dominance is not common, at least overtly. There is probably a hierarchy within the clan that is accepted by all its members. Their sleeping arrangements suggest this. The main sett is usually located in the most favourable place and main setts are distributed throughout an area according to some system of spacing. Hans Kruuk found that, in the area he studied, main setts were never less than 300 yards apart. There are several holes, or outlying setts, close to the main sett. The badgers spend the daytime sleeping in their holes and large adult boars are often found sleeping in the main sett while the females and young males spend much of their time, in summer at least, sleeping in the smaller outlying holes. The clan marks out its territory with its droppings which are deposited in the latrines that badgers make around the edges. The territory adjoins the territory of the neighbouring clan but does not overlap it. Within the clan territory each animal has a range, the females sometimes having exclusive ranges in which others do not forage, while the males have ranges that encompass those of the females. Unmated males, who live by themselves, have the smallest ranges. Kruuk measured them at just over 50 acres for a sett occupied only by 'bachelors', while other setts varied in size from 116 to 170 acres. Males from two adjoining and shared ranges covered about 250 acres in their search for food.

They are creatures of regular habits, patrolling their ranges by well worn tracks, and parts of the range that are some distance from the sett will be visited only every few nights, as though according to a rota. Cross Park may well lie within the range of badgers living on the Moor and several members of a clan may visit it. Their entrance may be through the large gap and slide in the eastern corner of the field. That was in regular use by some creature, but one that left no telltale strands of hair caught in the twigs by which it could be identified.

The first mole had moved into the field by the end of the month. There were two molehills close to the edge of the adjoining field to the south-east, and one by the wide headland on the south-western side of Cross Park, about at the centre. Ploughing destroys mole tunnels so that the entire network must be dug again. Now that at least one mole has entered Cross Park it will not be long before it has established itself with an elaborate network of tunnel traps that it will spend much of its time patrolling for the worms and insects that find their way into the labyrinth.

The local papers were carrying stories about efforts to save the oldest church building in Cornwall, St Piran's Oratory, at Perranporth, which is disappearing under the blown sand. Several Cornish churches have a habit of vanishing in this way and then reappearing centuries later when the sands shift again. The pretty little church of St Enodoc at Rock was buried for a long time. Funds were being raised to dig out the Oratory, and people were suggesting that while they were about it they might as well excavate the entire site, which is believed to conceal a complex of monastic buildings which date from about the tenth century.

Our village church, the one with the letter from Charles I displayed in it, is much more recent, but very fine. Many Cornish churches are dedicated to obscure saints, but none can rival this one. He is not even listed in the book of Cornish saints and no one seems to know anything about him. His name was Meubred, or in its latinized version Meubredus, and sometimes he is called St Meubredus Martyr. There is no other church dedicated to him, but there is said to be a picture of him in the window of a church a few miles away. The story told of him in the fifteenth century was that he was the son of an Irish king who lived nearly a thousand years earlier and that his body lay in what was then the chapel on the site of the modern church.

Certainly people were living here in the fifth and sixth centuries when the Cornish saints were evangelising. There are several inscribed stones from that period in the parish. The name of the village is derived from two Celtic words meaning 'fortified camp'.

The chapel or oratory built in the time of the saint survived and no doubt it was enlarged to become a church, which the Normans took over as part of the castle that the first lord, Richard Fitz Turold, built. He and his heirs continued to live in the castle until the fourteenth century. After that it fell into disrepair and nothing remains of it today. Richard Fitz Turold also acquired another chapel about a mile away, deep in the valley, called Lady Vale Chapel. He tried to give this to the Abbey of St Mary de Valle, near Bayeux, intending that a cell of monks should live on his land. The Abbey considered the offer and found it not worth the cost of maintenance and so they persuaded Fitz Turold to force it upon the Monastery of Tywardreath, which he was also busy founding. So it became the Chapel of the Monks of Val, served by the Priory of Tywardreath. At the Reformation it was nationalised and passed into the possession of the Duchy of Cornwall.

The chapel of St Meubred lasted until the late fifteenth century. In the reign of Henry VII it was demolished completely and rebuilt, and it is this fifteenth-century church that serves the parish today, together with the Methodist chapel beside the village school. The older building has contributed bits to the new, in the Easter Sepulchre, the font, and as isolated stones, but the new building has been preserved very well, mainly because it has been restored whenever the need arose, rather than improved or modernised. In fact in 1822 the then rector, Thomas Grylls, refused to comply with an order from the rural dean to have the roofs tunnelled in plaster, on account of the woodwork being, in his words, 'handsomely furnished'. The church is built largely of granite, its square tower being constructed in three stages with set-back buttresses. It has eight bells, five of which were re-cast and three added in 1895 by the Rev Athelstan Coode, and a chiming clock was added to the tower as a World War I memorial. The list of rectors goes back to 1271. During World War II the church came close to being demolished when a jettisoned bomb exploded against the wall beside the road. It destroyed the windows in the chancel and these were replaced by some good modern stained glass.

April

When you look at a field of grass, the chances are that what you will see will be simply a field of grass. That, after all, is what the farmer wants you to see, and what he wants to see himself. Really, though, it is not so simple.

We use the word 'grass' very casually, and we know what we mean, but to a botanist there is no such thing as 'grass'. There are 'grasses', if you like, members of the family Gramineae, or Poaceae if you went to a different school, and something like 5,000 species have been identified as members. We take them for granted because there are so many of them. About one-third of the land surface of the Earth is dominated by grasses, either actually or potentially, and the grasses comprise one of the largest families of flowering plants, a family that is of the greatest importance to man. Cross Park, which is one patch of green amidst many, is growing lamb and wool. At present it just happens to look like grass. The other patches round about are growing milk and beef, and they happen to look like grass, too. Pasture grasses are now an important crop, highly commercial and increasingly a product of advanced technologies.

Pasture grasses are only the start, of course. Wheat, barley, oats, rye, rice and sugar cane are also grasses. So is the common reed (*Phragmites communis*) that makes the finest of all thatch, and so is the bamboo you use to tie up climbing plants in the garden. Sedges, on the other hand, which look very like grasses, are not grasses, although they are close relatives. It is a bad mistake to underrate the grasses just because they are so commonplace.

We can all recognise a member of the family when we see it, at least in the sense that it is not very difficult to distinguish between a grass and, say, a tree or a flowering herb. All the grasses share certain features. They have erect, jointed, tubular stems that are either hollow and empty like cereal straws or pithy like sugar cane. The leaves are wrapped around the stem like sheaths, usually open on one side, and the blades bend away from the stem to form two ranks, arranged alternately first on one side and then on the other. There is often a small membranous organ called a 'ligule' at the point where the blade bends away from the stem.

Grasses produce flowers as small spikelets, arranged in groups. Many annual grasses are self-fertile, but the perennial species usually require cross-pollination. They rely on the wind to achieve this and, because they have no need of insects, grass flowers are small and undistinguished. Not for them are the bright colours and seductive perfumes of the herbs that grow among them, although hay fever victims may wish they were dependent on insects, for it is windborne grass pollens that cause their summer misery.

The importance of the grasses derives from their structure. All members of the family produce fibrous, branched and widely spreading root systems. In some species, if you were to dig up a single plant with all its roots intact and then lay the roots end to end, they would extend for several miles. Such elaborate root systems bind together particles of loose soil, helping to reduce soil erosion, and they penetrate heavy soils to help air and water to circulate through them.

Many species also produce horizontal stems. In some grasses these lie below the surface and are called 'rhizomes', and in others they lie along the surface and are called 'stolons'. In both cases the vertical stems that rise from nodes along the horizontal stems are no more than branches, and adventitious roots grow downward from the same nodes. Grasses with such horizontal stems can and do spread, and so they are often used to stabilise sand dunes. The species you are most likely to see around the British shores is marram grass (*Ammophila arenaria*), which produces a tough rhizome and which can withstand the very arid conditions of the sand dunes. Despite its strength, marram cannot compete against many other grasses that invade the land it has stabilised, so that as the dunes become covered with a layer of humus the marram is displaced by other species. It has not gone. It can remain dormant for years, and should the new vegetation die back the marram will re-emerge.

It sounds odd to describe the sea shore as 'arid', but the similarity between coastal sand dunes and those of the desert is not coincidence. Sand does not retain water and much of the water it receives comes from the sea and is salty. Salt water is worse than no water at all and everyone knows that if you drink sea water it will make you thirsty. This is because if two solutions of salts of different concentrations are separated by a semi-permeable membrane, such as the wall of a cell, pure water will cross the membrane from the weaker to the stronger solution until the two concentrations are equal. The process is called 'osmosis' and its effect is to drain water from living cells into any strongly saline solution to which they are exposed. Some plants and some grasses, including marram, use water very efficiently and can survive on a tiny amount. One of the ways they achieve this is by rolling their blades into tubes, with the stomata (by which water is transpired and lost by evaporation) on the inside, shielded from the drying sun and wind.

All of these characteristics make grasses useful, but one of them contains the real secret of their agricultural success. Because their main stems lie on or beneath the surface, and the vertical stems are only branches, if those branches are removed the plant simply grows a replacement. This means not simply that grasses can be cropped perpetually, but that within quite wide limits the more severely they are cropped the more vigorously they grow. They are improved by cropping, and since most of their competitors cannot withstand such treatment, repeated cropping encourages the grasses to dominate the habitat. You could say that we owe our way of life to that fact.

Cross Park is growing one of the ryegrasses. The long, cold winter delayed the crop's growth, so that during April it began to leap ahead for the first time, but by the end of the month the longest blades were only about three inches. The ryegrasses are members of the barley tribe, the Hordeae, as are wheat, rye and barley itself. They are native to northern Europe, although rather less common in the north and west of Scotland, and they grow wild on waste land, in hedgerows, and in old pastures in most places below about 2,500ft. Because it has been sown as a ley, meant to last for several years, the Cross Park grass is most probably perennial ryegrass (*Lolium perenne*). The most common alternatives, Italian (*L. multiflorum*) and *L. m. westerwoldia*, the Wester-wolds variety of Italian ryegrass, are annuals. This is not the native wild perennial ryegrass, of course, but a cultivated variety of it. If you are an expert you can identify the cultivar by the date it flowers.

It is an aggressive grass, which is another of its attractions. Once established it will suppress any wild grasses that attempt to compete with it. At the same time, it will tolerate white clover and certain other cultivated grasses. Modern pastures, though, consist of only one or two species of grasses rather than the countless number that used to make up the traditional meadow. This is because the farmer wants a crop that will grow evenly, so that all the plants in the field reach the peak of their condition together and can be cut to make hay or silage that is far more nutritious than the winter feed his grandfather made.

Many farmers sow perennial ryegrass in spring, but provided conditions are favourable late summer or autumn sowing can be successful and has the added advantage of supplying a protective cover of vegetation so the soil is not left exposed during the winter. The danger is that if the grass grows too tall before its first winter it may be damaged badly by very cold weather. The remedy to that problem is to allow the sheep to crop it before it comes to any harm. Apart from that, the varieties of perennial ryegrass that are native to Britain actually need cold weather. Like many plants, their production of flowers and seeds is governed by the length of daylight, but cold weather is needed to start the mechanism working. The plant will not believe it is spring unless it has experienced winter first. It will spread vegetatively without ever flowering, but in the wild it needs to seed in order to start new colonies elsewhere. If it does experience a winter, and the Cross Park grass can have been left in very little doubt, it will begin to form flowers as soon as the days are more than thirteen hours long.

It was still young, though, and there was room beneath it for other small plants to establish themselves, some of them opportunists that flower early in the hope of completing their reproductive cycle before the grass overwhelms them, some of them to live as ground-hugging survivors, like the plantains, and many to vanish, for it is not only for this year that they must endure the competition from the grass, but for several years.

A botanist friend, Barbara Garratt, walked the field with me on the 3rd. It was one of those cold, showery days that seemed to have displaced the Cornish spring, and for part of the time we bowed our heads not only to stare at the ground but also to shield ourselves ineptly from the sleet. The search was by no means exhaustive and since many of the woody species had not produced leaves, and few plants were in flower, identification was often tentative and the list full of gaps. All the same, Barbara found more than fifty species in the field and the hedges surrounding it.

In the field and on the inside of the hedges she found: brown bent grass (*Agrostis canina* spp. *canina*), false oat grass (*Arrhernatherum elatius*), daisy (*Beleis perennis*), shepherd's purse (*Capsella bursa-pastoris*), hairy bittercress (*Cardamine hirsuta*), mouse-ear chickweed (*Cerastium vulgatum*), pignut (*Conopodium majus*), hawthorn (*Crataegus monogyna*), cocksfoot grass (*Dactyllis glomerata*), foxglove (*Digitalis purpurea*), male fern (*Dryopteris filix-mas*), goosegrass (*Galium aparine*) which is also known as cleavers, hairif and sticky willie, hedge bedstraw (*Galium mollugo*), ground ivy (*Glechoma hederacea*), ivy (*Hedera helix*), cat's ear (*Hypochoeris radicata*), holly (*Ilex aquifolium*), nipplewort (*Lapsana communis*), field forget-me-not (*Myosotis arvensis*), annual meadow grass (*Poa annua*), polypody (*Polypodium vulgare*), blackthorn (*Prunus spinosa*), bracken (*Pteris aquilina*), oak (*Quercus robur*), creeping buttercup (*Ranunculus repens*), blackberry (*Rubus fruticosus*), common sorrel (*Rumex obtusifolius*), various willows (*Salix* spp.) that had not yet produced identifiable leaves, red campion (*Silenes dioica*), hedge mustard (*Sisymbrium officinale*), chickweed (*Stellaria media*), dandelion (*Taraxacum officinale*), Dutch clover (*Trifolium repens*), gorse (*Ulex europea*), navelwort (*Umbilicus rupestris*), ivy-leaved speedwell (*Veronica hederifolia*), common field speedwell (*Veronica persica*), and field pansy (*Viola arvensis*). On the outside of the hedge that runs beside the road on the lower edge of the field, Barbara found: yarrow (*Achillea millefolium*), black spleenwort (*Asplenium adiantum-nigrum*), hard fern (*Blechnum spicant*), broad shield fern (*Dryopteris dilatata*), bluebell (*Endymion non-scripta*), herb Robert (*Geranium robertianum*), hogweed (*Heracleum sphondyllium*), ribwort plantain (*Plantago lanceolata*), celandine (*Ranunculus ficaria*), greater stitchwort (*Stellaria holostea*), and common valerian (*Valeriana officinalis*).

By the end of the month the stinging nettles (*Urtica dioica*) were producing their first small, tender leaves in one or two places in the hedge on the south-eastern side of the field. I noticed them while walking the field with another naturalist, David Brewster. We discussed the possibility of dating the hedges, a subject that Barbara and I had raised earlier. It was something I had meant to do, but although a technique has been devised for the purpose, somewhat controversially, it is far from certain that it can be applied directly to Cornish hedges.

The technique was devised by Dr Max Hooper. He looked through local records to find the dates on which hedges had been planted and so accurately dated a large number of hedges. Then he examined his dated hedges to discover how many species of woody plants, such as trees and shrubs but excluding bramble, they contained. The result of this work was his discovery of an apparent correlation between the number of species in a hedge and its age. Allowing for a wide degree of variation, it made it possible to distinguish a Saxon hedge from a Tudor hedge, and both of these from a Victorian hedge, although it cannot be used to tell a Georgian hedge from a Victorian hedge because chronologically the two periods are too close to one another. To date a hedge you mark out a 30yd length of it and count the number of woody species. The more 30yd lengths you can examine, the better, because they can be averaged to give greater accuracy. Only one side of the hedge is used, and it is best to avoid the corners, especially if these adjoin woodland. Ninety-five times out of a hundred, a hedge with ten

The hedge bank is a tangle of brambles, woody plants and other vegetation that provides cover for the entrances to burrows. None of the vegetation was planted, and the amount and variety suggest that this is a very old hedge

species in each 30yd length will be between 800 and 1,150 years old, and this can be interpreted as a rule of thumb that says each species represents a century.

The technique sounds rather rough and ready, and so it may be in use, but there was nothing rough and ready about the way it was developed. The work was thorough and very detailed, and many factors were taken into account. Not all botanists accept it, but provided it is used as no more than a very approximate guide with an allowance of up to 200 years error on either side, it can be useful. The trouble is that it is based on studies of typical English hedges, which were planted. Cornish hedges were never planted; they were built as dry stone walls covered with turf or earth. As solid walls that are often 8 or 9ft tall, they are more than adequate for containing livestock and providing shelter. The farmer who builds them does not gild the lily by planting trees or shrubs in them. This means that any plants you find there arrived by themselves, as natural colonists of an essentially unpromising habitat. They would have become established only with difficulty, although once they were established they would have been protected from grazing animals by their position. David and I found six species in a 30yd length of the hedge on the north-western side, suggesting that this hedge is 600 years old. When you allow the 200 years either way for possible error, though, the date becomes 400 to 800 years old, which is a little vague to say the least! We both felt that the hedge is much older than this rough dating would indicate.

Be that as it may, the field was beginning to promise delights for later in the year. The blackthorn is a wild plum, whose fruit, the sloe, is quite inedible but makes a splendid wine, with a flavour distinct from that of wine made from cultivated plums. It is a difficult wine to clear, but only the most unforgiving of purists would condemn it on that account. I have never made sloe gin, which has always struck me as a slight cheat unless you also make the gin itself. The nettles were almost ready to pick. We have tried cooking nettles, but we never took to them. Perhaps they are an aquired taste, like dandelion leaves. I have never acquired that taste, either. Both plants have other uses, though. At one time they were cultivated. Wherever the Latin name for a plant contains the specific *officinalis* this identifies the species that used to be grown by the old herbalists. You can obtain a green dye from nettle leaves, a magenta dye from dandelion root, and if you can refrain from fermenting them, sloes yield a blue-purple dye. The tough stems of fully grown nettles can be made to yield a fibre, rather like hemp, and dandelion roots, cleaned, chopped, baked and ground up, make a substitute for coffee. Valerian has been used as a sedative since the tenth century, yarrow is edible (if bitter), and Richard Mabey says that shepherd's purse fetches a good price in Chinese vegetable markets if you happen to be passing that way. Common sorrel, known in Cornwall as 'green sauce', can be cooked in many ways, not the least of which is as the principal ingredient for a sauce that is eaten with fish. Pignuts used to be very popular until they were displaced by imported peanuts. Like peanuts, they are not really nuts at all, but tubers, and you dig for them. They can be eaten raw or roasted and salted, and they grow almost anywhere in Britain, except on the chalklands and in the fens, but there is a catch. The tale is told of an ecology student who dug up and ate three of what he thought were pignuts; in fact they were the sweet-tasting tubers of hemlock water dropwort (*Oenanthe crocata*). Happily, he recovered from the coma into which his snack plunged him. Both plants are umbellifers, members of the carrot family, as is hemlock itself. It is not especially difficult to distinguish one umbellifer from another, but unless you are quite confident about it perhaps it would be advisable to leave the pignuts in the ground and stick to peanuts.

The foxglove is no less poisonous. It is the natural source of digitalis, used to treat heart conditions, but on no account is it to be administered in self-medication! The difference between a therapeutic dose and a fatal one is very small. Its properties were first publicised by a Dr William Withering of Birmingham in 1785. He identified it as the active ingredient in a concoction that was used by an old woman of his aquaintance to treat dropsy. She, and Dr Withering, used it as a diuretic.

The field was beginning to emerge as a community. It is a community in which humans have long played a part, for it is not so very long since many wild plants were collected by country folk for food, flavouring, dyes, fibres or medicines. Wild plants played an important role in the rural economy and it is possible that some of them in fact escaped centuries ago from cultivation, like the daffodils that bloom by the roadside.

The animals were active, too, foraging among their expanding food source. Sometimes you could catch a glimpse of a vole disappearing into the cover, and the entrances to their burrows were clearly visible as neat, perfectly circular holes in the banks. Probably these are made by the bank vole (*Clethrionomys glareolus*), which is often above ground by day as well as by night. Its burrows are shallow, joined into a network, and there are usually many entrances. The field, or short-tailed, vole (*Microtus agrestis*) is rather more nocturnal and likely to be found further into the field. The two voles are similar in most respects, but they have adapted to different diets so they do not compete. The bank vole eats nuts, which it opens with some difficulty by gnawing untidily at the shells, as well as roots and a variety of fruits, but it cannot manage really tough, fibrous grasses. These are the speciality of the field vole, and wherever the grass is long and tussocky you are likely to find small tunnels through it, around the clumps. The field vole makes these, mainly by chewing its way along, and then continues to use them as pathways by which it can move about without exposing itself to predators. The field vole has very small ears, a tiny tail, is usually dark in colour, and has a habit of sitting on its haunches to eat. The bank vole has a longer tail, about half the length of its body, and is reddish in colour.

The voles share their habitat with the mice, and all these small animals are vulnerable to agricultural poisons. They are safe at Cross Park, because that is growing grass, but on fields sown to cereals they can find themselves in serious trouble. Nowadays cereal seedgrains are almost invariably dressed with a fungicide. Mercury compounds are used for this purpose, and dieldrin is used, but only in autumn-sown cereals, to reduce its effects on wildlife. Dieldrin is one of the most poisonous and most persistent of the organochlorine pesticides and its use is very restricted. Mercury is no less dangerous, though, and there have been many cases of human deaths in different parts of the world resulting from the accidental consumption of dressed seedgrain.

The bank voles, which seldom venture far into the field, are less at risk from dressed seed than are the field mice (*Apodemus agrarius*). A study of their behaviour made a few years ago by three scientists working for the Nature Conservancy Council found the mice ate the seed almost as soon as the farmer had sown it. The amount of dieldrin in their bodies increased by 68 times, and the amount of mercury increased by 11 times. The concentrations went on increasing for two weeks after the sowing and some mice were killed outright. Others may die later, because dieldrin dissolves into body fat and is stored there. If the fat should be metabolised as the animal loses weight, perhaps because food is scarce, the poison can be released into its bloodstream. It is not only the mice that are in danger, but the owls, kestrels and other predators that hunt them.

The study also made another curious discovery. It was found that the mice were distributed unevenly about the field, suggesting to the scientists that there may be two populations, one living close to the edges and another living in the open field. What is more, the further the mice were in from the edge the larger they were and the more males there were in proportion to females.

Beyond a doubt, though, the hero of the month was the mole. I say 'the' mole because so far as I knew there was but one, and he (or she) had been working hard. Moles do not like farmers any more than farmers like moles. Ploughing destroys all their tunnels, so as soon as the quiet time of year is over and the spring shows signs of returning, the digging must begin all over again. Moles do not dig tunnels for amusement or to provide them with a pathway from one side of your lawn to the other, but to obtain food. If they want to travel they are perfectly well able to move across the surface, and sometimes you may be lucky enough to catch them doing so. Some of them spend quite a lot of time above ground at night. They are good swimmers, too, when the need arises, but they do not swim for enjoyment, either.

Moles will eat any small creature they come across while tunneling, but if you are a mole what you really want is a tunnel into which food drops of its own accord, so that you can spend your working hours in nothing more exacting than patrolling. Where the tunnel system is good and well maintained, young moles often inherit it when old moles die, and it can pass through several generations of owners, most of whom never dig at all because they have no need to do so. They are creatures of regular habits. Molehills have been known to appear in precisely the same place year after year. Presumably this is because old tunnels are cleaned out annually by their houseproud occupant. They live alone for most of the time, just patrolling their tunnels.

The Cross Park mole made its appearance at the end of March and during April its tunnels and hills advanced to about one-third of the way across the field, starting from the gate in the middle of the hedge on the south-eastern side. It sounds absurd to say that the mole came in by the gate, but that is what it appeared to do, and in all probability that is exactly what it did. Its tunnels were very shallow. You could see them as distinct ridges running almost straight from one hill to the next. Had the mole entered under the hedge it would have had to tunnel much deeper to pass under the wall. There is no point in making work for yourself!

Moles are prodigious diggers. I was tempted at one point to try to dig this one out, but abandoned the idea at once, partly because I had no wish to disturb the creature, and partly because it can dig much faster than I can. Moles are not at all easy to catch.

When it runs, the mole holds its hind legs in the 'knees bend' position common to most small mammals. When it wants to dig, however, it can swivel its legs around so they project more or less at right angles from its body. In this position it can use its hind legs to brace itself against the sides of its tunnel while it digs with its front claws, swivelling its humerus and possibly extending its elbows. It can spread its digits to make its 'shovels' larger. Usually it digs using first one claw and then the other, but if the soil is soft it can proceed much faster by using both together and advancing through the earth with a kind of breast stroke. Its habit of bracing itself against the sides of its tunnel explains the fact that mole tunnels are always oval in shape, and wider than they are high.

Although it may surface at night, the mole has little regard for day and night. When it wants to come out, it first sticks its snout above ground, then waits, quite literally sniffing for trouble. If the coast is clear, out it comes, but if not the snout vanishes and the hole through which it projected is filled at once. The mole has a timetable of its own, with an 8 hour cycle, during which it spends about 3½ hours resting and most of the active period patrolling, unless there is digging to be done. It has a nest in which it sleeps for anything from a little over two hours to more than 4½ hours at a stretch, but it also takes short naps in its tunnel for anything up to 20 minutes. It is most probably hunger that wakes it. In old permanent pasture, moles take fewer naps than they do in arable land. This could be because permanent pasture provides them with more food, so that they need to do less digging to extend the tunnel system, and so they expend less energy. Where tunnels need to be extended to trap more food, a mole can spend from one-third to two-thirds of its 4½ hour active period digging. The tunnels can be extensive and an animal has been known to cover a total distance of about half a mile as it patrolled back and forth during its working 'day'.

By the end of the month the sheep had trampled down many of the molehills and the grass had grown sufficiently to hide the ridges made by the shallow tunnels, so that the activity of the mole was less obvious, although it could still be traced if you knew where to look. It would be interesting to see how far into the field it travelled. You can discover how active a mole is if you do not mind tormenting the creature. You use a small stick to make a hole in one of its tunnels and wait to see how long it takes the mole to plug it.

Most people think of moles as pests because as they tunnel they destroy any plant roots that lie in their path. They do some good as well, by eating some animals that do even greater damage to crops. They are hungry fellows, like all small mammals. A mole needs 4 to 5oz of food a day and in the course of a year it may eat from 40 to 80lb. Its favourite food is juicy earthworm, which is highly nutritious (should you ever feel tempted). About 85 per cent of a worm's body weight is water, but of the dry weight about three-quarters is protein, and there is very little fat, so that worms might be ideal for a slimming diet. Any worm the mole finds but cannot eat immediately, it stores. It bites off the last few segments of the worm and leaves the remainder in its larder. For some reason that is not really known, a worm that is mutilated in this way does not tunnel its way to freedom but waits, alive and therefore fresh, for the mole to return. Apart from worms, moles will eat all sorts of soil insects, including beetles, wireworms, leatherjackets and cutworms.

If you want to keep a mole in captivity you will have to feed it worms, although some scientists at the Zoology Department of Royal Holloway College kept moles apparently happy for some time on a diet of chopped hedgehog meat mixed with porage oats and earth. It will also require good accommodation and one type of mole housing that seems to work consists of several box-like cages connected by long tubes all joined to make junctions, with branch lines, very like the network the mole might make for itself. I suppose you should feed it by dropping morsels into the tunnels. I imagine that constant patrolling with never a worm to be found might make a mole highly neurotic. The tubes themselves should be tough. Zinc-coated woven wire is best, about a millimetre thick, with 0.5 centimetre square meshes, and the tunnels should be about 5 centimetres in diameter. Vacuum cleaner hose might be suitable. Really, though, moles make indifferent pets and are much happier left to their own devices in the wild.

Proverbially blind, the mole is not actually blind at all, although its vision is not good. It cannot see things that move quickly. Just as we cannot see a bullet in flight, so the mole may not be able to see a running animal. It can hear low-frequency sounds. Its principal sense organ is its snout, and a very sensitive and highly complex piece of equipment that is. It has a sense of smell, of course, and whiskers like those of a cat—and it has them in its tail as well as around its nose. The snout is covered with many small protuberances packed with nerve endings. These may be sensitive to touch, pressure, scent or heat. No one really knows, except the mole, and it says nothing.

The teeth of the mole determine its lifespan. Many animals have this problem. When the teeth wear down beyond a certain level it becomes increasingly difficult for the animal to eat and eventually it dies from starvation. For this reason no mole can expect to live for more than five years; most live for two or three.

The badger may have visited the field again. It was difficult to find footprints. The soil became too hard when it was dry, and when it was wet prints were washed out rather quickly by the rain, so that by the time I saw them they were usually very indistinct. David Brewster, who has been observing badgers extensively, took one look at the large slide in the north-east corner of the field and identified it as typically that made by a badger. That was at the very end of the month, though, and the slide had not been used for some time. On the 25th, a few days earlier, I had found footprints along the north-western hedge that may have been made by the front feet of a large badger. Badgers are quite numerous in Cornwall, and many are being destroyed because it is claimed that the badger population forms a reservoir for bovine tuberculosis that is transmitted to cattle. Most probably it was the cattle that passed the disease to the badgers in the first place, but that has not saved the badgers. The prints I found ran from the lower end of the hedge as far as the gate that is rather more than halfway along it, and they ran in both directions, as though the animal had gone one way and then returned. Perhaps it tried to leave the field by the lower gate on to the road. If that was its customary route it may have been closed to it, because the farmer had placed a band of wire mesh across the lower part of the gate.

At the end of the month there was a sudden and dramatic reduction in the amount of rabbit activity. All but a few of the burrows looked deserted. There was no freshly turned earth near them and in many burrow entrances small plants had begun to grow. There were almost no rabbit droppings. I found no clear explanation for this. Had anyone been killing rabbits I would hardly have expected them to enjoy such spectacular success, and anyway I would have expected to find some traces. There should have been some trampling of the ground, or at least some spent cartridges. Had the rabbits succumbed to a new virulent form of myxomatosis there would have been at least one or two corpses, and most probably a few sick and disorientated animals wandering in the open. The most likely explanation is that the females were heavily pregnant, and inactive for that reason. If this is so, then the rabbits should reappear shortly. Even then, though, what were the males doing?

The sheep were brought into the field on the 19th and they were still there at the end of the month, although by that time they had cropped most of the grass. The farmer planned to leave them there for only a few days more and then to manure the field to stimulate a vigorous growth of grass for cutting later in the year.

Despite the winter, the lambing seems to have been good. Many of the ewes had twins and all of them looked healthy. One little chap

The Devon Longwool ewe and her lamb. The breed is popular locally but is little seen in other parts of Britain

looked like an orphan that had been fostered on to a Devon Longwool mother. It had a black belt around its middle, which was unusual, and it looked like a Down breed, with tight, close wool and a generally heavier build than its companions.

There were hazards, though. Sheep scab was still a problem and the Ministry had ordered that in the autumn, between 3 September and 11 November, all sheep must be dipped again. On 20 April the Ministry issued a high-risk warning of nematodirus disease in lambs. Sheep are susceptible to parasites of all kinds, and this disease is caused by one of them, a worm whose eggs are deposited by the sheep to hatch in the grass from which the larvae are collected again as the sheep graze. The dry weather last autumn and the cold winter had prevented the eggs from hatching, so there was an unusually large number of them just waiting for warm weather. The Ministry predicted a peak of infection in the first week of May. Lambs are especially vulnerable and if nursing ewes become infested they lose condition, produce less milk, and their lambs eat more grass to compensate so that their risk of infection increases. The Cross Park lambs should be safe, though, at least while they remain in Cross Park, because no sheep have been stocked in the field for several years and therefore there can be no accumulated eggs.

The winter was said to have been the coldest since 1963, and on the 30th there were six inches of snow in parts of Scotland. It was milder than this in Cornwall, but still cold for the time of year and there was a good deal of rain, as well as more wintry showers. Easter, though, was said to be the warmest since 1949, as warm air from the Sahara was swept across the country by south-easterly winds.

On the morning of the 17th, the starlings decided it was nesting time and all of them were busy collecting materials. That was in our garden, close to sea level, but up in Cross Park the birds were becoming more active, too. The sparrows had organised themselves into a small, excitable flock, feeding together on the ground and then taking to the air and wheeling around the field as though starting in alarm at some imagined danger. The skylarks were there, too, leaping suddenly from the ground to climb almost out of sight, their song proclaiming to the world my invasion of their territory.

Nor was avian activity confined to the small birds. On the 21st I saw a cock pheasant in the field. When it saw me it ran off through the gate on the north-west side in the direction of the scrubby trees where it makes its home. Perhaps, having seen it once, my ear was specially tuned to its cry on my subsequent visits. Whether that is the reason or not, I have heard it several times since that sighting. Some years ago,

A barn that is believed to have been built from stone taken from the ruined chapel that used to stand over the Holy Well. Any carving is invisible because the barn was built with the decoration facing inwards

when I lived in Suffolk, pheasants were a very common sight. They are not exactly rare in Cornwall, but they are seen seldom enough to make them something of a novelty.

They are not wild, strictly speaking, and although they have become naturalised over the centuries, legend holds that they originated in Asia Minor, from whence they were brought into Europe by the Argonauts, whose journey was ancient history in the time of Homer. It was the Romans who brought them to Britain, so it is said. Today they are raised carefully in order to be shot, but they manage to get themselves listed in inventories of wild birds.

No one pretends that guinea-fowl are wild birds, although there seems little doubt that that is how they regard themselves. I saw them first on 1 April, five of them in a group, feeding on the Moor. They were there on several of my subsequent visits to the field, and on the 10th they were feeding in the field itself. They hail from Africa and southern Arabia, but they have acclimatized themselves with no great modification in their behaviour. They feed on the ground in small parties, and roost in trees at night. They are noisy creatures, screaming hysterically whenever they believe they are being threatened, but running for cover if the threat becomes real. They can fly, but not strongly. They are kept for meat by enthusiasts, and possibly for show, and although they have been domesticated for a very long time, they are never really tame. Indeed, this is one of their attractions. They look after themselves and require very little from humans by way of accommodation or feeding. In parts of Africa, and perhaps in other places, too, they are kept as 'watchdogs' because of the great commotion they make if they are disturbed. Provided they can be prevented from wandering far and wide, as the Cross Park guinea-fowl seem to do, they may make better guardians of fruit trees than the more conventional geese. They are noisier but less aggressive.

The guinea-fowl can do little harm. The real enemy to the stock farmer is the domestic dog that is out of control. On the 25th I entered the field, and heard a voice shouting loudly, but incoherently, in the distance. There was a man walking, far away on the Moor. Then I saw why he was shouting. His dog entered the field by the top gate in great excitement and at once the sheep were thrown into a panic. They all ran to the far corner of the field. The encounter ended there, because the dog returned to its owner, but even the most inoffensive hearthrug of a housepet is descended from the wolf, and sheep know it. Dogs can do appalling damage.

The insects were beginning to make an appearance early in the month. There were a few carabid beetles and ants and by the end of the month the flies were emerging. Down in the lowlands the bees were working among the spring flowers. The hunters of insects were emerging, too. By the 10th there were several sheet and orb spider webs in the hedgerows, the sheets appearing first, and the number of webs increased during the month. On the 30th I saw many small, dark brown, short-legged spiders, all belonging to the same species, but one I could not identify. Every few yards along the north-western hedge there was a solitary individual moving back and forth busily at ground level. These early spiders were emerging from hibernation and staking out territories for themselves. They were the survivors from last year, and before much longer they would be seeking mates. After that there would be a large increase in the spider population.

Many of the webs were built across the entrances to rabbit burrows, adding to the forlorn appearance of burrows that seem to be, but that may not be, deserted. An emerging rabbit would demolish the web instantly, of course, but that is of little consequence to the spider, which makes a web designed to last for only a day. Many spiders actually eat their own webs at the end of the day, when their usefulness has ended, and all of them begin the day by building a new one.

I am not certain that the small spiders I saw patrolling the base of the

Leaf miners tunnel inside leaves, making delicate white patterns on the surface. The miners themselves are the larvae of insects, and there are many species that feed in this way

hedge build webs at all. Many species do not, and there may be something like 40,000 species of spider in the world as a whole. All spiders produce silk, but originally it was used to make protective cocoons for the eggs. Spiders do not go through a larval stage, but hatch as complete miniatures of their parents. These 'spiderlings' often use their silk to help them disperse, climbing to a high place and paying out a long line of silk that eventually catches the wind and carries them where it will, to a new habitat. The use of silk to make traps came later, evolutionally. The most primitive of spiders lie in wait for their prey, or in some cases chase it. Rather more advanced forms use single strands of silk as drag lines to catch them if they should miss in their attack and fall, and to provide them with a quick route back to their original position. The sheet web, which in its simplest form consists of single strands laid over one another more or less haphazardly, offers the obvious advantage of catching any passing insect and holding it until the spider is able to deal with it, but it requires a great deal of silk. It has been adapted by some species to make tunnel traps, tents, and underwater diving bells that contain air for a strictly terrestrial spider that feeds on aquatic animals. There are no true trapdoor spiders in Britain, but trapdoor spiders use silk to line their burrows and to form hinges and trip lines. The hinges are attached to the trapdoor itself and the trip lines warn the spider waiting immediately below the door that a potential meal is passing its way. The most sophisticated use of silk is the beautiful orb web, built with great economy to provide the maximum net area with the least use of silk. Every orb-web species of spider builds to its own pattern, and despite its complexity, the web is made quite quickly.

I walked around the field on 21 April, in intermittent light rain, and as I was leaving I met an elderly man who lived in one of the cottages by the road and who had grown curious about the odd-looking fellow in the tweed hat and wellies. We started talking as I changed back into my shoes and put away the photographic gear in the boot of the car. He told me that Cross Park used to be called 'Big Cross Park', and that the small field beside it, which was sold a few years ago along with the house built on it, used to be 'Little Cross Park'. He could remember when Cross Park Field—the big one—was a football pitch, used by the village team, which played in the Bodmin League. The players changed in the western corner that is now all overgrown, and the game was played on the upper part of the field, where the ground is fairly level. That must have been half a century ago. He remembered the arrival of the first tractors, during the 1939–45 war, and he remembered, too, that before they had tractors, and all field operations depended on horses, the time spent feeding, harnessing, unharnessing, grooming and cleaning was unpaid. The rig had to be at work by eight in the morning, weather permitting—and it usually did—and the work involved in preparing it and putting it away afterwards was considered to be for the worker's own benefit, not the master's. Everyone was poor, of course, including the master himself in most cases. The old man told me of farm owners working in the rain with no more protection than a piece of sacking thrown over their shoulders, and two more pieces tied with string around their knees. No one could afford to buy a coat.

The old kind of farming was picturesque, and the old men who remember it remember it happily, but despite their nostalgia none of them would wish to see it return.

May

There are moments when the sheer beauty and tranquillity of the countryside can almost overwhelm you. It is as though the peace of the place had a physical quality, a weight or force like the rain or sunshine, to soak you and absorb you into itself. Nor is it the peace that comes when the senses cease to be assaulted with continually changing impressions, the peace of sensory deprivation. The place is alive, intensely, but quietly active, vibrant with hedgerow rustlings, birdsong and the hum of insects going about their business.

I had paused while this feeling came over me and I was suffused with well-being, a desire to jump for joy, but to do so without moving, for any sudden, violent movement would break the spell. The church clock, down in the valley, chimed the half hour, and the place assumed a sudden timelessness emphasised by the clock, whose sound might be heard there at any half hour of any day or night in any year. Time passed, but its passing meant nothing in a field where the centuries were marked by the appearance of a few invading plants and no creature counted the seasons. Interference from outside had made little impression here. The hedge by which I stood was already ancient when the church was built and the clock, installed little more than a half century ago and so to all intents and purposes spanking new, had learned quickly to merge its distant chime into the medley of natural sounds and to become part of them. It provides a counterpoint to birdsong, but its numbering of the hours is of little interest in a place where the regular cycle of birth, reproduction, death and rebirth is measured across aeons of geological time.

To the plants and animals caught up in that cycle, timelessness brings no possibility of respite from activity. Where eternity exists in a perpetual present, the business of living must be pursued with relentless urgency. There is food to be found, nests must be built, mates must be located and courted, and each time the man with the big

77

The scars left by the mechanical trimmer last through the winter but are lost amid the new foliage of spring

boots comes too close the sky must be torn asunder with a great, fluttering leap into the air and a long, noisy stream of invective that is part threat, part scream of terror, part warning to others, and that he will hear as the song of the lark. He will wonder at its beauty and, when he is done wondering, perhaps he will ponder its real purpose and the energy that is expended each time a bird about the size of a starling launches itself vertically upwards and produces a sound that can be heard for a quarter of a mile.

The larks had nests in the field. When disturbed they rose, usually two of them a few yards apart, and always from the same area. I tried to find the nests, rather half-heartedly for I had no wish to cause more distress than I could help and I feared that too clumsy a search might lead to a careless footstep and the destruction of invisible eggs. The nests are very well hidden. The grass grew well during May, but even while it was still short and sparse the larks managed to conceal them with skill of the same order as that they use in diverting what they suppose to be aggressors. They do not leap directly into the air, which would pinpoint the location of the nest for the benefit of any real enemy, but run along the ground first and rise from some distance away. Everyone knows they do this. So, I suppose, does every predatory bird and mammal. Yet it is virtually impossible to catch them at it, mainly because their early warning system makes them aware of the invader before the invader is aware of them, so that their short run can be performed secretly, invisibly, and in an unobservable direction from the point from which they erupt into the air so unexpectedly that they have a good chance of startling, and so diverting, any creature that intends to harm.

Despite the operatic power of its voice, the lark is not the noisiest of birds, and certainly not the noisiest if you relate its decibel output to its body size. The wren wins that contest with ease. There was a wren sitting high in the hedge, drowning out all its rivals with its long musical recital that continued for several minutes with barely a pause to take breath. Perhaps it is its vocal power, with which it seems to lay claim to a large territory, that has led the Germans to call it the 'king of the hedge' (*Zaunkönig*) and the Dutch to call it 'king of winter' (*Winterkoning*). It cannot be its size or appearance, for at about 3¾ in the wren is much smaller than the sparrow, and its colour is drab. Whenever you hear a chorus of birdsong to which many species are contributing, it is quite likely that much of the song you hear is made by wrens. They are said to be the most common of British birds, which is a startling statement to those who are more familiar with the urbanised house sparrow, feral dove, or starling, but an explanation of their ignorance may be deduced from the wren's taxonomic name, *Troglodytes troglodytes*, the 'cave dweller'. It is not especially secretive, but it lives in dense thickets and spends much of its time on the ground, rummaging for insects among the litter, and if you caught a glimpse of one disappearing you might mistake it for a mouse. It seldom flies far, more commonly proceeding by short hops. This may be a sign of evolutionary success, for flying consumes large amounts of energy and a bird that can find sufficient food and shelter on the ground within its own range has little reason to indulge in long, exhausting flights. There is an irony in this. Since the beginning of human history men have envied the bird its freedom, have marvelled at the skill and apparent ease with which it moves through the air, have sought to emulate it and, after many centuries of dreaming, have succeeded at last in making flying machines that obtain their lift from the forward motion of their aerofoil surfaces rather than from anything so crude as a lifting gas. Yet for all this time and more, the birds themselves have been willing to abandon flight whenever an opportunity to do so presented itself, and for the very reason that today is leading us to look rather closely at the way in which we live: the energy cost. Flying is hard work, even if you have hollow bones, huge muscles, and wings that can wrest every last aerodynamic advantage from the air. The less flying you do the less fuel, or food, you need.

That was the hot day, the day I watched the wren and absorbed the peace of my surroundings into my own mood. It was the day for shirt sleeves. I say 'the' day for shirt sleeves because it was the only such day I experienced, at any rate up to the end of May. It was the 15th, and a summer's day.

It was the first summer's day, and it was the last for some time. It was more than usually welcome, for May began with the coldest weather since records were first kept in this country, in 1931, and with more snow than had been seen for many years even in those places where snow on May Day is not unknown. In parts of northern England and Scotland up to four inches of snow fell on 1 May as air swept south from the arctic. In southern England there was frost, black ice, and snow on the higher ground in some places. Dartmoor received a light sprinkling, but Bodmin Moor escaped. There was snow at Exeter, and Plymouth saw snow in May for the first time for more than thirty years.

The cold start to the month continued and intensified the cold, wet weather of April that had delayed farming operations over most of Britain. Heavy soils were wet and cold, which delayed the planting of potatoes and spring cereals. There was almost no growth of grass in most regions, and in many places short-term leys had suffered badly, with much grass killed outright. This meant that livestock made little progress and there was some poaching of the pastures when cattle were turned out to graze, as they had to be because their stores of winter feed were exhausted. Difficulties of this kind usually spill over from one season and one year to the next, and recovery can be slow. Where winter feed has been eaten, cattle have to be turned on to the grass. If the pasture cannot sustain them, farmers have no choice but to turn them on to grass that is being grown for conservation. This may well mean that less hay and silage is made during the summer, which reduces the winter feed supply for next winter. That is when the farmers must make some very complicated calculations. If the coming winter is short, all may be well, but how can you know? If the problem is extensive, so that many farmers are short of winter feed, prices will rise during the autumn. The farmer who decides to pay the higher prices and buy in feed must hope for high meat prices next year so he can cover his costs. This is a gamble, and the alternative is to reduce the size of the herd to a level that can be fed with the resources available. If many farmers take this comparatively safe course, and it seems the most plausible, the higher slaughter rate may bring lower meat prices next October and November. It does not end there, of course, because if the slaughter rate increases in late 1979 the size of the herds will have to be increased again during 1980, so that the rate of slaughter will be reduced in proportion. Cheap meat in the autumn may mean expensive meat for much of next year. Whatever happens to the consumer, though, it is all bad for farmers. If they kill animals early they receive less money, partly because the animals have not attained their full finished weight and partly because the increase in supply reduces prices. During the following year they will have fewer animals to sell and so their incomes will be lower than they would be in a better year. If they decide to wait for next year, however, and finish their animals on the grass of spring and early summer, they must hope that prices rise sufficiently to cover the additional cost of buying in winter feed.

It is not difficult to see why severe famines often take several years to reach their full intensity and then continue for three, four or even more years while the farmers recover. The British farmer has a good life in many ways, but any idea that the permanence and apparent stability of the landscape and biological rhythms with which he is, or should be, temperamentally attuned bring with them financial security is wholly illusory. The British countryside has seen generations of farmers come and go and it has broken the hearts and bank balances of more than a few.

The bad spring weather had caused some mortality among lambs in the more exposed parts of the country, but not, so far as I could see, around Cross Park. In any case the losses were not severe and since the fall of lambs had been somewhat higher than usual over the country as a whole there was no marked effect on the size of flocks.

Once the cold spell at the beginning of the month had ended, there was no more violent weather until the end of May. For most of the time it was mild, though probably cooler than usual for the time of year, often showery but with dry weather for several days at a time, occasionally misty early in the morning.

The pattern broke on the 28th, when I was soaked to the skin trying to explore parts of the high Moor. What promised to develop into occasional light showers when I set out turned into continuous heavy rain driven by strong winds, and the Moor revealed itself as bleak and inhospitable. It was not the worst of it, however. From the 28th to the 31st the south of England was drenched by heavy rains. Cornwall escaped the worst of the flooding, but in Dorset and Somerset it was severe, and complicated by landslides and fallen trees. Some roads were under water, but in Somerset the village of Martock, between Ilminster and Yeovil, was cut off entirely by water 3ft deep, and in other villages nearby, and at Bridport in Dorset, people were being evacuated, often from upstairs windows. A caravan containing a sleeping family on holiday at Charmouth was swept into the River Char and might have been carried out to sea had it not collided with and lodged against a tree. Its occupants were unhurt, but cold, wet and frightened. The Bath and West Show, at Shepton Mallet, was nicknamed 'The Bath and Wet' by a local newspaper as the ground beneath it was churned into a quagmire; the final dampener to what should have been the agricultural and social event of the year for many rural communities came when the poultry tent collapsed, and that on the first day of the Show. The human spirit is indomitable—it needs to be—and the show recovered, more or less. The rain ceased and the ground began to dry, but history does not record the fate of all those gaudy chickens whose tarpaulin universe fell in upon them.

The showing of poultry is trivial, of course. Exotic breeds, developed for their fine plumage and groomed like coronation horses, contribute nothing useful to the production of food or of anything else. They lay so few eggs that they do not even contribute much to the production of one another. Yet they are small, easy to rear, and pretty, and the showing of them brings much pleasure, and not a little prestige, to country people. It is not everyone who can win prizes with the finest bull in the county, but anyone with the love, the eye, the skill and the patience, can own a prize-winning bird. The poultry tent is the place where farming and rural life become democratic, where Jack can be better than his master. For that it is important, and for the decorative value that the sight of so many fine feathers brings.

It transpired that the Yeovil area had received the equivalent of the entire month's rainfall for a normal May in just twenty-four hours—and that was additional to that month's normal rainfall, not in place of it.

In Cornwall it was bad enough and if my clothing did not absorb a full month's rainfall on that Bank Holiday Monday it certainly felt as though it did.

Despite the weather, there was other evidence that summer had arrived. I heard my first cuckoo on 7 May and on that day the small birds were busy collecting nesting materials. The may-blossom was out on the hawthorn around Cross Park by the 8th, and on the 14th I saw my first martins and swallows. Something someone said filled me with

The may came out,
aptly, in May

sudden doubt as to the correct time for clout-casting. Do you ne'er cast a clout ere may be out meaning in blossom, or ere it be out, meaning finished? My grandmother, with whom I lived for several years as a small boy, would never allow me to leave off my winter woollies until the may was out. It was one of several matters about which she was very insistent. It might be unbearably traumatic to learn after all these years that she had misread the old country saying, but since I was never sure how she was interpreting it, hers being a somewhat capricious regime—or so it seemed to me when I was seven—perhaps it does not matter. In either case, clouts should have been well and truly cast by the end of the month, which marked the finish of the hawthorn and the blossoming of the blackthorn.

It was a month for birds. I wondered several times whether it was only my fancy, or a phenomenon peculiar to this part of Cornwall, or whether, in truth, the magpie population was increasing? I could not remember seeing so many of these rather spectacular birds in past years. A magpie was a rare enough sight up in Cross Park, to be sure, for they live among the trees down in the valleys, but I passed many on my frequent journeys to and from the field.

On the 8th a skylark, careless of danger or ignorant of it, allowed me to walk to within a few yards of it. I could see it clearly and almost photographed it, but the sight of the camera was too much. It could not betray so blatantly the furtive nature of its kind and once it had flown it did not return to pose again.

The pheasants from the nearby copse were seldom far away, and the hen was out feeding as well as the cock. I heard them often and saw them several times. The guinea-fowl returned, too, briefly and noisily, on the 16th. The chaffinches were still busy, and at least one greenfinch, and the buzzards were very active. There was often one, and sometimes a pair, circling slowly over Cross Park or not far from it.

Directly or indirectly it was the buzzards—dramatic enough in themselves—that provided two of the moments of real excitement during the month. The first came on the 16th, the day of the guinea-fowl, when my attention was caught by a large bird circling slowly nearby. It was a buzzard and as I watched it moved off toward the Moor. It was then that I saw another bird coming towards me. Silhouetted against a flat, white, cloudy sky at first it looked like a crow, but it flew like a bird of prey. It was evidently not a buzzard and so I took it for a kestrel, but it was not a kestrel either. For one thing it was much larger. It flew over me in a long, fast glide, moving east-wards, and a moment later it was followed by what must have been its mate, an apparently identical bird, also gliding. Its wings were long and shaped like those of a harrier, with the primaries clearly visible at the tips, but its tail was slightly forked and no harrier has a forked tail. Indeed, as I discovered when I looked up the bird in reference books, the only bird of prey with a notched tail is the kite. What is more, the birds I saw had only slightly notched tails rather than deeply notched ones. The nearest kites to Cornwall are supposed to live in the mountains of mid-Wales, but they are red kites, with deeply notched tails. The bird with the slight notch is the black kite, which lives in central France and Germany and all over Europe to the south and east, but that is not a common visitor to Britain. I checked my sighting by describing it to Frank Smith, a naturalist who lived in Wales for a number of years and who has seen many kites, and he knew of no other bird that could answer my description. The word travelled fast among local naturalists so that I became a little embarrassed by it in case I had been mistaken. By the end of the month I had not seen the birds again and neither, so far as I know, had anyone else. If you draw a straight line due east from Cross Park you will cross the Channel coast somewhere near Teignmouth and the French coast somewhere near Etaples. Perhaps they were going home?

Then, on the 25th, there was further excitement. As I arrived at the field I saw a pair of buzzards being mobbed by half a dozen rooks. I knew this could happen, of course, and that even the awesome golden eagle is sometimes attacked by small birds—and loses—but I had not expected to see it. The rooks were in no danger. Twist and turn, climb and dive as they might, the buzzards were too large and too sluggish to out-manoeuvre the smaller, nimbler birds. The buzzards were forced to land in the field to the east of Cross Park, took off again, were mobbed again, and eventually, as the attackers began to withdraw, sensing perhaps that justice had been done and, most spectacularly, had been seen to be done, the engagement ended with just one rook against both buzzards, and the retreat of the buzzards. In aerial combat, large size and heavy armament guarantee a marauder no immunity from defeat by a faster, more manoeuvrable adversary. The lesson is hardly new!

My visit to the field on the hot day, the 15th, had been to examine the traps. Paul Chanin, a zoologist friend, had borrowed twenty-three Longworth traps for me. There should have been twenty-four, but one came without its tunnel. Such is life. He showed me how to set and bait them and we put them out together on the morning of the 14th. We used four sites and placed six traps at each of the first three and five at the fourth. We began in the western corner, the bottom left corner as you enter the field, and a place of rocks, rubbish and good plant cover. Our second site was about one-third of the way along the north-western hedge, beside a telegraph pole that made the site easy to find—which was important, as I was to discover. The third site was a little way along the top, north-eastern hedge, beside the feeder that in its time has carried hay for animals. The fourth site was in the bottom, south-eastern corner, which is another place of rocks and plants. I made a diagram of each site and marked the position of each trap carefully. Even so, my search for one or two of the traps became slightly desperate when I returned the next morning to examine them.

The Longworth trap is an ingenious device, a little more than a foot long when assembled. It has two parts. At the rear end there is a nesting box, about four inches square in cross-section and about six inches deep. At its open end there is a hinged flap and, next to it, a hinged strip. The second part of the trap is a tunnel, smaller in cross-section than the nesting box so it fits inside its mouth. The hinged flap folds down pointing to the rear of the nesting box and lodges against a flange on the rear of the upper side of the tunnel and the strip folds down pointing forward and lodges in one of a series of notches on the roof of the tunnel. The tunnel can be wedged in position firmly, but can be opened easily by releasing the strip from its notch, moving the tunnel far enough into the nesting box to free it from the flap, and then withdrawing it. The tunnel itself has a wire across it that an animal must cross as it leaves the tunnel to enter the nesting box. As it does so it depresses the wire, which releases a catch and allows a trapdoor to fall shut at the entrance to the tunnel. The trapdoor cannot be opened from inside and there is an adjustable spring that can be used to vary the weight needed to drop the door so the trap can be set to catch some animals but not others. For carrying, the tunnel fits right inside the box so that the trap occupies the minimum of space, which is an asset to the serious student who may need to set fifty or more of them at a time. They are efficient at catching small mammals without causing them any injury, the length of the tunnel being sufficient to avoid the risk of catching even the longest tail.

The trap is set by placing hay in the nesting box for bedding and adding a fairly generous ration of oats to provide the prisoner with a hearty meal. The trap is then placed close to a track. You can find the pathways used by small animals if you search carefully. Grass will be pushed aside, often to make a tunnel, and if there are field (short-tailed) voles in residence the tunnels will have been made by an animal that literally eats its way through the undergrowth. If you are very lucky you may even find a mouse's feeding platform. This is usually some distance above the ground and it may have been made from an abandoned bird's nest. The mouse will have made it more or less flat and you may find the remains if its meals there. It is a place to which mice take their food to eat in comfort and safety.

The trap should be placed at right angles to the track so that the small creature that uses the track must pass by its inviting entrance. In practice this is not always possible, and in a hedge it is rarely possible. You have to place the trap as best you can. Then it must be covered, especially around its entrance. It may look small and harmless to you, but to a mouse it may be very alarming. As Paul explained it to me, the sudden appearance in your garden of a strange object the size of a house might alarm you, and entering it to explore the interior might not be the first thought to cross your mind. So you disguise the trap. We made rather a good job of it, which is why I had difficulty finding some of the traps the next day. After that I left part of the nesting box exposed, to reveal just a glimpse of shiny aluminium. The final step is to sprinkle a little food by the entrance to persuade the passer-by to pause, but not so much food that the passer-by gorges himself and loses all interest in the second course.

When you compare the trap with the house that appears suddenly from nowhere, the courage and insatiable curiosity of small animals is

Field mouse

startling. They cannot resist the temptation to explore and investigate, and so they are caught.

We caught nothing unusual, only field (wood) mice, bank voles and common shrews, but I was surprised at the number of visitors we attracted and detained. Paul said that with 23 traps I might expect to catch 8 or 9 animals a night and that anything more than this should be considered a bonus. In fact, the four trapping sessions yielded 18 bank voles, 18 mice and 6 shrews, a total of 42 animals. Their distribution also intrigued me. The most densely populated parts of the field appeared to be the north-western hedge, where I caught 10 voles, 4 mice and 3 shrews, and the bottom, south-eastern corner, where I caught 10 mice and one vole. The western corner, which seemed to offer conditions just as favourable for small mammals, yielded 2 voles, 2 mice and 3 shrews and so, apparently, was much less densely populated. Nor was the top hedge so productive as the north-western hedge that I would have thought offered rather less cover. I caught only 5 voles and 2 mice there. I found, too, that of the two more productive sites the one in the hedge yielded 10 voles and the one in the corner, among the stones, yielded 10 mice. So the field came to resolve itself into 'mousy' and 'voley' areas.

Of course, it is impossible to draw any useful conclusions from such a small and brief sampling. Indeed, it is difficult enough to draw conclusions from much more elaborate studies. You have to allow for the animals themselves. Like humans, they are individuals, and each is a little different. To some, a night spent in the trap, followed by release, will be remembered as a horrendous experience to be avoided at all costs in the future, so that such an animal, once caught, may never be caught again. Another individual, however, may remember a big feed and a warm, dry bed, so that the shock of finding itself unable to escape and the further shock of being released by some great smelly giant will not have been too frightening. That animal may return to the trap again and again.

Then there is the problem of the faulty trap and the cunning visitor. Traps may receive a nudge from the wind that closes them, and I found one trap shut in this way, its contents apparently undisturbed. I also found the same trap emptied completely of food and bedding by an animal that had not only succeeded in crossing the trip wire without shutting the door, but had eaten the food and then managed to drag out the bedding, again without being caught. Doubtless there is some hero or heroine of the hedgebank who sleeps snug and warm and who regales his or her fellows with tales of intrepid derring-do and the outwitting of man. It was a bit humiliating to feel I was being laughed at by a mouse, but I recovered my self-respect by blaming the trap.

Nor are these the only events that prevent the animal behaviourist from treating small mammals as though they were inanimate. Small, timid individuals may enter traps to seek refuge from bullies, their fear of the trap being less than their fear of more aggressive members of their own community. Occasionally the bully may manage to follow the victim into the trap, with unpleasantly gory results (mice can indulge in cannibalistic behaviour under such circumstances). This is the time of year when machismo reigns in the mouse world, and aggression is rife. Alternatively, a dominant individual that loses a contest may go into a trap just to sulk. All such behaviour adds to the difficulty of using trapped animals to estimate total populations, despite the fact that proper scientists mark trapped animals so they know if they catch them again.

Once caught, the animals must be released, but not before you have had a chance to look at them. It is easy to tell whether a trap is occupied, because if it is the door will be shut. The procedure then is to pick up the trap, hold it upright so the door is at the top, then open the door gently to see whether the prisoner is in the tunnel or the nesting box. It is best not to be over-confident. Paul suggested that if the trap should feel rather heavy it might be wise to shake it gently and listen. If I heard an angry hissing noise, I would know that my unwilling guest was an exceedingly cross weasel, with exceedingly sharp teeth, who would have my finger off as soon as look at me. I cannot remember too clearly what I was supposed to do then, but it seems likely that if I were to open the door in the approved manner I would receive a faceful of weasel teeth. It did not happen, because I caught no weasels. There may be weasels living in the gaps between the stones of which the hedges are made, but I have neither seen nor been bitten by them. A weasel's typical victims are not necessarily toothless and timid. Small though they are (and so, for that matter, is a weasel) mice and voles will bite if they are handled carelessly. They do not bite, however, if you place your hand completely over them without gripping them. The correct way to hold any small mammal is by the loose skin at the back of its neck, which renders it helpless and therefore harmless. You can pick up a mouse by its tail in order to get a better grip, but the practice is not recommended. In many species there is a serious risk of stripping the skin from the tail, which causes pain and exposes the mouse to the risk of infection. What is more, mice have been known to turn around, climb their own tails, and bite their tormentors. I cannot say I blame them. If you grip a mouse by its tail, hold it only by the root of the tail. Their courage is formidable and talk of 'timid mice' is nothing short of defamatory. You can, and with larger or more aggressive animals you must, sedate the prisoner with a whiff of ether—never chloroform, which is very harmful and often kills its victims. That, actually, is the way to treat a weasel.

I chose the easiest solution and gently tipped the contents of the nesting boxes into a plastic carrier bag, where I could observe them without handling them at all.

I suppose the first thing that impressed me about these small creatures was their neatness. It sounds silly, or sentimental, to describe them as neat, but they are. Each one is spotlessly clean, its fur smooth and well groomed, its eyes bright. The mice, large-eared, two-toned and long-tailed, seemed more elegant than the slightly rougher looking voles. The shrews were quite different, with dense grey fur that stood up straight and very small eyes. Their snouts, too, are unlike those of the rodents, being extremely mobile and having, at the tip, a pink sensory apparatus that looks every bit as powerful and delicate as it is.

The shrew is tiny, and the pygmy shrew (that may live in Cross Park but that is too light to trip the traps) is still smaller. They eat almost constantly just because they are so small. Their problem is that their surface area is immense in proportion to their total volume, so they lose heat all the time and can maintain their body temperature only by burning immense amounts of fuel. They are unspecialised creatures that possess features found in many quite different animals, implying not that they were assembled from spare parts collected more or less at random, but that they carry prototype components that were retained by their many descendants. The very first mammals that dodged about the forests while the great reptiles slept included creatures very like the modern shrew, and we may be descended from them. The little shrew should be treated with some veneration.

There were, inevitably, a few deaths. Shrews cannot survive long in traps because of their need for food. We had adjusted the traps, or so we thought, to prevent shrews from being caught in them, but in the event four of our shrews were dead. One that was not was extremely hungry. When I released it, it moved no more than a yard from me before it began feeding. I could hear it munching. Two voles and one mouse were dead. The mouse may have been dying anyway, a victim of the high spring mortality among mice, and it looked as though one of the voles was at the point of death when it entered the trap. The food was untouched and the bedding undisturbed. One very lively mouse had a good memory. As soon as I released it it bounded away straight to the place from which I had taken its trap, and resumed eating the oats I had used to lure it. It was as though it remembered there was food it had not had time to finish.

So they left, the small creatures, the voles scurrying for cover in the banks, the mice travelling with great leaps, the shrews vanishing almost at once beneath the grass. They were not the only animals in Cross Park, of course. I caught a glimpse of a field vole on the 21st, as it disappeared between some stones, and the original mole was now one of three moles working away in the field, although the newcomers were so far away that the pioneer could not be aware of them. There was one along the north-western hedge, and one along the north-eastern hedge. Like the first mole, they seemed to be very active at first, producing many hills as they excavated their first tunnels, then there was much less evidence of them. They may resume digging later, for that is what the first mole did; and during the latter part of the month it was busy extending its network of tunnels.

There was an increase in rabbit activity, too, some of it by young animals just beginning to leave the burrows in which they were born. Almost as soon as they emerge above ground they begin to try out their paws at digging, and there were several small, shallow scrapes left by them.

As Paul collected his traps and left the field, on the 18th, Barbara

Primroses, protected now because so many were picked by visitors, only to wilt within a few hours. The Cornish hedgerows are full of them, and, left unpicked, their blooms continue to delight the eye for weeks

Garratt arrived to examine the plants. Her new list consisted of sycamore (*Acer pseudoplatanus*), sweet vernal grass (*Anthoxanthum odoratum*), betony (*Betonica officinalis*), false brome (*Brachypodium sylvaticum*), wild turnip (*Brassica rapa*), sticky mouse-ear (*Cereastium glomeratum*), creeping thistle (*Circium arvense*), hazel (*Corylus avellana*), smooth hawksbeard (*Crepis capillaris*), beaked hawksbeard (*Crepis vesicaria* spp *taraxacilfolia*), scaly male fern (*Dryopteris pseudo-mas*), sun spurge (*Euphorbia helioscopia*), common hemp nettle (*Galeopsis tetrahit*), cut-leaved cranesbill (*Geranium dissectum*), dove's foot cranesbill (*Geranium molle*), perennial ryegrass (*Lolium perenne*), bird's foot trefoil (*Lotus corniculatus*), field woodrush (*Luzula campestris*), pineapple weed (*Matricaria matricarioides*), changing forget-me-not (*Myosotis discolor*), silverweed (*Potentilla anserina*), barren strawberry (*Potentilla sterilis*), primrose (*Primula vulgaris*), pedunculate oak (*Quercus robur*), goat willow (*Salix caprea*), grey willow (*Salix cinerea* spp *oleifolia*), elder (*Sambucus nigra*), annual knawel (*Scleranthus annuus*), groundsel (*Senecio vulgaris*), field madder (*Sherardia arvensis*), prickly sow thistle (*Sonchus oleraceus*), hedge woundwort (*Stachys sylvatica*), scentless mayweed (*Tripleurospermum maritimum* spp *inodorum*), wall speedwell, (*Veronica arvensis*), germander speedwell (*Veronica chamaedrys*), thyme-leaved speedwell (*Veronica sepyllifolia*), common vetch (*Vicia sativa*), and common dog violet (*Viola riviniana*).

What interested Barbara was the single plant of annual knawel. This used to be common, but it seems to have disappeared from many areas

91

since the beginning of the century, so that now it is quite scarce. It is a small, rather undistinguished looking plant. Its odd-sounding name seems to be Saxon, and the modern German name for it, *Knäuel,* also means 'hank', 'skein', 'ball' and 'knot', so perhaps the name refers to the irregular, tangled branches it produces.

I was suitably impressed, but the delicate, tiny field pansy impressed me more. It is very common, and very beautiful, and it is the flower Oberon pressed to obtain the drops of liquid that he sprinkled on Titania's eyelids as she slept so she would fall in love with the first thing she saw when she awoke—which was the ass-headed Bottom, of course.

As we left the field I saw the largest Devil's coach horse beetle (*Ocypus olens*) I have ever seen. Indeed, it may be one of the largest anyone has ever seen. I did not measure it, but I guess it was 1¾ in long, which is a good deal larger than such animals are supposed to be.

Beetles are difficult to identify and most of them have no common names. I found two seven-spot ladybirds on the 25th and several other beetles I could not identify. Later we found a colony of weevils living in the south-eastern hedge.

That was on the evening of the 21st and I had gone out with Frank Smith in search of the moths that live in Cross Park. It was an enjoyable, not to say slightly hilarious, evening, that we had to abandon at 11.15 because, very clearly, there was not a single moth to be seen anywhere. Frank had brought the elaborate equipment without which no field lepidopterist can pursue his craft. We began by walking slowly along all the hedges while Frank tapped at the vegetation with his stick to knock its inhabitants into the net he held below. This produced three or four minute, pale-coloured moths and, of course, the weevils. Then we set up the light. This consists of a powerful electric light bulb on a stand that holds it about two feet from the ground, with a white disc like a shade over it. The bulb is powered by a small generator placed some distance away. The lamp was positioned more or less at the centre of the field on a large, white sheet, and Frank made a shady refuge at the base of the stand using egg trays. We switched on the light and waited for the moths to swarm to it. We waited with great patience but in the end we had to admit defeat. We planned to repeat the exercise in mid-summer.

The hedges were coming into full leaf. The sycamore erupted early in May and by the end of the month the oak leaves were beginning to appear and, with them, the first small leaf galls. When Barbara came to the field on the 18th the grass had not begun to flower, but by the end of the month many grass flowers had appeared.

June

Just because we found no moths or butterflies in May, it does not follow that the invertebrates were skulking in dark corners. The gaudy, delicate Lepidoptera need calm air, and the butterflies sulk when the sun does not shine. They are summer things and their preposterous flutterings are for the delight of children, lovers and mid-summer curates pondering their sermons. Other creatures, more robust or just more phlegmatic, take the weather as it comes.

The snails were mating. There are something like 35,000 species of snails, slugs and limpets in the world as a whole, and several hundred of them live in Britain. They are molluscs, relatives of the mussels and other bivalve animals you find on the beach and distant relatives of the octopus and squid. Snails are not bivalves, and they are not octopus or squid. They are gastropods, a class whose name suggests quite wrongly, that they walk on their stomachs like Napoleonic infantry-men. Most molluscs reproduce sexually, with a distinct male, a distinct female, and no doubt about who is who, at least among the molluscs themselves. The gastropods are different. Many of them, and all the snails you find in Britain, are hermaphrodites.

Life as a hermaphrodite, you may think, is simple if solitary, a narcissistic existence that ignores the world outside. The snail, you may imagine, falls in love with its own image reflected in the tiny pool of water held in a curled leaf, and fertilises itself. Most of them can fertilise themselves when the need arises, but for most of the time, the need failing to arise, reproduction is a great deal more complicated. The hermaphroditic snails court one another and they mate. It is a ponderous business, or so it seems to us. Doubtless the gastropodic heart pounds and the eye flutters, dewy and enticing atop its stalk as ardent Tristram pursues his Iseult to the farthest end of the cabbage patch in a moment suspended in time that is eternity, and that is lost forever in an instant. For the snail the delicious agony is doubled, since

Snails mating. Snails are hermaphrodite, but they reproduce by cross-fertilisation. To do this, two individuals circle one another, drawing closer and closer. When they are almost touching they fire darts at each other. These darts can penetrate deep into the body, but one can be seen sticking into the skin of the darker snail (on the right), about level with the front end of the shell. Soon after this, copulation occurs, with each snail performing both male and female roles

male is female and female is male and if you allow the tummyfoot emotions you must go on to allow that each individual experiences the full range of sentiments that among ourselves are shared between the lover and his lass.

To the snails involved it may be over in a moment, but to the human observer it is a slow, deliberate wooing, and if you plan to watch it you will do well to bring a stool to sit on and some sandwiches. The pair meet, stalked eye to stalked eye, and the ritual begins. Usually the two snails circle one another in decaying orbits, drawing closer together with each circuit until they almost touch. (Where they have met high upon a twig such orbiting may present difficulties, and in this case the snails must improvise.) Then there occurs the first extraordinary event in the whole improbable romance. They fire darts at one another, quite literally. The darts themselves are tiny splinters of a chalky material and they are discharged from organs designed for the purpose. They

94

are fired with some force and often penetrate deep into the body of the beloved. Those whose muzzle velocity is low may remain sticking from the body of the recipient. I saw a courting pair, very handsomely banded, one of which had a dart projecting from its body. So far as I can discover, no one knows the purpose of this duel. The metaphorical daggers that are thrown by human eyes have no immediate amatory effect, but perhaps we may imagine the snails to be somewhat sado-masochistic, so that they find the literal darts erotic. At all events, copulation follows. This is involved, but it does not require a long debate to allot sexual roles. Both snails play both parts simultaneously, each inserting the equivalent of a penis into the equivalent of a vagina. A few weeks later both snails lay fertile eggs.

We should not make comparisons, but we do. We sentimentalise over nesting birds, we admire the agility of flying insects that mate on the wing, we respect the parental care that is lavished on their larvae by the social insects, and we overlook the remarkable snails. We dismiss them as simple and rudimentary because they are soft-bodied, and as ugly and repulsive to the touch because they keep those bodies moist— as they must do or they will die—yet there is a beauty in them, too. I admired the courting snails and left them to their curious pleasures.

The butterflies and moths put in their appearance later in June. The Speckled Yellow and Pretty Chalk Carpet were there and there were others of which I caught no more than a fleeting glimpse in the tall grass, or that I saw but could not identify.

The flies were there in great profusion, and among the blacks and reds and yellows and greens there were the robber flies, the *Asilidae*, fearsome hunters of the air. Some of them lie in wait for their prey; others catch insects in flight. I saw one, with its victim gripped firmly beneath it, settling down to its luncheon. Despite their hunting prowess —and some of them will attack and kill a bee—the robber flies do not bite humans. They are not like the horse flies, whose males feed exclusively on nectar but whose females feed on mammalian blood. The cleg (*Haematopota pluvialis*) is one of the horse flies, and one of the nastiest of that delinquent family. It flies in absolute silence, unlike most flies which have the decency to buzz at least faintly, and its victim only knows it has arrived by its very painful bite.

The most voracious of all insect hunters are the dragonflies. Despite their dramatic appearance, they never harm humans but they are the terrors of the insect world. They fly very strongly and catch their prey in flight. All six legs are grouped together at the front of the body to form a kind of basket into which flying insects are swept, to be torn to pieces by powerful mandibles and so devoured. I saw a big Emperor dragonfly (*Anax imperator*) by the hedge on the lower side of the field. That was on 18 June, but later I discovered that two Emperors patrolled the hedge on the north-western side. They are sometimes called 'hawkers' because they hawk along their beat, often beside a hedge, picking off any fly that mistimes its take-off. I saw an *Aeshna grandis*, too, rather smaller than the Emperor, and brown, working in the field.

Dragonflies are semi-aquatic in that they spend their larval stage in water, as do their smaller and flimsier cousins the damselflies. The dragonfly is the largest of our insects and one of the most ancient. Its ancestors (one of which had a wingspan of 2ft 6in, making it the largest insect the world has ever known) perfected flying many millions of years ago and hawked their beats among forests that have become our coal measures. They can travel as much as three miles from the nearest water in their search for food. The damselflies are more limited and are not really strong fliers. You expect to see them flitting about over still water, settling frequently. Their nymphs are smaller than those of the true dragonflies, though they are just as voracious. The dragonfly nymph stalks its prey along the bottom of ponds, seizing it by means of a lower lip that folds back on itself like a penknife and that can flick forward with great speed. It will take something the size of a tadpole, or even a small fish. In late spring you can see the nymphs hauling themselves out of the water on to leaves, to lie wet and limp, suddenly defenceless during that critical period in which they dry, metamorphose, and emerge in their full imago splendour to complete the final and shortest stage in their lives. A nymph may live for three or four years. The imago lives but for a summer.

You might expect to find a large dragonfly far from water, but you would not expect a damselfly to wander so far afield. I saw one on the 11th, a pretty, red *Pyrrhosoma nymphula*. It was much later that I found the water in which these insects were able to breed, nearby but concealed, a slightly haunted place.

On the Moor above the field there is a disused quarry where great boulders of granite are heaped together. From a distance the place looks used, its piles of stones appearing neat and orderly and clean. In fact they are lying in confusion with plants growing among them. Many are covered with lichens and mosses, which prove that they have lain untouched for many years. They may well provide a breeding ground for reptiles. The old stone hut looks clean, it is true, but it is a ruin, abandoned when building stone became more expensive than red bricks imported from Bedfordshire.

Beside the stones and hidden by them is the quarry itself, a great bite

The cross that once stood in the Cross Park can just be seen peeping over a hedge on the neighbouring farm, provided you know where to look

taken from the land to leave a depression surrounded by sheer rock walls at one end and steep grassy banks at the other. It contains the pool in which the insects breed, a patch of dark water hung over by rock and plants, difficult of access and mysterious.

Other insects were appearing. The field provided nectar for countless bees, which came in all shapes and sizes. There are about 250 different species of bees in Britain and more than twenty of them are social insects. These include the bumble bees, and there are several of them, known by the colour of their 'tails' as 'buff-tailed' or 'red-tailed'. Early in the year the bumble bees you see are likely to be queens, for it is only they who survive the winter. They are large and unhurried as they move about collecting bits of dry grass, moss and other materials to build their underground nests, often in holes abandoned by mice or voles. Each queen works the nesting material into a tight ball and when it is finished she begins to collect food—pollen and nectar. She makes this into 'bee bread', places it in the middle of nest, and lays up to a dozen eggs on top of it. She covers the eggs with wax, builds waxen walls around them, and then a roof, so that the eggs are contained in a closed cell. Next she makes a food store, a honeypot of wax in which she deposits honey to tide the family over periods of bad weather. Her preparations complete, she sits on the cell, incubat-

97

ing her eggs just like a bird. After about five days the eggs hatch and the larvae begin to feed on the 'bee bread', the queen adding more food as it is required. In about two weeks the young bees are ready to emerge. They are workers and their only task is to collect food for themselves, for the queen, and for subsequent batches of young which the queen continues to produce by laying eggs in cells she has made. Later in the year male and female bees emerge and mate, and new queens fly away in search of winter quarters in which to hibernate, their fertilised eggs ready to be laid the following year. All the other bees die.

Bumble bees can carry astonishing amounts of pollen in their pollen baskets on their hind legs. Most bees can carry up to one-quarter of their own weight in pollen and individuals have been found carrying more than half their own weight. You can see them, huge masses of pollen on their legs, still going from flower to flower and collecting more. They work in close collaboration with the flowers, and the hedgerows around Cross Park, as well as those in it, began the month by producing masses of red campion and bluebells. Later in the month the bluebells were gone, the campion was fading, and the foxgloves were opening their bells. The bees that work the campion do so by gripping the flower from the front, leaning over it, and piercing the base of the bell to obtain the nectar. The petals open wide, to lie at right angles to the axis of the flower, so that by gripping at the front the bees receive and deliver their pollen. The larger bell of the foxglove is a more difficult proposition. The bees must enter and climb up the flower, disappearing completely for a moment as they do so. To guide them, the foxglove provides a guidepath, a pattern of more or less circular markings along the lower inside part of the bell that encourages the bees to follow them into the inviting interior. The principle is precisely similar to that used at international airports which provide markers to entice passing aircraft to land, that their passengers may savour the delights of the transfer lounge and the duty-free.

Not all bumble bees are bumble bees; the very hairy ones are quite likely to be homeless, or cuckoo, bees. They are similar to bumble bees in most respects, but profoundly different in one: they parasitise the bumble bees in much the same way as do the cuckoos after which they are named. Technically they are 'brood parasites'.

The cuckoo bee queen overwinters, as does the bumble bee queen. She emerges rather later than her bumble bee host, so that by the time she is on the move the bumble bee queen has made her nest, laid her eggs, and the first few workers have emerged. At this point the cuckoo bee queen invades the nest. If the bumble bee queen catches her at it there may be a fight, which the cuckoo bee wins, but as often as not the

Foxglove, showing the 'guidepath' of markings on the inner lower side of each bell

host never discovers she is being deceived. The new workers can recognise an intruder and they may object. The cuckoo bee subdues them. They cannot harm her because their stings cannot penetrate her very hairy skin. She can kill them with ease if they become too obstreperous. If they live, they learn to tolerate her presence. She lays her eggs and from then on the bumble bee workers devote all their energies to feeding cuckoo-bee young. Further bumble bee eggs are eaten at once. There are six species of British cuckoo bees (*Psithyrus* spp.) and each looks very like the one, or sometimes two, species of bumble bee that it parasitises. Apart from such parasites, bees have no real enemies; their yellow and black colouring warns all insectivores that they do not make good eating, and if the worst comes to the worst stings can be used.

The wasps were also beginning to breed. On the first of the month I saw the first small galls developing on the hedgerow oak. These were currant galls, and they were late appearing, no doubt delayed by the length and severity of the winter. They are made by a wasp called *Neuroterus quercusbaccarum*, a tiny insect whose adult length is no more than about five millimetres. Its life cycle is complex, involving two separate generations of insect, one sexual and one asexual. Each currant gall contains one grub. Later in the summer, its development complete, it will emerge as an adult wasp and it will be either male or female. The wasps mate and the females lay eggs on the leaves of the oak. These eggs develop into spangle galls and, again, each gall contains one larva. Just before the leaves fall from the trees in autumn the galls drop to the ground, where they continue to grow for a while. The grub spends the winter inside its gall, and pupates toward the end of the winter. It emerges as an adult wasp in early spring, but this time all the emerging wasps are asexual females. They lay eggs fertilised by parthenogenesis, which develop into currant galls and so from the asexual back to the sexual generation.

The system has distinct advantages for the wasps. Reproduction by parthenogenesis is much safer and more reliable than sexual reproduction. Since males are not required, all the adults can be females so that the number of egg-layers is increased greatly. There is no risk that some females will fail to find mates, or that matings will prove sterile.

Despite its efficiency, though, parthenogenesis suffers from a major disadvantage. Genes are not mixed. If parthenogenesis were continued over many generations each line of descent would begin to differ from all the others. By a process of genetic drift the insects would become more and more different. Many would exhibit disabilities acquired genetically and eventually it is possible that the entire species might become extinct. So the wasps—and there are many insects that reproduce in this way—have evolved to use both methods. Parthenogenesis ensures large numbers, and sexual reproduction ensures the regular random mixing of genetic material.

The plants leaped ahead as though eager to make up for the cold, wet, lost months of spring. By the middle of the month, on the 11th, I noted that the grass was about knee high. By the end of the month it was waist high. The raw wounds made when the hedges were trimmed had vanished completely in a riot of new foliage. The bracken was threatening to invade the field, especially from its lower edge by the road, and up on the Moor it enveloped and hid the great boulders that lie on the surface to give the bleak, unwelcoming look of winter.

The gorse was growing too, young and green. It had suffered badly in many parts of the country, this immigrant from more southerly climes that can barely tolerate our winters.

The young froghoppers were making use of the new plant growth. They have solved the problem of transferring from an aquatic to a dry land environment by taking their water with them. It is their nymphs that produce 'cuckoo spit', the small masses of froth that you see on plants in summer. The nymph, which lives inside the froth, exudes a liquid from its anus and then forces air into it to make bubbles. This prevents the nymph from dehydrating and it also provides some protection from predators. The adult froghoppers are very common. Rummage in the grass or hedgerow plants in late summer and you will find hundreds of them. They are little bugs that look very slightly like frogs and that move about by making immense leaps. The most common is *Philaenus spumarius*, which is usually brown but occasionally black with white markings. *Cercopis vulnerata* is less common but prettier, being red and black—another colour system that labels the insect as being unpleasant to eat.

The rabbits were active. The unused burrows vanished behind the foliage, but the occupied ones were easy to find by the fresh earth at their entrances, and there were several new scrapes, all of them along the south-eastern hedge.

The moles were difficult to detect and by the end of the month their hills and tunnels were completely hidden by the long grass. It seemed, though, that the original mole was extending its system at the beginning of the month.

The big slide in the eastern corner of the field was used, probably on 31 May, and probably by a badger. Some great barrel of an animal had scrambled down and up it, and on moist ground along the south-eastern hedge I found one clear badger footprint. No doubt this was a routine visit from the owner of the range, but it was not repeated. As the month progressed, the slide promised to vanish amid the burgeoning plants.

As the grass grew, tracks appeared in it across corners of the field but, so far as I could see, not into the centre, which was becoming accessible only to animals small enough to move along at ground level. The tracks were almost certainly made by rabbits.

There was a good deal of warm, sunny weather during June, and it was needed. In most parts of the country all the crops were sown late. May had been cold and wet, with sleet in many places, and, although crops were beginning to grow well by the end of May, those that were sown in spring were late because they had been sown late. Bad weather never fails to delight us, and towards the end of June one leading newspaper solicited predictions from leading professional and amateur forecasters. They divided fairly evenly, the professionals being pessimistic and the amateurs optimistic. The professionals feared that the fine, warm days of June might represent the whole of the 1979 summer, with July and August being generally wet with short, unstable periods of fine weather. The amateurs believed the summer would be long and glorious. William Foggit, of Thirsk, said the first half of July would be very hot and Arthur Mackins, of Sussex, forecast a hundred days of glorious weather. Even with that promised hundred days, it was estimated that the bad spring weather would reduce the grain harvest by five per cent compared to that of 1978.

We remember the weather that impresses us and the long, warm days of late June made it possible to forget the few days at the beginning of the month that came close to bringing disaster to the Royal Cornwall Show.

The Show is the event of the year. People come from far and wide in their tens of thousands. These days, the big shows (and the Royal Cornwall is one of the big shows) are very commercialised. Some people complain at this. They object to the number of exhibits and stalls that have the merest silken strand of a connection with agriculture. Agricultural shows, they suggest, should concern themselves with farming and with nothing else. They should be places for the exhibition of beasts, machines, techniques—places where farmers can show off and learn at the same time.

The suggestion sounds rather solemn and it must be a minority view, or one that is not held very strongly, because it seems that the more highly commercialised the shows become, the more visitors they attract. Yet the view is respectable, in the sense that the modern agricultural show began as a strictly agricultural affair.

The shows are run, as they have been since they began, by agricultural societies. These are not so old as they may seem. The first of them was formed during the last quarter of the eighteenth century and by 1800 most counties had a society of some kind. Like all new movements, that which produced the societies waxed and waned in its early days and many of the societies were short lived. New ones were formed to take their place, and their size and popularity spread. The most prestigious of them all, the Royal Agricultural Society of England, was formed in 1838. It is responsible, to this day, for the largest of all the shows, the Royal Show. Like most shows, the Royal now occupies a permanent site, near Kenilworth in Warwickshire, but at one time it was held in a different place each year. The first Royal Show, in 1839, was held in Oxford. At that time the Society had 690 members. By 1848 its membership had increased to 6,400, and the show had visited Cambridge, Liverpool, Bristol, Derby, Southampton, Shrewsbury, Newcastle-upon-Tyne, Northampton and York. As recently as 1879 it was held at Kilburn 'near London', and it was described by Richard Jefferies, who covered it in his capacity as a

Royal Cornwall Show

journalist working for the *Live Stock Journal*. People came to the Show down Edgware Road and Maida Vale and so into the green fields of rural England, although the tram did run right through the showground, so Kilburn cannot have been entirely rural.

The societies and shows had only one purpose: the promotion of more modern, more progressive, more efficient methods of husbandry. The agricultural shows were where new ideas, techniques and technologies were displayed, new machines demonstrated, where farmers were lectured, exhorted and generally browbeaten. The success was considerable. Most of the agricultural advances made during the nineteenth century owed much to the shows which served to popularise them and to persuade essentially conservative farmers to change habits of a lifetime. It was at a show that the expression 'where there's muck there's brass' was first used. It was said by the fourteenth Earl of Derby in 1862 at the Royal North Lancashire Show in Preston, and what he is alleged to have said was 'muck is money', meaning animal manure.

With this history it is quite reasonable for people to feel that the purpose of an agricultural show is the promotion of better farming and that shows exist for this purpose alone. People cannot remain solemn for very long, though, no matter how hard they try, and country people need an annual occasion. Gradually the show has come to combine its earnest Victorian purpose with an air of a medieval fair. People bring things for sale and they are not necessarily things connected in any way with farming although, because of the nature of the market, they are things that are likely to tempt country people. If the nineteenth-century strictly agricultural show has a respectable pedigree, the medieval fair has one that is even more respectable.

So the Royal Cornwall Show has become something of a fair. You have to search to find the livestock and most of them have gone by the third day. This has caused complaints, because once the judging is finished the animals have a high entertainment value and people enjoy just looking at them. This year the Show was larger and more fair-like than ever. Indeed, it included a fair, with the big wheel, the helter-skelter, the roundabouts and the large inflatables on which small children scrambled and clambered and fell in ecstasies of uninhibited delight while a man with a whistle and a stopwatch made sure they did not overstay their allotted span in paradise. There were stalls and tents of all kinds selling saddles and ladies' dresses, paintings and wine by the case, kitchen utensils, solar panels, swimming pools and cookers. There was a regular shopping arcade and a large tent in which local craftsmen demonstrated their skills and sold their wares. The police had a recruiting stand and so did the Navy, while the Army let small boys play with real guns and awarded paper badges to those who scored well with air rifles. There were ice-cream stalls, hot dog stands, popcorn sellers and an electronic fortune teller labelled 'for amusement only'—such is the status we accord our prophets! There was show jumping to watch, gymnastic displays by the military, and a single small biplane that performed low-level aerobatics above the craned necks of the amazed crowd.

The crowd itself was huge and it was everywhere. It went into all the stalls, into the beer tents (of which there were several), into the refreshment tents that sold no alcohol and into the tents devoted to the activities of non-commercial organisations. The Open University had a tent, the county council had a maze of interconnected tents, the archaeological society and the National Trust had tents. The Cornish mining industry displayed its techniques but not its products and the Rare Breeds Survival Trust exhibited handsome Longhorn and Dexter cattle, Gloucester Old Spots and Tamworth pigs, Soay, St Kilda and North Ronaldsay sheep—the sheep that can live contentedly on a diet of nothing but seaweed that they wade into the sea to find. Agricultural and horticultural worthiness had not been abandoned. The Flower Tent was splendid and its exhibits were judged, like those in the

Poultry and Rabbit and Cavies tents. The Ministry was there to exhort, the Forestry Commission to itemise the delights and benefits derived from the growing of trees, with trees planted several years ago in their permanent mini-park of an exhibit. There were producers of feed additives, fertilisers, pesticides and gadgets, eager to demonstrate the phenomenal rate at which crops and animals can be induced to grow provided they receive sufficiently large doses of the magic ingredient. The intent to earnestness was there, but amid the general gaiety the intent eroded and their displays, too, became part of the fair, entertaining sideshows. The banks, dispensing free liquor from permanent buildings that contained chairs, made their own contribution to the hilarity of the proceedings.

It was an outdoor event, despite the tents, marquees and buildings, and outdoor events are dependent upon the weather. The British climate being what we rejoice in it being, there is always something better than an even chance that the show will be inundated, though it is not entirely unknown for shows to be held in brilliant, warm sunshine. The Kilburn Royal Show of 1879, for example, was held in wet, windy conditions and the combination of rain and trampling feet upon the grass produced the inevitable quagmire. In Richard Jefferies' words:

> Between the sheds are spaces that once were green sward, but are now poached mud. Pathways of planks—such as are used by navvies to wheel their barrows on—lead from shed to shed. Round some of these sheds hurdles have been laid down, so that it is possible to pass: but other exhibits lie in the mud, and for that reason are practically inaccessible to most visitors. Nor is the plank pathway to be traversed without care; for a slip, a false step, or an accidental push from a fellow-passenger may land you in mire six inches deep.

The Royal Cornwall is a three-day event. On the first day the weather was cloudy but dry. It did not rain all day and conditions were almost ideal. It was dry but neither too hot nor too cold. On the second day it rained more or less continuously from early morning until well into the night. At first all was well, for the ground was dry from the day before and well packed down by trampling. As the day wore on, however, conditions deteriorated. They deteriorated first in the car parks. By mid-morning, tractors were being used to push cars into the car parks. The mud was churned and kneaded and kneaded and churned and by evening the tractor owners, bourgeois opportunists to a man, were charging, variously, from one to five pounds a time to help stranded visitors to leave. That night the bulldozers worked by electric light to push aside the mud that was starting to flow into the stands and to locate firm ground beneath it. Tons and tons of sand were spread on the 'grassed' pathways that led away from the skeleton of concreted roads. The Saturday was fine, sunny and warm, but it was also the busiest day. The entrance fee was halved in the afternoon. You entered through the main gate on to a concreted apron that opens to either side into one of the main concreted roads. In front of you lies the first of the paths leading to the centre of the showground. It was brown, shiny and menacing yet rather beautiful in its way. Almost everyone wore wellingtons. A few people wore plastic shopping bags tied around their ordinary shoes. These bags, bright yellow and distributed free by the Abbey National Building Society, became a feature of the Bath and West Show, from which they spread to the Royal Cornwall by a kind of cultural diffusion. The mud covered your feet and was very slippery, so that the pathways became hordes of individuals all tending to slide quite gently in random directions. Knowledge of the conditions at the showground was widespread, but the number of visitors was high enough to surprise and delight the Society. Someone said that if the Show were held on the bleakest part of Bodmin Moor in the middle of winter, people would still come to it in their tens of thousands.

The showground has remained in the same place for several years now, on a permanent site just outside Wadebridge. It is an exposed place, sitting above the town, and for all but three days in the year it lies more or less empty and unsightly. It is used for motor racing, Caravan Club rallies and private parties, and sheep graze quite safely upon it, but I dare say an economist would consider it under-utilised. The bus service, sparse for 362 days of the year, blossoms into a continual shuttle service, and the roads through Wadebridge are jammed with an endless stream of traffic for those three magic days. The town itself feels empty of people. Even the local shopkeepers move to the showground, leaving depleted staff in town.

The bad weather at showtime seemed not to dampen spirits at Wadebridge, but up at Cross Park it brought a small catastrophe. With the grass growing strong but late, Geoff, the farmer, had built a silage pit. In former years he had made silage in an improvised clamp in one of his fields, but two ewes had died from drinking the silage liquor, which is probably the most noxious and most useless of all farm wastes. Now he was determined to do it properly and safely and his new pit, up on the edge of the Moor, was well away from streams and underground aquifers, and was accessible to few animals other than the horses that are turned on to the Moor in winter to fend for themselves by owners who cannot, or will not, feed them. Horses will take hay, but they will not touch silage. Geoff built his pit and lined it with concrete. Before the concrete had set hard, the rain soaked into the soil around and beneath it and accumulated because it could not drain. The soil swelled and the pit collapsed into rubble. It was expensive rubble, because the concrete is expensive. Geoff reckoned it cost him about £1,000 to rebuild.

Further east, they were cutting for hay at the beginning of the month. I had to go to London on the 4th and in Somerset and Berkshire I saw many fields that had been mown. In Cornwall they began the cut later and it was not until the end of the month that the tractors and mowers were out and the smell of newly mown hay began to fill the air. Even then Cross Park was not cut. Geoff was making silage in his new pit, hoping, perhaps, to pack in sufficient weight to hold the sides should the soil swell again. Cross Park he planned to leave until later and use its grass for hay. The grass used to make silage needs a rather higher moisture content than that used to make hay, so that if the weather seems set fair silage can be made first while the remaining grass can continue to dry for haymaking.

On the 21st the sheep were sheared. I remember, some years ago, watching some young farm students learning to shear sheep with hand clippers at the side of a road in Sutherland, while the farmer and one of his friends watched, drinking tea and eating drop scones when they could stop laughing for long enough. The electric clippers have revolutionised shearing without robbing the job of any of its skill. Usually it is done by itinerant shearers, many of whom come from New Zealand. They spend two or three years in Britain and then return home. Presumably they do the job to earn money and from the rate at which they work I would not be surprised if in their two or three years they manage to save enough to buy their own farms.

Two of these young men arrived at the farm early in the morning. They work in bare feet and once they have started work they do not stop. Sheep are passed to them and taken from them so they seldom even straighten their backs. By my reckoning, each of them can shear a sheep in under three minutes. They do it completely, taking off the fleece in one piece (to make a second cut reduces its value) and they seldom injure the animal. During that morning they sheared 140 sheep and so far as I know their only refreshment was a cup of tea at ten o'clock. Then they moved to another farm, where they sheared a further 100 sheep in the afternoon. Then, I suppose, they had their tea. In the evening they visited a third farm and sheared another 175 sheep before bedtime. They said their record, for the two of them, was 750 sheep sheared in one day. Allowing for meal breaks, but not for travelling from one farm to another, that seems to be an average of under two minutes a sheep, and the really startling thing about it is that it is not even close to the world speed record for sheep shearing. The shearers provide living proof that new machines, new techniques, need not erode human skills, competitiveness, or the pride a skilled worker takes in his or her work.

By the end of June, then, the fields around Cross Park were filled with naked sheep, many of them still suckling their unshorn lambs. Cross Park was filled with tall grass. Above it all, sitting high on the wind, there rode the buzzard. It was usually to be seen somewhere nearby, and occasionally it had a companion. It watched and waited, circling slowly with the infinite patience of the true hunter in a world where only men must make haste.

July

' 'Tis the king of trades.' I was talking to Cyril, the blacksmith, aged 78 and still working. The welfare people told him he should give it up. He would be paid almost as much by them, what with his pension and various allowances. ' 'Tain't right, though, is it?' he asked with the assurance of a man whose health is robust and whose needs are few. He does it for 'the extras', to keep the van running and to pay for little luxuries. At least, he says that is why he does it. As I watched him I wondered whether the real reason is that he cannot leave his work alone. He is addicted to it, hopelessly, after a lifetime of exposure. Quite simply, it is what he does. Sitting on a bench in the park with the old men is not what he does. It is not difficult to understand. I say he has been exposed to life in his smithy for all of his life, but that is not quite true. He went away once, during the war. So far as I know it is the only time he has left his home ground. He went to Sussex. He pronounces the name in the way another man might pronounce 'Malaya', say, or 'Uruguay'. The word has a kind of assumed familiarity, a confidence in pronunciation, that is meant to obscure the romance it connotes. It is said with a sort of self-deprecating inflexion. 'I have been there, but I do not mean to imply that I am superior to you because of it.' What 'Uruguay' is for some, 'Sussex' is for Cyril. It is another place, a place of different speech, different customs, different values, an exciting place but one remote from the real world and of no great relevance to the important matters of every day.

He regretted leaving, though, because in his absence 'they' ruined Bodmin. It had been a lovely town once, but during the war they took away the guns and some of the monuments and changed the whole character of the place. There are people who believe that the final departure of the garrison from what had been a garrison town for generations left Bodmin without a role. Part of the reason for its existence had been taken from it and, some say, it has never been

Cyril, the blacksmith, in his forge at the farm

replaced. That is not the way Cyril sees it. 'They' took advantage of his temporary and involuntary absence to desecrate the townscape of his childhood and he has not forgiven them for it. I do not suppose he will ever forgive them. His eyes flash with anger when he mentions it. The anger is good: it is good that he can find someone to blame, some excuse for the change he cannot accept. Had he not gone to Sussex he would not have been able to prevent it and his anger might well have turned to guilt, defeat, and resignation. O brave Sussex! You have saved the spirit of a Cornishman. We would not wish him withdrawn and introverted.

Introverted Cyril is not. I was talking to Geoff in the yard when he arrived in his little van, parked it, and walked past us with a cheery greeting of which I took little notice. Geoff told me who he was and pointed out the thin plume of smoke that began to rise from the smithy chimney within minutes. I do not like intruding on people and I entered the smithy with some diffidence and asked, very politely, whether he would mind if I watched him while he worked. His face lit up with pleasure and I was there for the rest of the morning.

He and Geoff built the smithy on the farm. He worked there in the

1920s and until he went to Sussex, but that was in Geoff's father's time. Cyril worked for him and for Geoff's grandfather.

He was coaxing his fire as he talked. The fuel for it costs a small fortune, and you can't be sure of getting it. Cyril hoards it, a secret burner, lighting his fire when he has accumulated enough. Hardly anyone knows how to work the fire these days, he told me. It's all arc. You get these lads in workshops who learn how to use an arc welder and they think they can do anything. Trouble is, they never know what metal they're using. They never get to know the metal. Clearly 'knowing the metal' is to a blacksmith what knowing the characteristics of different woods is to a carpenter. It makes sense. 'You take what happens when you want to weld a little thin piece on to a great big piece. The big piece will attract most of the arc because of magnetism. It will get hotter than the little piece. They'll look as though they're welded, but they won't be. You give the little piece a bit of a knock with the hammer and it'll come right off.' He loves metal. Today most things are made from steel. Steel is hard and difficult to work. Iron is better. Iron has a grain, like wood. If you look at an old piece of iron you can see that it flakes, in layers. That's the grain. 'We used all iron in the old days.' Cyril used to make fine scrollwork and leaves.

I think he had his own business at one time, or was a partner in a business. They made farm carts. Cyril could make a farm cart in one day, from start to finish. He would begin at eight, do all the cutting, drilling, welding, bolting; he would assemble the wooden sides and bottom, put on the shafts, and at five—you get the feeling that it was at five precisely by the church clock—the cart was ready for spraying. The business failed, though. 'Came unstuck!' he says, with a chortle of glee, or is it bravado? He could make a cart in a day, but it was not enough. The industrial revolution, the division of labour, the production line, destroyed Cyril's business, but they did not destroy Cyril. It would take more than a little thing like an industrial revolution to do that.

His life is not complete, though. He is a man born to teach. He ought to pass on the skills he has learned; he wants to pass them on, and he almost bursts with frustration because there are no youngsters to keep the trade alive. I was there for no more than an hour or two. He did all the talking and he was beginning to teach me. Perhaps I should enrol as his apprentice? I think I might enjoy that. He rushed me outside to see one of the best carts he ever made. He made it for Geoff. Fifteen feet long it is and 'Oh 'tis lovely, don't rock, steady as anything'.

He was there when Geoff took over the farm just after the war. It was

111

very run down then. Sam, Geoff's father, was a good man and tried hard, but it never seemed to work for him. The land would not do what he wanted it to do. Land can be like that. Geoff was young then, with a young wife. 'She was marvellous, mind,' says gossipy Cyril. 'Wouldn't let him buy a car. Has to get his tractor and implements first. I used to get a car from down the garage to take her to do her shopping.' Bit by bit they built the smithy, the barns, the sheds, and finally they concreted over the mixture of mud and manure through which you had to wade to get anywhere and so made the yard. The farm is healthy and prosperous today. It works for Geoff. Cyril claims no credit for the achievement, but he is very proud of it all the same. It is Geoff's farm, but it is also Cyril's life. They are close, those two men.

Geoff came in carrying a turf iron that Cyril may have made long ago and that was used when peat from the Moor was important to them as a fuel. 'They looked after their turf before they looked after their hay,' Cyril informed me. It is a way of saying that turf is about the most important commodity in the world. Spend a winter on the Moor with no fuel and I dare say most people would agree. Cyril showed me a small ploughshare he had made of a kind you never see now. It cut a single furrow about two inches deep and it was used after the cereal harvest to turn each furrow over on top of the ground next to it so that the stubble was buried and rotted down more quickly. They would leave it like that for a while and then cultivate. He made bigger ploughs, too, and implements of all kinds, he repaired things, and he shoed horses, a job that went on throughout the year. Each day was different and if Cyril had his time over again he would learn the same trade.

He made his own tools, of course. The blacksmith is the only tradesman who makes his own tools. Cyril rummaged in a corner to produce a hammer he made years ago.

It was not the hammer he used to make the gate parts that were the real purpose of his visit. If you look at a farm gate you will see that it is hinged to the gatepost by means of two spikes mounted vertically on brackets set horizontally into the post, which fit inside loops of metal that form part of the gate. It was these loops that Cyril was making, and he made them very fast, from square section steel rod. He cut off a length of rod with a cutter on one side of the workshop, pulling a huge lever that moved a blade and cut through the steel as easily as wire cutters sever flex. He heated his metal, placed it on the pick of the anvil, hammered it into shape, and bang bang bang it was done. 'You have to know the anvil,' he said, 'It can do anything.' He pointed out to me the different parts of it and told me their purpose. 'It's all in the anvil,' Geoff said, later. 'You have to know just which part to use. When I try it the work goes all over the place!' Cyril scorched his wooden rule measuring the length he wanted, from the end of the loop, and made a mark with a chisel. Then he returned to the cutter and snipped off the finished article, leaving it on the floor to cool. He went back to the fire and made a second and then a third. Each one fitted exactly over the others. They were the same shape and the same size. Apart from the length, he measured nothing, and he did not refer to the loop he had finished to guide him in making its fellow.

Then he interrupted himself to show me how to make a hot weld, heating, hammering, to make the scarf, a 'step' in each piece, then laying one piece above the other and hammering them together. It took him two attempts and when he was done the rod had been cut and joined again invisibly. He used no flux and no other metal, and he was very pleased with himself. He hadn't done that for years. He made the fourth loop from the welded metal. If that gate falls because its hinge breaks, it will be my fault.

He made a catch for the gate, a piece of round rod with a small loop at one end to fasten it to the gate and ending with a right angle bend to fit through the loop on the gatepost. The trick lay in the barb at the end of the catch, made by bending the last inch or two back on itself and hammering it into shape. The barb made it impossible for a sheep to open the gate by lifting the catch with its head.

I left him laughing and waving outside his smithy. Short of stature he is, thin as a rake but wiry, and happy as a small boy. ' 'Tis the king of trades.'

I had gone up to the farm to watch them shear the lambs. They are done separately from the ewes, and later. The two New Zealand lads were back, working at their frenetic pace. 'I don't know how they keep it up,' said Geoff. 'I don't know how they do it,' said Doreen. Neither do I. They just do. Lamb succeeded bewildered lamb and the shorn ones huddled in small groups about the yard while Geoff and his son swept up the wool and stuffed it into bags. There was no question of folding the fleeces neatly, the way they fold those from the ewes. They were bundled in anyhow. They will go off to the Board with the rest.

They are a breed apart, these shearers, and they see the world from a viewpoint denied to most of us. When the shearing is finished in Britain, these two will move over to the Continent and shear there. Others have gone to Israel, to shear on the kibbutzim. Some go to America, shearing in the north, picking cotton in the south, then go on to Brazil for the coffee harvest, and so home. The world they see is no place for the faint of heart or for the rich. It is inhabited by working farmers, peasants and labourers. They do see it, too. Once or twice a day they stop for refreshment, sitting on the ground, leaning back, with a sack around their shoulders to prevent cramp, and that is when they look up and see whatever it is that they see. They do not talk much. Conversations tend to be monosyllabic. They laugh readily, though.

That was on the 17th. They had started cutting the hay in Cross Park on the 4th, and by the 10th it was safe in the barn. At haymaking time everyone works from dawn to dusk, because it must be done quickly, while the weather holds. It is an anxious, sky-staring, nail-biting time, and the relief that comes when the last bales are under cover is physical. You can feel the weight being lifted.

Farmers have made hay ever since they learned to combine the grazing of livestock with the cultivation of crops. If you cultivate crops you must live in one place, but if you live in one place you cannot be a pastoralist, following the herds and flocks from one grazing ground to the next. Farming consists quite largely in the reconciling of the irreconcilable. The closest you can come to achieving the best of the two quite different worlds of the farmer and the cowboy is to reduce the number of animals so that some of the land remains ungrazed, then cut the surplus grass and save it for winter, when the grass stops growing but the animals do not stop eating.

You cannot just cut the grass and leave it in a heap in a corner. A living plant obtains its energy by photosynthesis, supported by mineral nutrients it takes from the soil in the form of a dilute solution. If you cut its stem and so sever its links with the soil, it will continue to respire for quite some time, and most of the energy used by any living organism is used in respiration. The cut plant will obtain its energy not from photosynthesis, but from its own store of sugars, so that its food value drops very quickly. The aim of grass conservation is to stop respiration as quickly as possible so that what is conserved is not so much the grass as the food value of the grass. Drying the grass is one way to achieve this.

The theory is simplicity itself. You let the grass grow until it matures and sets seed. Then you cut it and let it lie in the field to dry. Then you store it. However, if you just leave it to dry it will not dry evenly. It must be turned. Traditionally this was done by tedding, a word derived from the Welsh *teddu,* which means 'to spread out'. The tedder, who used to be a human being with a rake but more recently became a machine, picks up the swathe left by the mower—who was also a man once, wielding a scythe—throws it up and over and so allows air to enter. You seldom see farmers tedding these days; instead the mown grass is scattered using mechanical rakes that look like

The rakes, like demented coat hangers

demented coat hangers or large bicycle wheels whose spokes project far beyond the rims. The rakes do less damage to the grass than tedders, especially if it has rained recently and the grass is wet. They follow fairly closely behind the mower, because the faster the grass is dried the better. That is when the farmer stares at the sky. If the hay becomes really wet, and stays wet, it will start to rot, its food value dropping all the time. If it is stored while it is still damp, respiration will consume some of its sugars and the rest will feed bacteria that will decompose it. The bacteria will generate warmth, the hay will heat, and it may catch fire. Many a careless farmer, and many an unlucky one, has lost his barn because of a hay fire. There are one or two every year, wherever hay is made. They are destructive, because a hay fire blazes with great ferocity. The hay is ready to collect when the moisture it contains accounts for less than thirty per cent of its weight. At this stage, the grass becomes very brittle and it must be handled with care. The walls of its cells break easily, so that their contents are lost and what remains is the thin, papery, and almost useless cellulose.

Of all the methods for conserving grass, haymaking is the least efficient. The food value of the hay is about 35 per cent lower than that of the grass from which it was made. The technique survives because it is simple, well known, traditional, and cheap.

You can improve on it. It is possible to conserve grass and lose no more than about five per cent of its food value. The grass is cut when it is ready to cut, taken straight back to the barn, and dried rapidly by blowing hot air through it. The method was devised back in the 1920s, but it has never really caught on. This is due to much more than the natural conservatism of farmers. It is an expensive process. The farmer must buy a large blower that devours proportionately large amounts of fuel, and all this must be paid for out of the saved nutrients after those nutrients have been converted into meat or milk. It takes many pounds of hay to make a pound of beef.

There is a compromise—there is always a compromise in this industry of compromise. If the grass is cut and allowed to dry until the moisture content is about 45 per cent of the weight, it can be taken back to the barn and dried much more simply and cheaply. Less moisture has to be removed from it, and so the blower can be much smaller, and so less fuel is used. A suitable blower can be run off the power take-off from a tractor if the farmer does not want to buy a diesel or electric engine, and the waste heat from the engine exhaust can be used to warm the air. The nutrient loss will be about 20 per cent, or even less. It is called 'barn drying'.

Ensiling works on a different principle and it is slightly less efficient than barn drying. The cut grass is not dried completely. It is chopped, often twice, until it is like suburban lawn cuttings, and then it is left to wilt for about 24 hours. Conservation is achieved by packing it together very tightly to squeeze out all the air. It can be packed in an airtight silo, a tower built for the purpose, or in a clamp like Geoff's, where the tractor is run over it repeatedly to press the material down while the clamp is being filled. In this airless state the greenstuff ferments. It cannot heat, because the bacteria that cause heating require air. Other bacteria break down some of the sugars and make lactic acid. The acid prevents respiration in the grass and further decomposition by bacteria, so that the silage can remain for long periods in a sort of pickled state. There is a great deal that can go wrong, though. If the grass was too wet it will exude a liquor that is highly noxious. If too much acid is formed the silage will be unpalatable. If air enters, the silage will turn into tenth-rate compost.

By the 10th, then, the hay had gone and Cross Park had changed its appearance again. Already the new grass was growing and from the other side of the valley the field that had been buff-coloured was green by the third week in July.

About a third of the field mown, the cut grass lies in long, regular rows that must be moved if the grass at the bottom of each heap is to dry at the same rate as the grass at the top

After it has been trimmed, the verge looks devastated, brown with dead and dying vegetation where before it had been a riot of wild plants. This is the verge beside the road that runs below Cross Park; the field is on the other side of the hedge

It was the time for mowing. On the 4th they were cutting the roadside verges all round the village so that the air hung heavy with the scent of newly mown grass. These days everything that happens in the countryside is controversial. The councils used to spray herbicides on the verges to control plant growth. This led to many protests, and rightly. It caused considerable damage to one of the few remaining refuges for wildlife, it was unsightly, and as often as not the spray drifted into nearby vegetable gardens to cause havoc among the cabbages. So spraying was abandoned and mowing took its place. Not everyone is satisfied even now, for while the mower poisons nothing it damages wild plants, because that is what it is meant to do. Some conservationists would prefer no management, or a kind of selective management in which certain plants are cut back and others are protected. That would require armies of botanists who would have to be paid out of the rates, leading to rather predictable protests, while abandoning all management would create a haven for insects and small mammals, but before long the smaller and probably rarer plants would be crowded out by the more vigorous or taller species. Eventually, of course, trees would establish themselves, transpire great amounts of water, lower the water table, and, quite possibly, lead to the subsidence of the road. Once you start managing nature it is not very easy to stop. Sooner or later someone has to do something. I am glad it is not I who must decide who or what.

It was a bright, hot, sunny day. The fine weather that began towards the end of June continued for the first week in July, after which conditions became less settled. There was a good deal of humid, oppressive weather, sometimes with low cloud and drizzle that did not relieve the oppression, and towards the end of the month it became showery, with some heavy rain. July ended spectacularly in many parts of Britain. On the 29th and 30th it rained almost non-stop around Cross Park, but elsewhere there were severe thunderstorms. Lightning killed a six-year-old girl on a beach at Skegness and injured her sister. In Plymouth nearly 1.3 inches of rain overloaded a sewer and sent sewage washing over part of a park. In St Austell a pavement cracked under the pressure of water, a manhole cover was lifted off, and tarmac was torn from a road surface. Roads were flooded, drains blocked, the rain continued for 24 hours, and then the storms passed. The 31st was showery and breezy. In general, though, the month seemed to be dry. When it did rain people were saying 'The gardens need it', and perhaps they did.

The yellowhammers were there, singing noisily on telegraph wires and making flashes of bright yellow as the males darted into and out of the hedges. They nest fairly close to the ground and although they are only partially migratory you see them here only in the summer. 'Little bit of bread and no cheese', they sing, and when you have heard it you do not forget it. The corn buntings were there too, paler cousins of the sparrow, and the true summer migrants, the martins, were around in large numbers. They say this is a tremendous year for martins and certainly there seemed to be plenty of them. I expect that means something profound to those who read the rural omens. The buzzards circled slowly above everything, swooping occasionally and then aborting their attack to climb back to their stations and watch. They are forever watching.

On the first of the month I was looking at spiders with Mr Wheatley, who probably is Cornwall's leading authority on arachnids, the spiders and mites and their cousins the scorpions. He spent the weekend catching them for identification. He found about a dozen species, all of them common.

I have no way of knowing how many spiders live in Cross Park. To discover that would require a team of collectors to make a thorough sweep of the field. The total population is certainly large, although much smaller than would be found in an undisturbed meadow. An acre of English meadow was examined years ago and was found to contain 2,265,000 spiders. It is one of those numbers that is repeated in all the standard reference books. It proves that spiders like English meadows. In the world as a whole there may be about 40,000 species, and there are 570 species that live in Britain.

The success of the spiders is phenomenal and it is a success that was achieved many millions of years ago. Fossil spiders have been found that are almost identical to spiders that are alive today. They have had no reason to develop further. They improve not, neither do they learn. If you find a spider that makes a web with a mistake in it you can be sure that it has always made that same mistake and that it will continue to make it in every web it weaves until the day it dies. Learning is beyond the spider, which has nothing with which to learn. Its brain, if you can call it that, consists of a ganglion, a collection of nerve endings, where impressions are received from its sensors. It has plenty of those. Most species have eight eyes, although some make do with only six. Its chelicerae, the appendages with which it seizes its prey, are sensitive, and its 'feet', all eight of them, are sensitive to vibrations in ways that are not simply beyond our experience but beyond our comprehension. Not only can we not feel as the spider feels, we cannot really imagine what it would be like to feel in that way. Each of its hairs has its own nerve, and that, too, transmits impressions. The animal sounds sensitive, and it is, but it is incapable of learning. It is a very sophisticated machine, an automaton that reacts in perfectly predictable ways to the stimuli presented to it by its environment. It is a machine, but it is not a self-programming machine.

The spider is also beautiful and fascinating, and not in the least evil. It is a stranger to malice as much as to love and is no more capable of vindictiveness than it is of generosity. Moral judgements do not apply to it. It is a machine.

Most spiders are venomous but very few can injure a human, and none of those lives in Britain. The huge, hairy 'tarantulas' from South America are not poisonous at all, but because they are large they can deliver a painful bite to those who molest them. If a giant molested you, would you not hit back? The North American black widow and brown recluse spiders, and one or two of their South American relatives, produce a venom that is many times more poisonous than that produced by a rattlesnake, but they are so small that they inject only the minutest dose. It can be painful and unpleasant, but it is seldom fatal to humans. The true tarantulas are also quite small and come from the region around the town of Taranto, in Italy. They used to be blamed for a peculiar form of madness that afflicted the locals and that caused them to dance a furious dance called a tarantella. Whatever caused their malady it was not their spiders, because tarantulas are quite harmless.

Spiders need defending because they receive such a bad press, and many people are frightened or revolted by them. They are deaf to our complaints. They possess many senses but the one they lack is hearing. Spiders are deaf.

In Cross Park the lycosids were reproducing. These are the wolf spiders, dark-coloured spiders that live on or close to the ground. They do not spin webs, but they do produce silk. All spiders produce silk and they use it in innumerable ways. The female wolf spider drags her fertilised eggs behind her in a silken sac. Spiders are not insects, and their life cycle does not include a larval stage. The eggs hatch into spiderlings—tiny but fully formed spiders. As soon as they are free of the sac, wolf spiderlings scramble on to their mother's back, where they cling tight and remain still, like so many small pimples. Being machines, spiders do not make the best mothers in the world and Madame Lycosid does nothing to help her brood climb aboard. Either they make it or they do not, in which case they are left to their own devices which lead them, inevitably, to an early demise. Once on her back the spiderlings remain there until they have grown large enough to fend for themselves. Mother does nothing to protect them, but she does protect them simply by existing. That which would relish a spiderling sandwich may hesitate before crossing Madame.

By the time they leave home the spiders have become hunting machines, just like Mum, and they depart rapidly. Once off her back and in her line of sight they are potential meals so far as she is concerned. She is no less of a potential meal to them, but spiders are solitary creatures that never collaborate and not one of them is large enough to attack her. Off they trot to seek their fortunes. Many species of spiderlings migrate by flying. You can see them, at the right time of year, ballooning their way through the air.

The wolf spiders are not invulnerable. We lifted a stone to reveal a nest of ants, who began at once to remove their larvae from the chambers we had exposed. At the edge of all this activity there stood a female wolf spider, her egg sac still attached to her. She seemed hesitant, and well she may have been, for she was in considerable danger. She was more than a match for any ant, but unlike spiders ants do collaborate and unwelcome intruders are attacked by as many ants as are needed to remove the threat. Had she approached any closer she might well have been overwhelmed and killed. Our lifting of the stone diverted the ants and presented her with a line along which to retreat, and so she escaped unharmed.

The web-spinners were there, too, in the hedgerows, including the most common of British spiders, the diadem or garden spider, *Araneus diadematus*. Its appearance varies somewhat, but it earns its name by the white cross on its back.

The spider you see sitting at the centre of its web may be male or female, but when the spiders are courting the centre of the web belongs to the female. It is the males who visit her. Mr Wheatley showed us how to distinguish males from females. In front of its head a spider has a pair of appendages called palpi, that look like short legs, but that are not legs at all. In the male, the ends of the palpi are modified into bulbous structures that in most species are visible to the naked eye, and that look for all the world like boxing gloves. If the spider wears boxing gloves it is male. If not, it is female. That is all there is to it.

The Cross Park spiders were courting. The females sat in their webs and if you looked beneath leaves and twigs close to the edges of the web you found the males. Often there were two or three males waiting for a chance to cross the web and seize the prize. Provided you know the rules, and male spiders are hatched knowing them, the mating of spiders is much less hazardous than many people suppose. Males do get eaten by their mates now and then but it is not a very common occurrence. The male makes placatory signals, and this is what matters. He vibrates the edge of the web. All spiders are very sensitive to vibration, as I said, and the female can tell whether the twitching of her silk is caused by the wind or by the impact of something solid. If an object strikes the web the spider can tell its approximate size and whether it is animate or inanimate. It will not approach to investigate anything that has not announced itself as a meal. The male, then, vibrates the web to signal the arrival of a mate, an animate, interesting, and decidedly inedible visitor. If the female is not prepared to receive him she may do what spiders always do when danger threatens, and drop from the web very fast indeed, on the end of a thread. If he is invited to enter the web the male must then signal that he is a male of the same species intent on mating, not eating. He weaves a small pad of silk, deposits a drop of semen upon it, then sucks it into his palpi. Palpi charged, he approaches the female and inserts them into receptacles on her body. The palpi, the 'boxing gloves', and the corresponding female receptacles have a shape and size that is characteristic of the species, so that inter-specific breeding may be impossible, or possible only between closely related species. It is after he has discharged his palpi that he may be in danger, because now he is very close to the female, who is larger than he is, and the effect of his placatory signals is wearing off. He retreats quickly, and usually successfully, before she mistakes him for prey.

Spiders never eat, they only drink. Like many invertebrates they begin the digestion of their food outside their bodies, by injecting their subdued prey with digestive fluids that liquefy it so they can suck out the contents and leave the indigestible, chitinous exoskeleton behind.

They leave their own exoskeletons lying around, too, for they can grow only by moulting one inelastic outer covering and expanding quickly before the new one hardens. When you find what look like dead and dried up spiders in the corners of rooms, these are abandoned skeletons. It is a tricky business that causes many deaths, with spiders caught by limbs they are unable to extricate from half moulted coverings.

The day we looked at the spiders was also the day we found evidence of the weasels. Beside the gate at the top corner of the field, next to the Moor, the stonework is exposed and gaps between the stones that might have accommodated weasels had been worked into what were very definitely the entrances to tunnels. We found a dead rabbit, partly eaten, beside a hedge. A few minutes later, when we went back for a second look, it had gone. We had interrupted a weasel while it was feeding and it had returned to take its meal to more private quarters.

The dragonflies were there, two of them, each with its own section of hedge to patrol, but by the middle of the month they had disappeared. It is their mating time, too. On the pond at home the damselflies were laying eggs on the 5th, and soon after that they had vanished for another year.

Other insects were appearing. The flowering umbellifers each had their complement of soldier beetles, *Rhagonycha fulva*, and by the end of the month they, too, were mating. They are called 'soldier beetles' because of their generally neat appearance and their red thorax that looks like a soldier's tunic. Sometimes they are called 'blood suckers', which is a calumny. They do not suck blood, but they are carnivorous. What, then, are they doing spending so much of their time on flowers? The theory is that they feed on those other insects that visit the flowers in search of nectar, but you rarely see them except on umbellifers. Another possibility is that their larvae feed on the leaves of some umbellifers, most commonly hogweed, and if you look at hogweed leaves you will often find them eaten away extensively.

The cardinal beetle, *Pyrochroa coccinea*, is more splendid than the soldier and its name is richly deserved, for it is as brightly red as any cardinal. I found one on the 4th, flying from plant to plant. Its larvae live beneath bark. The longhorn beetles (*Cerambycidae*) also feed on wood. One emerged quite suddenly from beneath a head of hogweed flowers, climbed on to the top, and then flew away over the hedge. It was very large, and black with bright yellow markings, and it sported the tremendously long antennae that give the family its name.

A few pea galls had appeared, round, bright red and clean, on the leaves of the briar rose. They are made by a tiny gall wasp, *Diplolepsis nervosa*, a relative of those that parasitise the oak. By the end of the month the roses were shedding their petals and hips were starting to form. The campion, too, was nearly finished. On the advice of a botanist friend, I looked for, but failed to find, the dark blue fungus that sometimes infects the stamens of female red campion flowers. I gather it is not uncommon and it might well repay a thousandfold any biochemical study, for it changes the female flower to a male flower.

There were plants we had not noticed earlier in the year. Scabious (*Scabiosa columbaria*) was flowering here and there in the hedges, making little feathery patches of lilac blue to compensate for the decline of the campion and the foxgloves, which were forming seed, starting at the bottom of the stem. Tufted vetch (*Vicia cracca*) was there, and so was self-heal (*Prunella vulgaris*). This is a common enough plant, but one much favoured by ancient herbalists for the styptic, tonic and astringent properties it is said to possess. Like many herbs it cures almost anything, cleansing wounds and relieving headaches with equal facility and, says Culpepper, 'it is an especial remedy for all green wounds to close the lips of them and to keep the place from further inconveniences'. Make of that what you will. An infusion of it can be used as a gargle to soothe mouth ulcers and sore throats. So perhaps it deserves its name and really does enable the sick to avoid the ministrations of physicians.

The bryony (*Bryonia dioica*) grows where there are no rabbit burrows. It is not that it avoids the rabbits, but that the rabbits avoid it. It, too, has herbal uses, for coughs and other respiratory ailments and, curiously, for rheumatism and gout. In the middle ages it was said to be an antidote for leprosy. It has, or has had, many names. Long ago there were people who used to make the root, which is the part of the plant that is used, into the approximate shape of a human. They did this by digging to expose the root of a young bryony plant, taking care not to damage it. Then they made a mould around the root in the shape of a human so that as the plant grew the root was constrained within the mould, which it filled. At the end of summer, which is as long as it took, they would dig up the root and take it about the country to impress simple country folk with its magical powers. It was no midget, either. There are accounts of roots the size of a child. They called it a 'mandrake' or 'mandrake root' and it was said to scream if it was cut. This is the mandrake root that John Donne exhorts his audience to get with child.

> Go, and catch a falling star,
> Get with child a mandrake root,
> Tell me where all past years are,
> Or who cleft the Devil's foot,
> Teach me to hear mermaids singing,
> Or to keep off envy's stinging,
> And find
> What wind
> Serves to advance an honest mind.

I never heard a bryony plant scream and I bet Dr Donne never heard one, either. He was nobody's fool. In fact bryony is very poisonous indeed and on no account should anyone try to eat any part of it, including its pretty berries. It is best even to handle it with some care, for it is powerfully irritant.

The brambles flowered, began to shed their petals, and blackberries started to form. The thistles set their seeds and the wind blew them along the hedgerows, and short mid-summer hinted at autumn.

The lower hedge, bordering the road, was dominated so completely by tall bracken that nothing else seemed to grow there. It had become a place that promised no surprises. As I walked along it a cock pheasant erupted through the bracken, over the road, and into the field on the other side, with a loud and hideous cry uttered no more than two feet from my left ear, so that my heart pounded like Cyril's hammer. I am too old for such alarums.

Avoiding the deadly bryony and the more deadly weasels, the rabbits were active, leaving piles of fresh earth to mark their house-keeping. Their numbers are still lower than they seemed to be in winter. I saw no victims of myxomatosis, but I heard that the disease had struck again on farms a few miles away.

The rabbits had trampled the tall grass that still grew beside the hedges, where the mower had not reached, making tracks that ran for short distances and, here and there, larger trampled patches. The big slide, in the top corner, was blocked completely by bracken and other vegetation, but on the 26th I had the impression that some fairly large animal had used it. There was some disturbance—but no tell-tale hairs —a patch of trampled grass, and then a track that ran most of the way down the south-eastern hedge.

Beneath all the grass the moles were still at work. They vanished for a time as the hay crop hid them, and for a few hours the baler was parked right on top of the home of one of them.

I found a large frog not far from the moles, sitting in the wet grass a long way from water. We may marvel at the courage of men who embark on perilous journeys yet spare no thought for the migrating frog that sets out to seek its fortune, leaving the pond where it was born and spent its tadpolehood. Like all amphibians it has a skin through which it can breathe and drink, but which does not hold water. It is very susceptible to dehydration so that apart from the more obvious hazards of encounters with snakes, birds, and enemies of all kinds, it must find water within a very limited time or it will die.

The grasshoppers began to appear at the beginning of July and by the end of the month they were everywhere in the short grass, jumping away as you walked along, and singing loudly most of the time. It is the males who do most of the singing, by rubbing pegs on their legs against a hardened vein in their front wings. The females also sing, at least in some species, but their pegs are smaller and their song more muted.

The larks, several of them now, strutted through the grass and leapt into the air at the slightest disturbance, but they sang less often and less loudly. The business of singing had been taken over by the yellowhammers. 'Little bit of bread and no cheese.'

125

August

The young frog hopping his way through the regenerating grass on the lower side of the field summed up, by his presence—and he was not alone—the summer of 1979. He was far from the pond in the quarry where he is most likely to have graduated from his tadpole studentship, and between him and the culvert that is exposed on the opposite side of the road there lay the hedge, filled densely with bracken, a steep bank about eight feet high, the road itself, and a journey of perhaps 75 yards along the far side of the road, most of it on the road itself because the hedges that border the front gardens of the cottages afford little shelter. He was far from safety, yet he was safe, for his summer was wet enough to meet even his urgent need for moisture. It was a summer of squalls and steady rain, of torn skies and streets filled with tourists driven from the beaches, damply anoraked and miserable in their pleasures. There were fine days, but as August brought the whole sorry season to its welcome conclusion they will be forgotten or, if remembered, remembered only as light relief, brief respites from the general drabness.

August is the month that betrays summer and allows autumn to take hold of the year, and it is often wet. I suppose it is because the schools are on holiday for the whole month that we think of August as the height of summer, but it is not so, and they say that the original purpose of closing the schools and colleges in August was to release their inmates to help with the corn harvest. If so, that places August in autumn, almost by definition. On average, there are fewer hours of sunshine each day in August than there are in July. In the thirty years from 1941 to 1970, in England and Wales, there were an average 5.88 hours of sunshine each day during July and 5.48 in August. In the period from 1916 to 1950 there was, on average, more rain in August than in either July or September. The July average was 79 millimetres, that for August 81, and that for September 76. An average summer,

The flooded quarry, difficult of access and mysterious, the breeding ground for the aquatic species that visit Cross Park

Small frogs hop about by the hedge at the bottom of the field

The shorn lambs, chilly and rather confused, huddled in small groups

then, ends at the end of July; a bad summer is one in which July is also cloudy and wet, and a good summer continues through August.

The climatologists say that the climate of the northern hemisphere is a little cooler than it used to be when I was a boy. This makes its weather less stable, more difficult to predict, and more prone to long spells of unchanging weather, good or bad, that end violently. It was they, you will remember, who predicted a bad summer for 1979. The amateurs, who foretold a glorious August, were wrong, though it pains me to have to award the prize to their less colourful rivals.

July, on the other hand, had been dry, warm and sometimes distinctly hot. The farm crops made up some of the time they lost earlier in the year and by and large they looked healthy. There may be shortages of hay and silage during the winter, though. Regrowth after cutting was slow in most places, so there was little chance of a second grass cut. By the third week of the month the grass in Cross Park was almost knee-high, with a dense mat of clover beneath it, but if Geoff ever considered taking a second cut from it the idea was abandoned and the sheep were turned into it. These were the lambs, shorn a few weeks earlier, and their fleeces were growing thick again.

The month ran drearily, but it ended violently. It was not on the farms that it caused its greatest havoc, but on the seas to the west and south of Cornwall. The ocean-going yachts, racing from Plymouth to

Fastnet and back, set out from Ireland on their return leg and ran straight into a force ten, 70-mile-an-hour gale. That was on the 14th. The day was windy enough inland, but it was not until evening that news arrived of the storm that cost at least fifteen lives before it was done. Boats that cost a tycoon's ransom were tossed about like toys and smashed by 50ft waves. The rescue operation was said to be the largest ever mounted in the Western Approaches.

The most dramatic of events may go quite unremarked only a few miles away, among communities they neither touch nor concern. In Cross Park life continued in its own ways, only the butterflies and moths making necessary concessions to the weather. They do not mind a modest amount of rain, provided it is not heavy, although butterflies prefer sunshine and moths prefer complete darkness, but they do not like wind. They are weak fliers and a foolhardy foray in a stiff breeze can carry them far from home. That is not too serious a matter in itself, but becomes so should the wind deposit them far out at sea or in a desert. It is not a journey over which they have much control, which makes it doubly surprising that many species migrate, sometimes over long distances that take them from one continent to another. It must be a haphazard business that costs the lives of most of its participants, that voyage made more on the wind than on the wing.

Cross Park is often windy and its hedges are not rich in butterflies. There were some, though: elusive, tantalising creatures that flutter restlessly in and out of the vegetation, seldom settling for more than a moment. When, occasionally, one does come to rest in a position where it can be seen clearly it moves on, nervous as a bird, before I can draw close, as often as not vanishing over the top of the hedge into that other world from which I am excluded. One day I followed a Grayling almost the length of the field, not chasing it, not altering my pace, but hoping it would settle while expecting it would not.

Moths are more phlegmatic and in Cross Park they are more numerous, too. The little black and white mottled pyralids, whose foreign relatives include such notorious characters as the Indian Meal Moth, the Flour Moth and the Corn-Borer, were there, one every few yards along the hedges. Most of them were *Eurrhypara hortulata*, which are not pests.

On the evening of the 20th, Frank Smith and I made a second attempt to study the night moths by means of a lamp. We were more successful than on our first attempt, which says little, but by any reasonable standard our effort ended a damp failure.

It was a strange evening. The day had been fine and we arranged to meet at the field at half past eight. I arrived first, having driven through a little very fine drizzle, to find the higher ground moistened by patches of mist, and low cloud sitting firmly on the upper side of Cross Park. It isolated the field without really obscuring it, and turned the sheep into shadowy figures that came and went at a distance from me I could not estimate. The grass was coated with a film of water so that it was very quiet and wet underfoot.

Frank arrived and we set up the lamp just as it was growing dark. By about nine o'clock we were ready and waiting for customers, prepared if need be to spend the night there. As the darkness descended so completely as to make even the mist invisible except where the lamplight was reflected and refracted through it, our shadows were cast behind us as huge spectral giants, blacker than the surrounding blackness, only vaguely human, and, because the illuminated area was spherical, crouched forward in an attitude of menace. Now and then the wind would blow gently, but for most of the time nothing moved within our small illuminated sphere nor, so far as we could tell, outside it.

As it turned out, our stay was not to be long. During it we were visited by eleven species of moths, most of them represented by several individuals and some by half a dozen or more. The haul was less than impressive, but it impressed me.

The first arrival was a Ruby Tiger (*Phragmatobia fuliginosa*), a common enough moth and less spectacular than some of its tiger relatives in the Arctiidae family, but attractive for all that. It has a deep red body, which earns it its name, and some of the Ruby Tigers we saw seemed to be heavy with eggs. It spends its youth as a large and hairy caterpillar, as do the other tiger moths, feeding on low-growing plants.

It was followed by the first of several Antler moths (*Cerapteryx graminis*), brown moths with white patterns on their fore wings that are slightly reminiscent of antlers. The Antler belongs to the largest of all lepidopteran families, the Noctuidae or, if you prefer, Agrotiae. Most of them are brown or grey in colour, but many have brightly coloured hind wings. These serve a defensive purpose, as 'flash coloration'. When the moth is disturbed and flies off, the wings flash their colours intermittently. This makes the moths very difficult to follow and even more difficult to catch. It is said that the Yellow Underwing is one of the most difficult of all moths to catch in a net. We did not try to catch one so I have no way of knowing how difficult it would be, but we did see many Yellow Underwings (*Noctua pronuba*). They are fairly large moths whose hind wings are hidden completely by their drab fore wings when they are at rest. They, too, were due to lay eggs that will hatch into small brown caterpillars that feed through the winter on low plants and that can devour the winter greens if they are fortunate enough to be born in a garden.

The next moth to arrive was the Dark, or Black Arches (*Lymantria monacha*), a member of the Tussock moth family, Lymantriidae, and it was followed by a large number of Flame Shoulders (*Ochropleura plecta*)—large, that is, compared to the numbers of other species. It is not a big moth. It earns its name by its fore wings, which are purple-brown, or sometimes paler than that, with a stripe along the leading edge that gives the appearance of much brighter 'shoulders'. These moths belonged to the second generation of the year and their comparatively large numbers may have been due to the fact that they had emerged from their pupation only recently. Within a few weeks many will have fallen victim to predators. Those that survive will breed, the females will lay their eggs, and then all the moths will die. As with so many insects the splendid imago form enjoys only a brief life. The caterpillars, more or less brown, sometimes freckled, with an ochre-coloured, freckled line along each side and paler broken lines along the back, will hatch late in the autumn. They will spend the winter more or less in hiding, eating little for there will be little for them to eat. As the new spring produces fresh vegetation they will feed voraciously, on nice, tender leaves of lettuce and other crop plants if they can find them, for these require little chewing. Then they will pupate to become the first of the two generations of Flame Shoulders that are produced each year. By next August they will be dead and it will be their offspring that are flying to lamps, dodging the birds and bats, and breeding.

The Rustic (*Caradrina blanda*) which appeared next, was near the end of its life. It flies in Britain from June to early August in most years. Its eggs will have been laid. The caterpillars, which will feed through the autumn and winter until they pupate around Easter, are a grey-brown-olive colour, with a dark line along the back, and they eat dock, chickweed, plantain and other such herbs. The Rustic is not easy to distinguish from several other species, especially the Uncertain, Vine's Rustic and the Powdered Rustic, all of which have drab brown fore wings and paler hind wings. Compared with the Uncertain, which it resembles most closely, the Rustic has browner fore wings and less prominent markings, and is generally smoother in appearance.

The Snout (*Hypena proboscidalis*) is much easier to recognise because it has very long palps that extend in front of its head and give it its name. Its fore wings are marked with an attractive, though subdued, marbling pattern. It is one of the insects that depend on stinging nettle for food. In early summer its caterpillars are to be found eating the nettles; they are green with a dark line along the back and yellowish stripes along the sides, a brown head, and hairs, each of which rises from a raised spot.

Crambus tristellus, one of the Grass Moths, that appeared next is a member of the Pyralidae, the family of microlepidoptera that has about 200 British species. *C. tristellus* is small and pale and when it folds its wings it looks for all the world like a grass seed. So disguised, it spends its days resting almost invisibly at the top of a grass stem.

The Common Carpet (*Epirrhoë alternata*) is a pale colour with dark brown bars across its fore wings. It emerges twice a year, our visitor most probably belonging to the second generation. As a brown-green caterpillar it fed on the hedge bedstraw. Its own caterpillars, hatched from the eggs it lays in autumn, will overwinter, then emerge early next summer to lay the season's first brood of eggs.

The Lesser Broad-Bordered Yellow Underwing (*Euschesis janthina*) has dark brown fore wings and deep yellow hind wings with a broad black border. Its caterpillars will hatch in autumn, spend the winter feeding on various hedgerow plants including bramble and dock, and in spring, before they pupate, they will fatten themselves on the young growth of trees and hedgerow shrubs.

Our last visitor was the Small Square Spot (*Diarsia rubi*), a small moth whose name is derived from the pale, very approximately square, marks on its brown fore wings. It produces two generations a year. Members of the first generation, which flies in early summer, are larger than those of the second, early autumn, generation, but fewer in number. The caterpillars from both generations feed on dandelion, dock, grass, ragwort flowers and other plants that grow close to the ground.

A bird began to cry mysteriously above our heads, seeming to circle in the utter blackness, and we strained our eyes to catch a glimpse of it. We saw nothing, and apart from our certainty that it was not an owl or any other conventional bird of the night we failed to identify it. Indeed, I cannot be sure whether it was one bird or two, for its song was always moving, now close, now far, and sometimes it seemed to come from two directions at once, but that may have been no more than the confusion of our ears by mist and wind. Some weeks later I startled a lark that leapt into the air with a cry that reminded me at once of our strange nocturnal visitor. Was it a lark, shocked into the night air by our voices, or by some more sinister visitation? I suppose I will never know.

It was evident that the Small Square Spot was to be the last moth we would see. The mist had become suspiciously like drizzle and the drizzle had turned, unmistakably, to rain that by now was moderate and continuous. The wind had risen and moved round to the south, so that only the most reckless of lepidoptera would trust themselves to it. The squadrons were grounded and we were very wet indeed. I had been advised of a device that was guaranteed to keep my trousers dry: I had tucked my trousers inside my wellingtons but left my over-trousers pulled down over the outside of them. This, so the theory went, would prevent much dripping into the tops of the boots. It might have worked had the over-trousers been waterproof, but they were not. The effect, therefore, was to draw water by capillary attraction up the over-trousers as far as my knees and there to soak my trousers, in which the water moved down again, also by capillary attraction, into my socks. Far from enjoying dry legs I found the technique most effective for wetting the feet from above without removing them from their perfectly good wellingtons.

Thus the decision was taken to abandon the exercise. We evicted the moths that were huddling beneath the lamp and Frank's soggy egg boxes to keep dry and sent them fluttering into the night. We wrung the water from the sheet, agreed to try again another night, and squelched our way back to the cars.

There should have been countless numbers of Common Carpets, for their food supply was limitless. The hedges had changed their appearance quickly and dramatically. The reds faded as the foxgloves set their seeds and vanished, dull green and brown, into the background, and as the red campion flowers disappeared from all but a few places, and the hedge was covered with bedstraw. It grew in great festoons, tangled mats of it that reached the full height of the hedges, each mat several feet wide, so that in about half a dozen places no other plant could be seen. On the 6th the hedge bedstraw had flowered to smother the hedges in the white blossom of a false spring and by the 23rd it was finished and all was green again.

The wet weather favoured all those creatures whose skins are not so good at retaining moisture. The slugs emerged in force and many of them were very large indeed. *Arion ater*, possibly the largest of them all and sometimes six inches long, was able to feed placidly during the day. It is a very variable slug that may be one of several colours. Those in Cross Park were mostly black with an orange or red edge to their foot, or plain yellow. Many of them had a bump on their tails that became coated with small pieces of detritus of all kinds. Probably this was their enlarged and very active mucus gland. You may not find slug slime attractive, but the slugs themselves consider it among the sexiest of materials for nuptial wear. Indeed, you never see them wearing

133

anything else and they like it so much that sometimes they will eat it off each other's backs.

Life is not easy if you are a slug. For one thing the hand of man is turned against you, not to mention the foot of man. Do you find the pleasures of a slime-eating slug revolting? What business is it of yours? Have you ever asked a slug its opinion of your kinky underwear? Few people are able to grow genuinely enthusiastic over the slimy fraternity and I dare say most people would be happy to exterminate the lot on the ground that there never was a slug that was not addicted to cabbages and the larger the slug the more cabbages it can eat. All slugs are pests, therefore, and the only good slug is a dead slug. So we attack them with poisons, which they tolerate with a fair equanimity and sometimes actually enjoy, with salt, with traps into which they fall and drown, and with boots. You would think, said the slug, that the going was tough enough without having to endure the implications of such calumnies. For a start, a very large slug is not just a big version of a very small slug. It belongs to a different species and may not even be a close relative. You might just as well lump together horses and mice as larger and smaller versions of the same animal. After all, they both possess four legs, a tail and a somewhat similar arrangement of internal organs. They are different, for all that, and so are the slugs.

There are three families of slugs that live in Britain, the Arionidae, to which *A. ater* belongs, the Limacidae, and the Testacellidae. Some people count a fourth family, the Milacidae, as separate though closely related to the Limacidae, but probably it does not warrant the distinction and the slugs of the genus *Milax* are more properly included in the Limacidae. Slugs are simply snails that have dispensed with shells, and the three slug families are descended from three different snail families, so that while each of them has fairly close snail relatives each slug family is not closely related to the other slug families.

The testacellid slugs are unmistakable. There are only three species and they still have external shells, very small ones, carried at the rear end of their bodies. They are not very common but you may see one if you are lucky. Far from being pests, the testacellids are wholly carnivorous, feeding mainly on earthworms. They have no movable jaws, but their radulae are well able to grip their prey securely. All slugs and snails have radulae. These are the equivalent of tongues, but equipped with thousands of sharp teeth arranged in rows across them. The animal grips its food with its horny lips and then rubs its radula back and forth, pressing the food against the roof of its mouth and tearing it into small fragments.

Most snails and slugs feed on fungi, algae, lichens, mosses and rotting vegetation. They seldom touch healthy living plants. The attraction of cultivated plants is that by and large they are succulent, tender, and to a gastropod more like rotting vegetation than healthy plants, which, as every slug and snail knows, tend to be tough. They can thrive on a wide variety of foods, though, and they are able to digest cellulose. They do this by means of an enzyme they produce, rather than by playing host to a colony of bacteria as do ruminant mammals and termites. This ability means they can eat damp paper and cardboard, which is handy these days. It also means they can digest chitin, a hard substance found only in animals: the exoskeleton of an insect or arachnid is made from chitin. This suggests that all of them are potentially carnivorous.

Only some species of slugs are pests, the most serious being *Deroceras reticulatum*, the most common of all British slugs and *Milax budapestensis*. Both slugs are quite small and dark coloured. *A. ater* feeds on many things, but especially on decaying vegetable and animal matter.

There is one slug that seems actually to like humans. *Limax flavus*, a fairly large mottled yellow fellow, is more or less domesticated and prefers to live in or close to houses and farm buildings. Naturally, being a discerning creature, it prefers old houses to new ones. So far as I can discover its quite genuine affection for *H. sapiens* is not reciprocated and whenever it tries to settle for a quiet nap by the fire it is likely to be assaulted violently. Yet it persists and feels only the warmest of goodwill toward the ingrates who torment it.

Identifying slugs is difficult and some species can be named positively only by means of internal features that are revealed by autopsy. There are a few clues, though. The testacellids, as I have said, have a small shell near the tail that provides positive identification at least for the family and (because there is but one) the genus. It has no use for the vegetable garden, although it may devour a smaller slug now and then.

If you find a very large slug that wags its head at you aggressively when you disturb it, it is *A. ater*. If you do not flee in terror, which is what it would like you to do, it will contract itself into a dome. All the arionids do this and there are two more ways in which they can be distinguished. The first is from the position of their respiratory opening. All the shell-less slugs have a mantle, visible as a distinct raised section toward the front of the body. In snails and the shelled slugs the mantle is largely or entirely beneath the shell. The mantle houses their breathing apparatus—rudimentary lungs—and air enters through an opening that is clearly visible on the right side of the body. In the arionids it is towards the front of the mantle, in the limacids it is towards the rear. The final check is the presence or absence of a keel, a shaping to the body that brings the sides to an inverted V shape along the back. All limacids are keeled, all arionids are unkeeled. If the slug that you frighten contracts itself into a horseshoe shape I suppose you must be permitted to stamp on it. It is *M. budapestensis*, the only slug to perform this trick.

It is obvious from its name that *M. budapestensis* came to Britain from eastern Europe, but in fact all our slugs and snails are immigrants. The original population was killed outright by the last ice age. Since the glaciers retreated they have been returning, little by little because it takes a long time to work your way across a continent if you are not the fastest of runners.

This lack of athletic prowess is but one of the difficulties with which the gastropods must learn to live and it is worse for slugs than for snails. Imagine, if you will, that some tasty morsel tempts you into the open when, lo! you are espied by a bird, a large carnivorous beetle, a snake, a small mammal, or even a glow-worm larva. These are only a few of the creatures that dine regularly upon gastropods. You might say that the gastropods go to the gastronomes, and there are many gastronomes. If the enemy happens to be a carnivorous snail or slug you might make a run for it, but otherwise flight is futile. If you are a snail you can disappear into your shell and the one thing all snails can do quickly is vanish. Apart from their foot, the only strong muscles they possess are those that withdraw them in a hurry. Many of them shut themselves in by means of a door. That will deter many foes, but not all. The song thrush, for example, will carry you off to its 'anvil' and batter your shell to pieces. Some birds will simply swallow you shell and all. Still, it is better than having no shell. Apart from the testacellids, some slugs, such as the majestic *A. ater*, have a vestigial shell inside their bodies, but you cannot hide in an internalised vestigial shell. You had best contract youself into the smallest possible space, as your ancestors used to do in the days when they still had shells, and hope that your sticky mucus, supplied in generous amounts, will prove unpalatable. It is their sliminess that saves such slugs as are saved from predators. If you watch a bird with a slug you may see it wipe the unfortunate beast on the grass before swallowing it. Presumably the wipe removes some of the mucus. Still, there are compensations. Slugs can squeeze themselves into small crevices that no snail could enter with its cumbersome superstructure, and slugs can and do burrow up to three feet below the surface of the earth.

The burrowing is partly for concealment and partly to find moisture, and the mucus also conserves moisture. It is important because if you are a slug your most serious problem, apart from predators, is desiccation. Your skin just will not hold water, but the situation can be improved by covering the skin with a viscous substance. (Snails do this, too, although their need is not so great because their shells are fairly waterproof. Snails have been found in deserts, but not slugs.) You will be well advised to feed mainly by night or, at least, when the sky is overcast. Bright sunshine is bad for you. The world will be moister then, and at night the predators will not see you so well, so you are comparatively safe unless you have the misfortune to run across a family of hedgehogs, or a mole that has surfaced to take the evening air, and that is never averse to a quick snack.

Short of asking them, it is impossible to tell the age of the large slugs I saw in Cross Park. Most of the smaller species live for only one year, dying soon after they have laid their eggs in late summer or autumn. The large species, though, may take from two to four years to reach sexual maturity and some individuals may live for up to ten years. The eggs are laid in clutches of anything from twenty to a hundred or more according to the species, and more than one clutch may be laid during the season. The eggs are not guarded and many dry out or are eaten. Those that survive to hatch release animals identical to their parents, but much smaller, and they, too, are highly vulnerable to predators of all kinds. Out of each hundred young that are born, no more than five may reach adulthood and the human boot. It is, as I said, a hard life, and in addition to their large enemies, the gastropods have their own full complement of internal parasites and diseases just like other animals. So spare a thought for the humble slug and watch where you tread. He may be slow on his foot, but for a mollusc he is not stupid. He has three nerve ganglia in his head, which is something, and his senses are highly developed. His longer, upper tentacles each have one eye at the tip, with a lens and retina. Their field of view is restricted but they are good at detecting quick movements. The shorter, lower tentacles are very sensitive to smell. He retracts his tentacles by pulling them inside out, like the fingers of a glove.

The sheep dunged the field, their dung providing food for its own hierarchies of organisms. There were usually some Yellow Dung-Flies (*Scatophaga stercoraria*) in attendance, either laying their eggs which will hatch to produce dung-eating larvae, or hunting their own food, which consists of the smaller animals that feed on the dung. The Yellow Dung-Fly is a predator, although it is quite a close relative of the ordinary Housefly (*Musca domestica*).

On the 23rd I surprised a weevil as it sat on a twig, all unsuspecting and doing nothing in particular. There are more than 500 British species of weevils. They look like small beetles, but they have one important distinguishing feature in the long snout-like structure in front of their heads. The antennae grow from the sides of the snout and have 'elbows' so that the upper part can be folded back into grooves, or 'scrobes', in the snout itself. The eyes are on either side of the base of the snout, or 'rostrum', and although it looks like some kind of nose in fact it is a mouth with mandibles at the tip that can bore through wood. Weevils feed on plant material and some of them may bore holes in wood to deposit their eggs. Many weevils are covered in tiny coloured scales, which makes them bright and cheerful in appearance. The one I saw was *Apion miniatum*, bright red and slightly larger than a ladybird.

The ants were busy in their colonies beneath the larger stones. The ants are related to the bees and wasps, being members of the same section, Aculeata, of the same sub-order, Apocrita, of the same order, Hymenoptera, which is a convoluted way of saying they have evolved from a common ancestor and share many features, including their 'wasp' waists, their social habits, and their stings. However, only a few bees and wasps are social, and not all ants can sting. The sting, where it exists, is a modified ovipositor, and so is possessed only by females. Ant venom consists mainly of formic acid, and some ants that cannot sting can squirt formic acid at their foes. Many more ant species, which can neither sting nor squirt acid, can nevertheless deliver a painful bite with their tough, sharp mandibles.

Beneath a stone the ants were busy moving their grubs from one part of the nest to another

The ants are the most highly developed of all insects. All of them are social, but they exhibit many kinds of social organisation, both economically and politically. Curiously, their evolution parallels human social development. The most primitive of ants are hunters. They seldom make permanent nests and when they do their colonies are small. More commonly they make temporary 'camps' which they use while they are breeding. They feed on such small creatures as they can overpower and that they find in the surrounding range. The next step in evolutionary development is the equivalent of pastoralism and the ants at that level look after aphids, eating their honeydew and augmenting this with vegetable material that they collect in the wild. Some pastoralist ants keep their aphids in their nests with them, feeding the aphids by attaching them to the roots of plants that project through the walls of the nest. Most British ants, and there are about 36 species of them, fall into this category. The most highly developed of all ants are farmers and live in tropical America, where they gather plant material which they make into compost on which they grow the fungus that is their only food.

Among the British ants there are many political systems. The red ants that you may find in the garden, *Formica sanguinea*, operate a slave economy. They raid the nests of other ants to steal pupae, which they carry back to their own nest and tend. When the adult ants emerge, they work for the red ants. *F. sanguinea* can look after itself should it fail to obtain slaves, but some slave owners are much more helpless, relying on slave labour to build their own nests.

Most of our ants live in societies that are rather like constitutional monarchies in which the queen or queens—for there may be several—perform the important task of breeding while most of the population consists of workers who collaborate very closely with one another. This co-operation relies on the frequent communication of information. You can see worker ants passing messages by rubbing their heads together and making complicated movements with their antennae.

Some ant species are winged, some not, but it seems that most species produce winged and sexually mature forms at certain times of the year. These ants fly off to mate, usually in the air, and because the timing of the nuptial flight is determined by the weather all the nests in a particular area will release their winged ants at the same time. This can produce great clouds of flying ants but, more important to the ants, it ensures widespread cross-breeding among different colonies. After mating, the ants land, the males die, and the females break off their wings and seek a refuge in which to spend the winter. This may be within an existing nest which then has, and tolerates, an additional queen. Alternatively the young queen may seal herself up until the spring in some small hole, feeding on her bodily reserves, which include the wing muscles she no longer needs. She lays her eggs in spring and then feeds her young with her own saliva. As soon as they grow up the youngsters take over all the work, building a new nest and leaving their mother to lay eggs and produce subsequent generations. A queen may live for several years and, though ants come and go, colonies of them are very stable and can survive for long periods.

The Cross Park ants, visible on the penthouse level of their nests, were busy moving grubs from one place to another, which appears to be an endless activity. I am amazed at the mechanics of the ant as much as by its social organisation. Worker ants move very fast. If you work out the time it takes an ant to travel so many times the length of its own body, and then relate this to a mammal, you can see just how fast they run. When you take account of their weight it becomes evident that their energy consumption must be colossal: they use energy much more efficiently than any warm-blooded animal that must burn great amounts of fuel just to maintain its constant body temperature.

The moles were burrowing, or clearing out their existing tunnels. The most active of them all was the first and original Cross Park mole, who lived by the gate half-way along the south-eastern hedge. Its home was not well sited. Machines that wished to move to the next field could not avoid driving over its tunnels and the sheep trampled there and must have caused the collapse of tunnels very frequently. It must have been most annoying, but the mole persevered.

Although the large slide in the eastern corner was still overgrown, it looked on the 23rd as though some large animal had passed that way within the previous twenty-four hours or so. The ground was covered completely with vegetation and so retained no footprints, and I cannot tell whether or not the traveller was a badger. There were still no tell-tale hairs caught on twigs so far as I could see. I would like to think the badger had patrolled its range, if for no other reason than to reassure me that it was still alive. The gassing of badgers, which had been proceeding steadily for a long time, aroused a storm of controversy on Dartmoor, where the conservationists were well organised and active. The official Ministry argument is that bovine tuberculosis passes from affected cattle to the pasture, from the pasture to badgers that pass through it, and from the badgers back to the pasture and so back to the cattle. It means that while it is possible to test cattle for tuberculosis and to destroy those that are affected by the disease, for as long as the badger population provides a reservoir for *Myobacterium bovis*, the organism that causes tuberculosis, healthy cattle will continue to be reinfected. Badgers that contract tuberculosis die, usually slowly and nastily, so that in killing them the Ministry is really doing them a favour. The badgers do not harbour disease in most of Britain. It is only in the south west that the problem is sufficiently serious to warrant action. So the officials search for badger setts, test the faeces they find for *M. bovis* and if it is present they kill all the badgers in the vicinity. The conservationists argue that this policy has led to more or less indiscriminate killing of badgers. So battle is joined, becomes heated, and, as is usual in such cases, the truth of the matter is an early casualty and it is increasingly difficult to discover just what is happening and whether or not it is justified. I would not wish any human to be infected with tuberculosis from milk, but all the same I hope the Cross Park badger has not fallen victim.

Many of the rabbit burrows were in use, suggesting that at least the rabbits were healthy. Myxomatosis has emerged again on farms not very far from Cross Park but it seems not to have spread.

It was a month for the insects and other invertebrates, though, rather than for the birds or mammals. The first of the marble galls appeared on the hedgerow oaks. There were few common wasps in Cross Park, although there were many of their relatives. Elsewhere it was a good year for them and hospitals were busy treating stings, in some cases caused by attacks on humans by whole swarms.

By the end of the month the grass was flowering again. Among it I found one isolated plant of a particularly fragrant mint. There are several native wild mints. They hybridise with one another and with cultivated mints, so that their identification is notoriously difficult. I suspect this one of being either Water Mint (*Mentha aquatica*) or Corn Mint (*M. arvensis*) or, more probably, a hybrid of the two. The hedge bedstraw finished flowering. The foxgloves set and released their seeds. A few remaining red campions brought specks of colour to the hedges here and there and the scabious continued to flower, small and discreet, close to the hedge bottoms.

The leaves on some of the trees began to dry and curl and, very slowly, the year began to die.

September

It was the month in which the Large Blue butterfly, *Maculinea arion*, became extinct in Britain. Its final disappearance was announced by the Nature Conservancy Council on 12th September. It continues to live in central Europe, but never again will we see it in this country. It used to live in Cornwall: the Cornwall Naturalists' Trust has it for its emblem. The last colony to survive was in Devon, and it is the loss of the Devon colony that removes it finally from our shores.

The Large Blue fell victim to myxomatosis, in a roundabout way. Its fate demonstrates dramatically, if sadly, the extent to which quite unrelated creatures depend on one another. When first they hatch, the tiny caterpillars of *M. arion* feed on wild thyme. They are camouflaged to look like thyme flowers, which helps keep away the many insectivores to which a plump little caterpillar would make a tasty morsel. As they grow they moult their skins and after the third moult the caterpillars leave the thyme and crawl off through the grass. There they are discovered by foraging ants, which inspect them closely, stroking them with sensitive antennae in the process. This stroking excites an *M. arion* grub and makes it secrete a sweet substance that the ant tastes and likes. Persuaded of the value of its find, the ant then takes the caterpillar back to its nest. It is an arduous business because the caterpillar is much bigger than the ant. It hunches itself to make the task a little easier (the ants have never learned to drive it, nor the caterpillar to follow the ants) and one way or another the ant humps its cargo all the way home. Once inside the nest the ants make a great fuss of it, feeding it on their own larvae and stroking it constantly to obtain the sweet exudate. The caterpillar grows and grows until it is three times its original size. As the autumn begins to turn into winter the caterpillar hibernates, and with the return of spring it pupates. Then, in June or July, depending on the conditions, it crawls to the entrance of the ant nest, pumps its flabby, damp wings full of blood to extend them, waits until the wings have dried and hardened, and takes to the air. The adult butterflies mate, the females lay their eggs on thyme plants, the adults of both sexes die, and the cycle begins all over again.

Britain has always been at the edge of the range of the Large Blue and it was rare even in the eighteenth century, but the final blow came with the decline in the fortunes of the wild thyme. Thyme cannot compete with grasses, which overwhelm and suppress it, but it could thrive in places where rabbits and sheep ate the grasses and kept them short. As sheep farming became less fashionable the number of sheep was reduced and so the thyme became more dependent on the assistance of rabbits. When myxomatosis spread through the rabbit population, a Great Lagomorphic Pestilence, rabbits died in their thousands, grasses flourished, thymes died, and the Large Blue butterfly found itself short of plants to feed its larvae. It teetered for some years, then finally became extinct. It was a victim of myxomatosis. It was also the first butterfly to become extinct in this country since about 1848, when the Large Copper (*Lycaena dispar dispar*) disappeared. Today a small colony of the related *L. dispar batava* is maintained at the Woodwalton Fen nature reserve in Huntingdonshire, but the true Large Copper has gone.

In Cross Park the rabbits escaped this year's myxomatosis and were fairly active. There was much fresh burrowing in the banks and in one or two places the soft earth thrown out by the rabbits had been used by smaller animals, probably bank voles, to make their very round burrows. They were burrows inside burrows. Indeed, it was a good time for burrowers of all sorts, for the moles, too, were throwing up their hills industriously beside three of the four hedges that surround the field and one adventurous—or desperate—mole had worked its way about a quarter of the way across the field. For some reason the top side of the field seems less attractive to them, but elsewhere I guessed there must be about half a dozen animals scuttling back and forth like carnivorous shuttles and ducking each time my heavy foot threatened to bring down the roofs of their galleries.

There were a few butterflies, too. There was no Large Blue, of course—in any case, there is no thyme in Cross Park—but I saw the common Meadow Brown (*Maniola jurtina*) and the Speckled Wood (*Pararge aegeria*). The Speckled Wood produces broods throughout the summer and into October; the Meadow Brown lives for longer and has fewer broods. The butterflies I saw in September were females, which appear later than the males. Unlike many species, including the unfortunate Large Blue, these common butterflies succeed by feeding on a range of grasses: that is why they are common.

143

The Crane Fly (*Tipula paludosa*). Although the larval form, the leatherjacket, is an important pest, the adult is quite harmless. It feeds only on liquids and its mouth parts are soft. The front of the head is extended into a kind of beak, and the fleshy labella, by which food is obtained, is at the end. Like all true, two-winged flies, the second pair of wings is reduced and modified into halteres, looking a little like drumsticks. One can be seen behind the wing of the Crane Fly. The halteres move rapidly in flight to help the Crane Fly to balance and to increase its aerodynamic ability

The *Bombus* bumble bees were still flying, especially the honey-coloured *Bombus agrorum*. I suspect most of those I saw were females, feeding before they began the search for places to hibernate in the hedges. *Andricus kollari*, the wasp that is responsible for the marble galls on oak, had mated and laid its eggs, for many new marble galls appeared during the month. They develop quite quickly as green spheres and then turn brown as the cells of which they are composed lose their chlorophyll, die, and turn into a substance very like cork.

The most abundant insect was *Tipula paludosa*, the Crane Fly or Daddy-long-legs. On the 5th I found them mating in the grass and throughout the month they were starting up at my approach and making their short, rather erratic flights from one patch of grass to the next. They are true, two-winged flies and *T. maxima*, the close cousin of the common *T. paludosa*, is the largest of all British flies, with a wingspan that can reach 2½in. Nearly 300 species of Crane Fly are found in Britain, and some of them are tiny. Certain of the gnats that hang in the air on warm, humid days are members of the Crane Fly family, the Tipulidae.

Some people are frightened of Crane Flies. It is a phobia similar to that which condemns spiders to the twilight regions of our culture and it is even less rational. At least spiders can bite, even if they never bite humans. The Crane Fly can neither bite nor sting. It lacks the necessary equipment so that even if an individual were to conceive a dark hatred for all humans there is nothing it could do about it. It feeds only on liquids, and its mouth parts are quite soft. People fear it, I suspect, because of its very long legs. I dare say spiders are feared because of their legs, too, which are sometimes long, sometimes hairy, and always too numerous for comfort. The octopus also earns our dislike by possessing too many legs. Are we jealous?

The Crane Fly is a serious pest, for all that the adult is innocuous. The damage is caused not by the fly but by its larvae, the leatherjackets that live in the soil and feed on the roots of grasses. No doubt there is an insecticide that would get rid of them, and no doubt this would increase the productivity of our grasslands, perhaps by a large amount. In Cross Park, though, they go unsprayed and I am not sorry. I enjoy watching them. Who are we to decide they have no right to share with us the grasslands they evolved to exploit? Who are we to deny their enemies the right to feast on them in early autumn when they are so abundant? Even the leatherjacket has its admirers. As it dines in the grass roots, it is but a millimetre from the tunnel in which the mole waits to dine upon it. Mind you, I imagine moles would manage quite well in a world that contained no leatherjackets, and in Cross Park it is fairly obvious that most leatherjackets will never encounter a hungry mole. Geoff will just have to do without some of his grass.

The tipulid gnats never bite or sting. There are biting midges: but they are not related to the Crane Flies. Their larvae live in water—as do those of some tipulids—which is why you find them in damp places, and the adults are tiny. All of them belong to the family Ceratopogonidae and the most common biter among them is *Culicoides obsoletus*. Actually, it does not 'bite' at all. No fly has jaws that can close to inflict a bite in the literal sense. What the biting midge does is to pierce the skin in order to suck blood, sending its victim rushing for soothing potions, scratching furiously as he runs. Luckily, only a few of the 130 British species of biting midges will bite humans, although they make up in numbers what they lack in species diversity. The rest feed on birds and other mammals if they belong to the genus *Culicoides*, and on insects if they do not. I shall reflect, the next time the crop of itching bumps appears, that the whole animal creation provides the meat on which these almost invisible creatures subsist. When our conceit persuades us we are the lords of creation, it may be morally beneficial to recall the animals that outnumber us by millions to one, and to whom we represent nothing more than a source of food.

There were other flies, too. The Flesh Fly (*Sarcophaga carnaria*) was there, and there were a few small sawflies. The Flesh Fly is a member of the same family, the Calliphoridae, as the bluebottle and green-bottle. Its larvae feed on decaying meat but they differ from those of most of their relatives and, indeed, from those of most insects, in that the eggs hatch within the female's body. The larvae enter the world alive and active, and the species benefits by the fact that no other creature can eat the eggs without also eating the adult female.

The sawflies are primitive members of the Hymenoptera, not flies at all but relatives of the bees and wasps. They earn their name from their ovipositors which, in most species resemble saws. The female uses the saw-like ovipositor to cut a slit into the stem or leaf of a plant to make an opening into which the eggs are laid. Other species have a stabbing ovipositor that bores a hole, and the Horntail (*Urocerus gigas*) can bore a hole in wood. It is these ovipositors that have become stings in the more highly evolved bees and wasps, but sawflies are quite inoffensive to humans.

There were hoverflies, too, the mimics of the insect world, many of which look very like bees or wasps. Some hoverflies carry this mimicry to the length of curling over their abdomens to make stinging movements, but it is all pretence. They cannot sting, nor yet bite, for the adults feed only on liquids, principally nectar. The mimicry is defensive, Batesian mimicry, in which a harmless and edible species profits from its resemblance to a dangerous or poisonous species. Many of the hoverfly larvae—though not all of them—are carnivorous and they are much admired by perceptive gardeners who can distinguish them from their Hymenopteran models and who realise that their grubs enjoy nothing more than a leaf groaning beneath its edible load of fat, juicy, tender aphids.

The sheep, just over forty of them, grazed the field for the first half of the month, their dung providing a happy hunting ground for the predatory Yellow Dung-Flies.

The other invertebrates also prospered. The large diadem spiders lay in wait every yard or two along all the hedges and it seemed that their webs seldom remained empty for long. On the 11th I found almost all of them feeding, as though I had chanced upon them during a meal break. There were other spiders, too, and other web designs. Smaller spiders made smaller orbs and here and there along the hedges, about three feet from the ground, there were the tube webs, probably of *Agelena labyrinthica*. I could see the spider inside its tube but I could not examine it closely without both destroying the tube and sending it scuttling to invisible safety. It belongs to the same family as the House Spider, *Tegenaria atrica*. The tube-web spiders begin their spinning in mid-summer, with tubes close to the ground. By autumn, when the spider is mature, the tubes are much further from the ground and more elaborate. In addition to the tube itself, and its fastenings to the twigs that support it, there are threads that form a loose tangle above it. These have nothing to do with support. They are to trap passing insects, which fall on to the top of the tube and summon forth the waiting spider. Closer to the ground, suspended loosely across the tops of the grass, there were hammock webs, made by members of the Linyphiidae family. The webs were quite large, covering several square inches, but their owners are 'money-spiders', the small, dark-coloured, inconspicuous creatures that fail to frighten even the most dedicated spider-hater. The spider sometimes sits on top of its hammock, but more usually it hangs beneath it. There are threads extending from the hammock down to the ground which trap small insects as they walk through the grass. As they become entangled in the sticky filaments the hammock is jerked, and down drops the spider to inspect the catch.

Sometimes, and especially in autumn which is the real season for spiders, the weather conditions stimulate all the spiders into making webs at the same time and suddenly there are webs everywhere. There were days like this in September. The 11th, when the spiders were almost all feeding, was one of them.

On the ground the new brood of lycosids, the wolf spiders, scuttled about in search of food they must chase because they never mastered the art of web making. In fact, the whole evolution of the spiders could be seen without moving so much as a step. The most primitive of them were the ground-dwelling wolf spiders. The hammocks and tubes represent an intermediate stage, and the orb webs are made by the most advanced spiders of all. It is not simply that the orbs are beauti-ful, although they are, but that they provide the largest trapping area for the smallest amount of silk, making them the most efficient of webs. Economists might study them and so learn not to confuse activity with useful work.

Both males and females were active. On one web I saw a female run towards a male that had ventured on to her web and so drive him away. She did not attack him, though, and he was in no great danger. On another web both male and female were fussing about with a crane fly they had caught, apparently sharing their meal. After a few moments the male left, so far as I could tell of his own volition, for the female made no move that I could interpret as a threat and he did not hurry. After that the female settled down to feed, while the male moved about the edge of the web and the adjacent leaves in what looked like a fidget of indecision. There was no conflict, and at no time did it seem possible that the female would attack her partner.

Running about among the foliage of the hedges were the animals that compete with the Crane Flies for the title of Daddy-long-legs: the harvestmen, harvesters or harvest spiders. They belong to the order *Opiliones* and although they are arachnids they are not spiders. They belong by themselves, great button-bodied, gangling things whose principal method of defence, should flight fail them (and they can move fast), is to shed a few legs, which grow again quite quickly. The long legs have other uses. For one thing they make their owners ant-proof. A harvestman can stand on tip-toe, as it were, and so place itself out of reach of a swarm of ants that otherwise would overwhelm it. They do not produce silk and so they cannot make webs. In the autumn they lay their eggs in crevices, and then die. The eggs hatch the following spring to release—because they are arachnids and not insects—individuals that are tiny versions of their parents. They are quite round in shape but although they have no neck or waist the button-shaped body does have a front and back. They have eyes, though how well they see with them is not really known. They explore their environment with their long legs and it may be that their sense of touch is more important to them than their vision. They are carnivores, hunting for small insects, small spiders and mites, and they are not above eating one another.

Harvestmen are said to bring luck. They can retract and extend their legs in a movement reminiscent of that of a scythe. Some people believe they help the farmer to cut his grass or corn. Others, or perhaps the same people, believe they improve the pastures for the benefit of sheep. At all events you are not supposed to kill them.

How do such old wives' tales begin? Is it, perhaps, that the harvestmen are more noticeable than the small creatures they hunt, but that their prey is more plentiful where the vegetation is lusher? This would mean that harvestmen would be more numerous in fields that will produce good yields so that the harvestmen were credited with creating the environment that in fact they were merely exploiting. Well, it is a theory. Sometimes I watched the harvestmen running about from twig to twig and the small insects ducking out of their way.

I did not see a harvestman make a catch. The spiders were doing much better.

The mite-eating harvestmen might have profited from an inspection of the Lousy Watchman I found on a flat stone on the northern side of the field. It is a dor beetle (*Geotrupes stercorarius*) and like all members of its family (Geotrupidae) its favourite food is dung. It prefers cow dung, which you can find on the Moor above the field, where farmers turn their cattle on to the common grazing. In Cross Park it would have to make do with very inferior sheep droppings. Perhaps it was an adventurous beetle with a gourmet taste for exotic feeding places. It earns its name because it goes through life infested with mites. If it could come to some arrangement with the harvestmen, both might benefit.

The male and female Lousy Watchman work together to dig tunnels in the earth beneath cow pats, then they pull dung down into the tunnels and the female lays her eggs in it. The adults also feed on the dung and they work with enthusiasm, pulling down far more food than they or their offspring can eat. It may sound revolting, but it is very useful to the farmer. The beetles work the dung into the soil and so help to recycle its plant nutrients. The more quickly animal manures can be incorporated into the soil, the better, because they rapidly lose their nitrogen to the atmosphere. In a sense they are colleagues of the slugs, which also consume wastes and so return nutrients to the soil. *Arion ater* was still there, munching its methodical way across the landscape, a great giant of a slug.

On the 24th I saw two *A. ater* mating beside the hedge on the south-eastern side of the field, two slug bodies locked together in their ponderous embrace. There was little sign of movement. Impassioned they may have been, but animated they were not.

September 15th was the day on which the Ministry made its annual declaration of war on the Warble Fly, *Hypoderma bovis*, urging farmers to douse their cattle with insecticides in autumn and to treat infested cattle in spring. The Warble is becoming less common. The adult is marked with black and yellow bands and is about half an inch long. It flies with a very characteristic whining hum. Cattle are said to recognise the sound of it at once and to be terrified. This is curious, if it is true, because the adult fly does not sting. Indeed, during its short life it does not feed at all. What it does is to lay its eggs on the legs and bellies of cattle. These cause trouble enough, but is it possible that the animals can associate the sound of the fly with the discomfort they experience months later? It seems improbable. Perhaps the cattle mistake the sound of the Warble for that of one of the other flies that do sting? If they run from it they are saved by serendipity. When the Warble eggs hatch, the grubs bore through the host's skin and make their way either to the spinal canal or to the wall of the gullet. They reach this resting place by about December and stay there until February. Then they start moving again, this time making for the back of their victim. By this time the larvae are fat and all spiny. They lie just beneath the skin on the back and bore holes through it to breathe. The tissues around them become inflamed and swollen and this causes the lumps that are called 'warbles'. When they reach their full larval size, the grubs climb out through their breathing holes and fall to the ground, where they pupate in the soil. Cattle infested with them suffer agonies of irritation. They lose their appetites, which makes them grow more slowly and if they are dairy animals their milk yield drops. When eventually they are slaughtered, the parts of the carcase that harboured the grubs have to be trimmed away, which reduces the value of the meat, and the hides are of little value because they are punctured with small holes. The Ministry reckons that the Warble Fly costs British farmers about seven million pounds a year.

All the same, the life cycle of the parasite is fascinating. That of the liver fluke is even more so, because it requires not one host but two, and its numbers are controlled mainly by the weather.

The fluke itself is a flatworm, a trematode, called *Fasciola hepatica*, and grows to a full size of about an inch long. It lives in the liver of its host, in the small bile ducts, and it may move into the body of a cow, sheep or rabbit. It has close relatives that parasitise humans and cause such diseases as schistosomiasis, which is very common in hot climates. In farm animals, fully grown flukes that have dwelt in the liver for three months or more cause a general loss of condition, a wasting away, and eventually death. A sudden infection of the liver by many young flukes can cause the sudden death of an animal that appeared to be perfectly healthy.

The adults lay their eggs in the small bile ducts and the eggs are excreted. Everything now depends on the ground being wet, because when the eggs hatch in the dung, the minute larvae, called 'miracidia', must swim off in search of their first host, which is a small aquatic snail called *Limnea truncatula*. If there is no water the miracidia cannot swim, and if there are no snails they cannot get the start in life that they need. It is a chancy business being a flatworm. If they are lucky, they enter deep into the body of the snail, where they spend about ten weeks and change their appearance several times as they develop. By the time they emerge they are 'cercaria', tiny creatures that look a bit like tadpoles. In fact they consist, more or less, of a small version of an adult flatworm, plus a tail. They swim about in search of a suitable blade of grass, attach themselves to it, then secrete a protective covering for themselves which hardens and turns them into 'cysts', each about the size of a pinhead. Now they need a herbivorous mammal to come along and eat their blades of grass. Inside the second host its digestive juices dissolve the walls of the cysts and out pop young flukes. They bore through the gut wall and make their way to the liver, where they burrow around in search of the small bile ducts in which they settle.

The complexity of its lifestyle is marvellous, but that is no reason for encouraging it. The Ministry of Agriculture keeps a close eye on the weather and conducts searches in wet pastures, mainly for the snail that is the first host to the parasite. From this it calculates the risk to livestock and issues its warnings in September. This year the fluke population is depressed in all but a few places, one of which is north-west Devon. The drought of 1976 destroyed countless numbers of flukes and snails. This meant the animals were infested less heavily and so when the wet weather returned there were fewer eggs to take advantage of it. Each year since 1976 fluke numbers have increased, but it has been a slow increase. The wet spring and summer of this year should have allowed the flukes to return to something like their original numbers, but they were unlucky and the rains came at the wrong times. The wet spring led to an increase in the population of *L. truncatula*, but in June, just when the fluke eggs should have been hatching, the weather turned dry again and most of them died. More eggs hatched during August, but this was too late in the year for the flukes to develop fully and so produce eggs that could infect pastures before winter begins. The reason that fluke numbers are rather high in parts of Devon, and also in Cumbria and Powys, is that the dry spell in June and early July was less pronounced there.

Was it flukes that killed the rabbit I found beside the south-eastern hedge on the 17th? It seemed to be uninjured and it did not look as though a predator had killed it. Whatever did kill it, something took it away to eat, because the corpse did not remain there for long. The remains I found on the lower side of the field were certainly the work of a predator, though. Nothing remained but a few scraps of fur to tell that a rabbit had died there. The predator was probably a weasel, and it may also have been a weasel that took the rabbit whose death appeared to have been peaceful.

There are weasels living in Cross Park. The burrows made between the stones beside the gates are probably theirs. The burrows are quite small, but then, so are their occupants. The weasel, stoat, mink and polecat are close relatives and all of them are built to much the same design, but apart from the Pygmy Weasel, which lives in some parts of Europe, the weasel is the smallest of them all. An adult male may grow to about seven and a half inches, and individuals may be rather smaller than this, but seldom larger. Stoats are rather bigger. It may not be easy to tell a weasel from a stoat: the weasel has the shorter tail, but unless you see two animals side by side this is not much help. Nor is it much help to assume that stoats can be distinguished in winter because their coats turn white. It is true, but it is also true of most weasels. There are two more reliable clues, provided you get a good look at the animal. The stoat has a very distinct black tip to its tail, even when the rest of its coat is white. The weasel may have a few black hairs, but not what you would call a tip. That is the first clue. The second is the line where the brown back meets the pale underside of the animal. If this line is marked clearly and straight, the animal is a stoat, if it is irregular and waving, the animal is a weasel. If you see a group of them hunting together, they are certainly stoats. Weasels are usually solitary.

Mustela nivalis, the weasel, is a fierce beast. It will attack anything it perceives as either a threat or a meal, including a human. Our great size may frighten it, but the weasel believes that attack is the best form of defence, and usually it is right. It is wrong to say it has an uncertain temper: its temper is remarkably constant, and always bad. It is easily vexed. If you manage to trap one, or get one in a corner, it will hiss and spit furiously, and if you try to pick it up, hero or innocent that you are, the attempt may cost you a finger.

You would think, would you not, that such an aggressive, bad-tempered creature would be constantly at odds with its fellows, so that the world of the weasels is one of perpetual warfare? You would be wrong. Weasels are very tolerant of other weasels, provided they are not crowded together too closely. Carolyn King, a zoologist from Oxford, spent much time studying the weasel population in a woodland habitat near Oxford. She found that they do not even mark out and defend territories in the true sense. Their behaviour, it seems, is regulated largely by the number of males in the area. If there are too few there is no social cohesion and if there are too many they may begin to establish territories and become aggressive. Mostly, though, both males and females have ranges in which they hunt, and these ranges often overlap. They use scent to mark them, as a form of indirect communication, and where two males share part of the same range they avoid one another. The size of a range varies greatly from one individual to another, and, of course, it depends on the abundance of food. Males have the larger ranges. In the Oxfordshire woodland the males worked from 14 to 40 acres each and a few worked as much as 60 acres. The females worked from 2½ to 10 acres. If you relate this to Cross Park, where food for weasels may be rather less abundant than in an old mixed woodland, it seems likely that the weasel ranges will be larger and that weasels living in the field will hunt quite widely outside it. This difference in range sizes between males and females is common among carnivorous mammals. Feral cats arrange matters in the same way. It serves the interests of both sexes by allowing the males to wander far and wide, partly in search of females, while the females remain closer to their nests and their young.

Not all the Oxford weasels had ranges. There were non-residents as well as residents in the woodland, and it seemed that each group preferred its own way of life. When a resident died, or vacated its range, the range was never taken over by a non-resident but always by a neighbouring resident. There was no hurry to occupy it, and often several weeks would elapse before the neighbour began to patrol it. Should a non-resident have wished to take up residence, there were always some vacant ranges available. The non-residents were rather smaller than the residents, but they seemed to manage well enough.

Weasels are supposed to hunt mainly by night, but they do come out during the day. The Oxford weasels were trapped more often by day than by night, so perhaps the belief in the animal's nocturnal habits is founded on a myth.

You can read some history in the distribution of these small animals. In Iceland there are neither stoats nor weasels. In Ireland there are stoats but no weasels and in mainland Britain there are both stoats and weasels. Does this tell us something about the way animals were migrating as the last ice age ended? It may, if you suppose that the stoats were moving ahead of the weasels. As the ice sheets and glaciers were melting, sea levels rose, and one by one what are now islands became cut off from the continental land mass. Iceland became an island before the stoats reached it, but stoats did reach Ireland before the Irish Sea rushed in and prevented the weasels from making the crossing.

The campaign to halt the gassing of that large relative of the stoats and weasels, the badger, made a big advance. The slide in the eastern corner of the field had been used when I inspected it on the 24th, but probably by rabbits rather than a badger. The Cross Park badger may have been killed or have moved away, but such badgers as remain are a little safer than they were, at least for the time being. So loud had been the conservationists' protest that on the 25th the Government announced that, except in areas already cleared of bovine tuberculosis, which it proposed to keep clear, the gassing of badgers would cease while Lord Zuckerman examined the problem. It was pointed out that apart from being a former Government Chief Scientist, Lord Zuckerman is President of the Zoological Society of London and President of the Fauna Preservation Society, and Peter Walker, the Minister of Agriculture who made the announcement, promised that the results of the Zuckerman Review would be published. If I were a badger who read the papers I would take the opportunity to pack my bags and leave, before they find that their gassing programme was nothing like intensive enough.

It was on the 24th that I saw the only reptile I have encountered in Cross Park. At a place on the north-western hedge, where something—probably a sheep—had pulled the vegetation and earth away from the stone core of the hedge, a small female lizard was basking in the sun. She was a Common, or Viviparous Lizard, *Lacerta vivipara*, about four inches long. She showed no sign of alarm as I stared at her rudely, but she was gone a little while later when I returned to the spot.

The Common Lizard is distributed widely all over Europe. It is even found in Ireland, though it is less common there. It is an adaptable creature, like many reptiles, and despite its name it is not really viviparous: like the Flesh Fly, it is ovoviviparous—it produces eggs but retains them inside its body until they hatch. The young are alive when they leave the body of their mother, but it is not true live birth. To be truly viviparous, like the adder or any mammal, the food store in the egg must be supplemented by nutrients supplied directly by the mother. In the 'Viviparous' Lizard the developing young are wholly dependent on the contents of their eggs. In fact, the female can lay the eggs and let them hatch by themselves. Members of the species that live in southern Europe, where the weather is warm, do this. Further north there are distinct advantages in hatching the eggs inside the body. It means they can be carried about to the warmest places. They are warmed when the mother basks in the sun and when the weather is cold she protects them by moving herself into a burrow or other sheltered place. The trick has enabled the Common Lizard to thrive all over Europe. It is better still to be truly viviparous, though. The adder lives inside the Arctic Circle: no egg-laying reptile could do that. Once the young lizards have hatched, of course, they are on their own. Apart from the crocodilians, reptiles are not strong on motherhood.

The Common Lizard is a little drab, but if you look more closely you see that it has attractive markings. It is a pretty animal, if unassuming. Like most lizards, it feeds on insects. In fact, as a group, the lizards are the most important insectivorous vertebrates in the world. They eat

The Common, or Viviparous, Lizard (*Lacerta vivipara*)

more insects than birds or even bats. In hot countries people are quite happy to allow lizards to live in their houses with them to mop up surplus insects.

It is odd that we find lizards—well, most of them—attractive and yet snakes are awesome and alarming. There are more snake gods than gods in the shape of any other group of animals. Yet snakes and lizards, which comprise the order Squamata, are so similar that it is almost impossible to produce a clear definition of one group that does not include some members of the other. I think it is all to do with legs. Things that have two legs are all right. Things that have four legs are at best lovable and at worst tolerable. Things that have far too many legs are alarming (butterflies, in this sense, have no legs, only wings, which makes them like two-legged birds) and things that have no legs at all are appalling. People who encounter a harmless slow worm for the first time are often horrified by it, but when they learn that it is not a snake but only a legless lizard, they become much more tolerant of it. They regard it as a creature that ought to have four legs, but that lost them, perhaps in an unfortunate accident. We are not alone in this. Many other mammals also avoid snakes and legless lizards. The lizards have not lost their legs by accident, of course. There seems to be an advantage in losing them. Snakes are more highly evolved than lizards and many lizards have legs that are tiny and weak. The skinks, for example, are lizards that may be losing their legs. The Common Lizard, though, has very definite legs, and feet which it plants defiantly upon its world, and it shows no sign of wishing to be rid of them.

I left the Cross Park lizard basking on her stone and I did not see her again. The meeting with her sent me off into the long, wet grass at the top of the field to see whether there might be a wandering grass snake weaving its way in search of a frog snack, but if there were any snakes in the grass I did not find them. I had to make do with the lizard. The frogs that might have fed the snakes were still to be found, but they were all on the lower side of the field. There were no snakes there, either.

The robins were making a tremendous noise. I noticed it first on the 11th and they kept it up for more than a week, not only up in Cross Park, but in the valleys as well, and in my garden. The newly matured birds were marking out their territories by perching on trees and telegraph wires to shout defiance at their neighbours, who shouted back. Like victors in a war they were carving up the conquered territory according to the simple principle of possession being the whole of the law. Compared to these little belligerents, the weasel is a docile, amiable soul.

The days grew shorter and sometimes, early in the morning, there was a chill in the air that suggested just the merest touch of frost before dawn. It was fine and by mid-morning the sun was often shining warm, but the trees were not to be fooled. The shortening days made them cut off supplies to their leaves and as the nutrients drained back to the centre of the plant the first of them began to brown the tips of their leaves and then to send them spinning down into the country roads. The bracken was starting to turn brown and die back. On the other side of the valley, bright in the morning sunshine, a farmer was baling up a second cut of hay, his tractor and baler moving slowly, methodically and silently back and forth across the yellowing field. It was harvest time. Where they were growing corn the harvest began in August and by the end of September it was more or less done.

It was harvest time, the time for the fruits. The blackberries in Cross Park began to ripen, but slowly, and the few sloes I saw were insufficient to flavour a bottle of gin or to make any wine. It was not a good year for them. Everyone knows about sloe gin, which is said to be

The first haws

The sycamore leaves began to wilt in September, and the first winds of autumn plucked from the trees such leaves as it could grab. On the north-western hedge, seen here, the hazel had not begun to wilt and, here at least, the ferns remained green

delicious, although I have never tasted it, and some know about sloe wine, which I have made and can recommend, but how many people make haw brandy? I have no recipe for it, but I imagine it is made like sloe gin, with equal weights of fruit and sugar to half fill a bottle that is then topped up with spirit and left to stand for a couple of months.

The first haws were ripe by the middle of the month, and a few late hawthorn flowers were still open and being visited by flies. The hawthorn is a very ancient plant. The 'haw' in its name comes from the Old English *haga*, which means both hedge and bush, as does the modern German *Hage* which gives the hawthorn its German name of *Hagedorn*. Before the late sixteenth or early seventeenth centuries most hedges were 'dead' and were made from walls, earth banks, or fencing. Did the hawthorn invade them spontaneously or was it being used to make living hedges in the days when people still spoke Old English? We associate it with May and with the pre-Christian rites connected with May Day, but it has Christian connections, too. It is said to have furnished the crown of thorns worn by Jesus at his crucifixion, and the Glastonbury thorn, which often flowers in winter and sometimes on Christmas Day, is said to have sprung from the staff of Joseph of Arimathea. The legend may or may not be based on fact. What is a fact is that *Crataegus monogyna*, the more common of the British hawthorns, does sometimes flower in winter. The Cross Park hawthorn is of this species, and so is the Glastonbury thorn. Henry VII adopted the hawthorn as an heraldic device because, so the story goes, after the battle of Bosworth a small crown that had become detached from the helmet of Richard III was found hanging on a hawthorn bush.

As the month drew to its close first the sycamore and then the oak leaves began to change colour. Oddly enough it was a time for young animals rather than old ones. The robins, shouting their challenge at real or imagined invaders, were asserting themselves in their world for the first time. The moles, tunnelling busily in their perpetual search for earthworms, were those born earlier in the year, just embarking on their subterranean careers. The burrowing in the banks was that of young rabbits beginning their housekeeping after a spring and summer spent making shallow practice scrapes in the soft earth to learn the feel of the soil in which they must spend so much of their time. The slugs were mating, and so were the Crane Flies. It was an active time, a time that was none too long if a million small, vulnerable creatures were to make themselves secure before the start of the long, cold, hungry nights.

October

A sheep, you might think, possesses a face poorly equipped for the expression of deep emotions. You could be wrong. I watched a ewe whose wild-eyed, desperate look conveyed an emotion concocted from panic, despair and a kind of tired resignation. She lurched backward, forelegs flailing, as a laughing man threw her into what she expected to be eternity, but which turned out to be a cold bath. The right way up now, her feet barely touching the bottom, she struggled to escape. She was held, though, pushed back each time she managed to move toward the ramp at the end. The men had what looked like long-handled brooms without the bristles and they used these to control her. Three times a boot pushed her head beneath the thrashing surface, and each time she succeeded in pushing the top of her back into the air the prodders ducked it again. She kicked and splashed and gasped, too breathless to cry out, for what seemed a very long time. When, at last, she was allowed to leave the bath she had to be helped by another man, stationed on the ramp, who half dragged her clear. Her sodden fleece was almost too heavy for her to carry and the battens set into the steep ramp afforded too little purchase for her hooves. The evil-smelling liquid streamed from her and as she shook herself another torrent was caught by the sides of the narrow pen and channelled back into the bath.

It was dipping time, and by no stretch of the imagination can sheep be said to enjoy the experience. The ram, larger and heavier than his ewes and the subject of much ribald merriment, almost collapsed, mouth open, blue tongue protruding, eyes rolling and breath rasping. He was grabbed, hauled clear, and recovered instantly.

For the half-dozen men conducting the operation it was an occasion for hilarity, the brief euphoria that comes from working hard amid high excitement. Like most farming tasks it was an annual event, but unlike many it was one that called for the collaboration of several workers and

159

Sheep dipping

that brought neighbours into contact. The men knew that no sheep
would, or could, come to any harm. The sheep were less confident.
One of the men believed the animals remembered the dip they had had
last year. That, he said, was why they stopped in their tracks at the
entrance to the pen on the dry side of the dip. The sights, sounds and
smells were familiar to them and they stopped and tried to turn back as
a man might do as he caught his first glimpse of the guillotine whose
high blade awaited him. It was as though they remembered the
experience but not their swift recovery from it. The recovery meant a
return to normality, and normality is not memorable. Only the dipping
remained, as an impression buried deep beneath their consciousness,
like a ghost to be raised whenever the circumstances that created it
were supplied.

The dip itself was made from concrete and blocks. Numbers
scratched in the side with a stick or nail while the concrete was setting
suggested that it was built in 1959. The central part consisted of the
bath itself, just wide enough for a full grown sheep to turn around and
about half as long again as a sheep. At the dry end there was a long
pen, rather wider than the bath, with a gate at each end and a third
gate in the middle. The batch of sheep were driven into the outer pen

and then, about a dozen at a time, they were moved into the forward pen. The gate behind them was closed, the gate in front of them was opened, and one by one they were manhandled, usually backwards, over the edge, which dropped sheer to the bottom. They left the bath by the ramp and into another pen. Its floor sloped sufficiently to ensure that the dip dripping from them flowed back into the bath, and it was closed by a gate at its upper end. There the dipped sheep stood until they had more or less stopped dripping, when the gate was opened and they were allowed to emerge into a small patch of waste ground used for the dip. There they huddled in tight little groups, until they were dry enough to be taken back to the fields.

It was an attractive spot and a beautiful morning. Dipping must be done on ground that is used for nothing else, to prevent contamination from the insecticide used in the dip. The farmer who has a suitable spot usually builds the dip and shares it with his neighbours. The sheep from Geoff's farm were being dipped just down the road, on the next farm, on a bit of useless, low-lying land infested with coarse grasses and weeds and surrounded by scrubby trees and hedges. It was useless for cultivation, but ideal for dipping, and because it was uncultivated and used only occasionally, it was very pretty. The weather on the morning of the 25th was still, sunny and warm, with an intensely blue sky from which the rains of the previous night had washed the dust. Small, puffy cumulus clouds gleamed very white. During a pause while more sheep were brought down the road, one of the men was glad of the shade of the trees to rest from the heat. It was one of those occasional autumn days that relieve the otherwise relentless progress into winter. It had rained almost ceaselessly for days, and the 24th had been wetter even than the days that preceded it. It rained for most of the night and at dawn it was still raining. Then the rain stopped, the clouds broke, and the dipping began.

The dipping was not, and cannot be, arranged to suit the weather. The blue sky was no more than a fortunate coincidence. In any case it did not last: the rain returned in the afternoon. The operation must be planned well in advance because the local authority has to be given three days' advance warning. Everything is subject to control and supervision. The dip must be made from ingredients approved by the authorities and an official must be present at the dipping to ensure that the dip has been mixed correctly, is being used correctly, and that the sheep receive an adequate dose. Each animal must remain in the dip for not less than one minute.

It is an elaborate ritual, but a necessary one, designed partly to protect the sheep and partly to protect the environment. The dip solution is poisonous and must be treated with respect. What happens to the remains of the dip after dipping is something of a mystery and a cause for concern. Each year British farmers have to dispose of something like 63,000 tonnes of spent dip. The water authorities are supposed to be informed of the place and time at which dipping is to take place, so they can advise on disposal and be prepared to deal with any pollution that results from it. Most of the time they are not informed, due to the obsessive secrecy that shrouds every part of government. The local authorities, which should notify the water authorities, regard the addresses of sheep farmers, the locations of their dips, and the dates on which each of them has decided to dip, as confidential. It is not impossible that by passing such information some official could be prosecuted under the Official Secrets Act and end his days incarcerated in some dank dungeon, remembered only as a spy and traitor, vilified by the society whose vital security he had endangered! There is a rumour spreading in some quarters to the effect that, while doubtless an alien power possessed of the addresses of all British sheep farmers could wreak havoc with the economy and deprive us of our woollies and our excuse for making mint sauce, when it came to it most such powers would shrink from so dastardly an act. I suppose, though, that the authorities worry about New Zealand saboteurs (disguised as shearers?) and French fifth columnists (travelling as tourists?). Was it they who spread the sheep scab, bustling about the countryside on sinister nocturnal errands with briefcases bulging with mites, keds, ticks, lice, blowflies and all the other parasites to which ovine flesh is heir, to ensure a thorough infestation with everything while they are about it? It seems unlikely, but you never know. After all, the extra-mural activities of intelligence services are made entertaining by their startling eccentricity.

The autumn dip is to prevent sheep scab, and it is compulsory. All sheep must be dipped between 3 September and 11 November. There is a good chance that, by persisting with the compulsory dipping programme, sheep scab can be eradicated. Up to the end of October there were forty-five cases of scab in Devon and Cornwall during 1979. For the past few years the incidence of scab has been increasing, but only in these two counties. Elsewhere it is declining and of the eight cases that occurred in other parts of Britain up to the end of October 1979, six were caused by infection from sheep moved out of Devon or Cornwall. The compulsory dipping applies to the whole country, though, not just to the south west; the only sheep that are exempt are those destined for slaughter during the dipping period. After they have been dipped, the sheep are kept separate from undipped sheep and they can be taken for sale to the market only if they have a certificate declaring that they have been dipped within the preceding fifty-six days. Even then, those that are to be sold are not allowed to mix with those due to be killed. The success of the programme everywhere except in the south west led to the relaxation of the restrictions from the end of the 1979 dipping period, from 12 November. Except in Devon and Cornwall, all the marketing regulations ended. You still needed a licence to move sheep out of Devon and Cornwall, even for immediate slaughter, and undipped sheep could not be moved out of the region at all.

The Ministry had declared war on the sheep scab mite, just as it declared war on the Warble Fly. Sheep scab is marginally less distressing to its victim than warbles, but it is bad enough. The mite causes intense itching, which leads to scratching. The fleece is damaged and sometimes ruined, and the wounds caused by the scratching can become infected. As they heal they cause the scabs that give the disease its name. It is unpleasant and affected sheep lose their appetites and much of their zest for life.

So there we were, on that sunny October morning, watching the sheep endure their moment of terror and discomfort in order to avoid much worse discomfort later. One by one they went protesting through the dip, each animal spending its statutory minute in the bath—although no one had a stopwatch. The two men from the ministry (or was it the County Council?) stood by, smoking cigarettes and gossiping about their work and their colleagues. Every now and then the dip had to be topped up with water from a milk churn. The churn was filled again by a piece of hose whose 'tap' consisted of a doubled-back end secured with a piece of binder twine. Then the insecticide, a dark brown liquid that smelled like creosote, was poured very carefully from the green drum into an aluminium measuring jug. It was the cause of some amusement. 'They sell this in the pubs in Bodmin.' 'It tastes like peppermint.' 'If you get it on your hands it burns.' 'If you get it in your eyes, that's really bad.' Some wore oilskin leggings, made these days from PVC, like fishermen, and wellington boots. Others, including one of the Ministry men, wore thigh-length waders. They were careful not to allow the insecticide to touch their skins until it was diluted in the water. After that they could not help touching it because they had to handle the wet sheep and there was a great deal of splashing. Despite this, their clothes remained perfectly dry. The operation was less casual than it looked.

The Ministry men decided to sample the dip. One of them leaned precariously over the edge to collect a specimen in a jar, which he took back to the estate car parked down the road by the farmhouse. He carried his rudimentary laboratory with him and in a few minutes he was back to announce, and approve, the concentration of insecticide. Sheep are dipped to combat other external parasites, but it is only the scab dip that is compulsory and it is only this dip that is supervised so closely.

The substance they took from the green drum consisted of carbophenothion and 32 per cent (water volume) of gamma HCH (hexachlorocyclohexane). It was a heady mixture whose resemblance to creosote ended with the colour and smell. When it was mixed with water it turned to a creamy buff colour, like a disinfectant. Carbophenothion is an organophosphorus compound and its use is very restricted. Apart from sheep dips its only other permitted use is for dressing winter wheat seed against wheat bulb fly. Even then, farmers are advised to use it only if an attack of the pest is likely, and never to use it on spring-sown wheat. Once seed has been dressed with it some care must be taken to make sure it is not milled by mistake and fed to animals—or humans. Gamma HCH is an organochlorine compound, much less poisonous than carbophenothion, but more persistent. It has many brand names, the best known of which is 'Lindane'.

The Ministry specify the insecticides that can be used and, predictably, this causes some anguish. Some individualists regard it, and probably most other regulations, as an intrusion on their privacy and an invasion of their right to do precisely as they wish. Quite apart from this apparent assault on private enterprise, the fear of pesticides causes problems all of its own. 'Pesticide' is the most emotive word in the agricultural vocabulary. It surpasses even 'factory-farm' in its capacity to make blood boil while spine tingles. A year or two ago someone challenged the dipping programme by refusing to dip his sheep in the approved manner. In due course he was taken to court, where he faced a magistrate who sympathised with his dilemma. I suspect, though, that the magistrate failed to understand the scientific arguments behind either dipping or the particular insecticides that are used. Of course it is true that wild sheep survive quite happily without being dipped. However, wild sheep—and there are none in Britain— do not have fleeces and do not live in large flocks. The fleece and the flock are both products of agriculture; if the benefits they have conferred include a higher output of meat than would be possible from the culling of a wild population, and wool that would not exist at all without domestication, the costs include the increased susceptibility of the sheep to parasites. If we farm sheep we must protect them, and so far no one has devised a better way to do this than by dipping.

Our friend in court argued that organochlorine insecticides harm wildlife. He was concerned about the gamma HCH. He is quite right in general, but in this case his choice of organochlorine was unwise. Gamma HCH is one of the least harmful in the group, mainly because it has an unpleasant smell and taste (it was the gamma HCH that made the dip smell of creosote) and few creatures will eat food contaminated with it. If they do, it does not seem to cause them any serious problems and it does not remain for long within their bodies. It does dissolve in body fats, like other organochlorines, but it does not accumulate seriously because it is released again and excreted. Be that as it may, our lone farmer stuck to his guns and eventually the Ministry modified its position by allowing the use of three recipes for dips that date from before the invention of modern insecticides. They employ such ingredients as lime, sulphur, carbolic acid, soft soap and tobacco. So now you can dip in one of these solutions. The disadvantage is that the sheep must be dipped twice, the second dipping eight days after the first. The sheep would not enjoy that, even if the farmer could spare the time—on our farm dipping took two days—to administer the insecticide. It might lead to a nationwide mutiny among the sheep as they refused to enter a dip they remembered very clearly indeed from a week earlier.

Apart from their visit to the dip, the sheep spent the whole month in Cross Park, chomping contentedly at the grass. They were back in the field on the 1st, and on the 31st they had gone again.

There were some mild days and some warm sunshine—apart from that we enjoyed on the morning of Dipping Day—as well as much rain during the month, and the insects made most of what was left of the fine weather. On the 1st, I saw a hawker dragonfly crossing the road away from Cross Park and vanishing over the hedge on the other side. There was an occasional caterpillar to be seen and a few late bees hurried as they visited the bramble flowers that still burst fresh along the hedges, some pink, some white, with additional, isolated buds to keep them flowering until the frosts would bring their season to its end.

The dung flies were mating on the 15th. They are very possessive, these small, brightly coloured flies. I saw intruders being chased away from patches of dung occupied by other individuals. The territories were small, but clearly there was a principle at stake. Sometimes the encounters were quite violent and the combatants came to blows. It is only the males that are coloured bright yellow; the females are rather greener and generally more drab than their spouses, but still pretty, considering the circumstances under which they live. They, or some other insect, were laying eggs. Every pile of dung was peppered with tiny white specks, eggs waiting to hatch into larvae that would tunnel into the dung, provided no predator seized them first.

Beneath the stones the woodlice were living their quiet, ancient lives. They are vastly underrated creatures, woodlice. Small boys attempt to keep them as pets—unsuccessfully, for they make dull pets—but otherwise they go largely unnoticed. They make some people cringe as all small creatures should do, but they are not really successful as strikers-of-terror-into-the-hearts-of-damsels. They look like beetles and many people take them for insects, which they are not. They are crustaceans, and it is that which makes them interesting. They are the only land animals living in our climate that are related to shrimps and, more distantly, to the crabs and lobsters. The great majority of crustaceans live in water and there they play roles very similar to those played on land by insects, so that sometimes they are called 'insects of the oceans'. The large crabs and lobsters, which are the most famous members of the class, are far less important to the ecology of fresh and salt waters than are the millions of smaller, less impressive creatures. It is as though we studied and admired the dragonflies and butterflies among the insects but overlooked the bees, wasps, aphids, ants and all the rest, which are far more influential and far more numerous.

Some of the woodlice curl up into a ball when they are disturbed. It earns them the name of 'pill bug'. Others are called 'sow bugs'. The armour plating and the habit of curling up for safety has been developed quite independently by other creatures. The armadillos do it, and so does the hedgehog, with spines instead of plates.

The little woodlouse may look a bit like a beetle, but it is very different from any insect. For one thing it has no neck, so that its head is not distinct. The head is fused to the first of its eight thoracic segments. Each of the remaining segments bears a pair of pereopods, or legs, and there are more leg-like appendages on its abdominal segments. This is altogether too many segments for an insect and far too many legs. The creature breathes differently from insects, too. Some woodlice have specially adapted abdominal appendages and others breathe through tufts of tubes that are visible as white spots on the undersides of their bodies.

They lay eggs, of course, but the young go through no larval stage: there is no such thing as a woodlouse grub. Most crustaceans carry their eggs around with them until they hatch, but the woodlouse is an isopod and the isopods (order Isopoda, subclass Malacostraca, division Peracarida, of the Crustacea) have taken this a stage further. The woodlouse has a pouch on the underside of its thorax, made from overlapping plates and fastened to the bases of its legs. The eggs are laid in the pouch and undergo their development there; the young emerge as creatures very similar to the adults but much smaller. While they are in the brood pouch the young are fed by a secretion from the adult. They are more advanced than they may look, with ovovivipary developed quite highly.

The woodlice, then, small, despised, and yet marvellously adapted to exploit a terrestrial environment that is and always has been closed to the vast majority of crustaceans, live out their lives beneath the stones. They are not the parasites the name 'louse' suggests. They feed on almost anything. Their main food item is decaying vegetation, although some of them will eat a living plant now and then, and they will eat carrion and, occasionally, some species will eat one another.

Amid the grass at the foot of the north-eastern hedge I found a film of a transparent substance, more or less rectangular in shape, and about ¾ in by ⅝ in in size. It looked like a small window, stretched taut between the grass leaves to which it was attached, as though some creature might dwell beneath it, protected and yet with a view of the world above. There was no such sheltering creature, of course. The 'window' had been made by a slug, perhaps one of the large *A. ater* that were still to be seen here and there. For a time the *A. ater* had been alone and I saw no slugs other than these giants. Now, though, the smaller species were putting in an appearance, and some of them were tiny. There was one, perhaps *Arion intermedius*, that I saw grazing placidly on some moss on the 31st. It was no more than ¾ in long, pale buff in colour, with a dark head and tentacles. It is a pretty slug, and very common.

It is difficult to imagine a slug as being anything but placid, but appearance can be misleading. Just because a creature loses its temper in what we would consider slow motion, it does not follow that it is any less angry or that its rage is any less impressive to animals that live at a similar speed. Some slugs are quite aggressive. If *A. ater* is disturbed in the performance of some important activity, it may twitch in angry frustration in its contracted position. *Deroceras caruanae*, though, goes much further when it meets other slugs of which it does not approve. It lashes its tail—slowly—and snaps at them. It is pretty wild stuff down there among the bellyfeet. It is a small slug, usually brown but sometimes grey or black, and you can identify it by what looks like a white ring about half-way along the right side of its body. This is the pale margin of the respiratory opening.

The slugs I saw seemed peaceful enough. The real garden pest was there, *Deroceras reticulatum*, and a slug I took to be *Limax marginatus* (also known as *Lehmannia marginata*). It is very soft-bodied even for a slug, and it can absorb large amounts of water. It is a great climber, especially in the wet weather it prefers, and can travel up walls and high into trees in search of the lichens and small fungi on which it feeds. Its party trick is to attach its mucus to a support, draw it out into threads, and then climb up or down it. The one I saw was on a stone in the south-eastern hedge and it was not performing acrobatics. It is a truly wild slug that will have nothing to do with humans or their crops and you will find it only in places that are fairly undisturbed.

Further down the same hedge, in two gaps between stones, there were snails all packed together. In one of the gaps I counted five, all with their shells touching, and there may have been more further inside. They were common enough, and so was their behaviour. *Helix aspersa*, the common garden snail, is very gregarious and it enjoys life in a gastropodic commune. It may be that the ones I saw were preparing to hibernate. They also survive prolonged dry periods by sealing themselves inside their waterproof shells in a state of suspended animation, called 'aestivation', that is not unlike hibernation. They are one of the largest of the native snails. The introduced Roman or edible snail, *H. pomatia*, is larger, but *H. aspersa,* its cousin, is no less edible. If you feel like trying them you should capture wild ones and keep them for a couple of weeks on a diet of fresh lettuce leaves, to clean them out. You eat only the foot, so that *aspersa* is much more fiddly than *pomatia*.

The oak apples appeared. I saw them first on the 22nd, as the oak leaves were beginning to turn brown and wither, so exposing the wood. Oak apples are much the same size as marble galls and they grow on the wood of the tree. They are made by *Biorrhiza pallida*, a gall wasp that reproduces alternately sexually and asexually. The apple gall is produced by a larva hatched from eggs that were laid as a result of sexual mating during the summer. It will produce a wingless, asexual wasp which will burrow into the ground and lay its eggs on wounds it makes in the roots of the oak. These will hatch to produce larvae that make root galls, and these in turn will give rise to next year's sexual, winged wasps. The oak is especially attractive to gall wasps, and to some other insects that make galls, but about half of all plant species are used in this way by some creature or other. The root nodules, made by *Rhizobium* bacteria on the roots of many leguminous plants, are galls. They are of great economic importance because the bacteria that inhabit them make use of atmospheric nitrogen, incorporating it into their own cell chemistry, and so make it available as a plant nutrient when they die.

The oak apple is not a fruit, but in this year, when everything seemed to be late, real fruiting continued to the end of October and beyond. Throughout the month those blackberries that had ripened hung dark and luscious on the brambles, but ripening was patchy, and many berries were still red and hard. The rosehips and haws brought small patches of bright colour to the hedgerows and high above the north-western hedge, well out of reach, great bunches of black elderberries dangled heavy to tempt the amateur cordial maker into foolhardy adventures with ropes and ladders.

Not all the fruits were edible. The bryony produced its berries and by the third week of the month they were turning from pale green to bright red. Many insects feed on them, including some bees, but most mammals avoid them. Bryony often grows over rabbit warrens, and the rabbits leave it strictly alone. Despite their cheerful red colour, the berries do not look wholesome. Many of the relatives of the bryony produce edible, indeed delicious, fruits: the bryony belongs to the Cucurbitae, the family of the gourds that includes melons, cucumbers and marrows.

There were still a few flowers, apart from those on the brambles. Occasional red campions bloomed low down in the hedges where they were sheltered from the wind and rain, and the scabious brought just a speck of blue here and there. In general, though, the hedges were turning brown. The bracken withered first, but remained upright in dense, dead stands. The oak followed it, but unevenly. Some trees were still entirely green while others had begun to shed their leaves. The sycamore was preparing to drop its leaves for winter. Whenever there was a strong wind, leaves would be swept away to scurry about the countryside, modelling the eddies and vortices that carried them, and yet by the end of the month many leaves still clung to their trees, so that people said that each warm day, each day that passed before the trees were stripped of their leaves entirely, postponed the onset of winter.

In the country as a whole the farming had caught up with itself and it was late no longer. The cereal harvest had been gathered in by the beginning of the month. Apart from the mixed corn, grown to feed stock, yields were a little lower than those of 1978. The wheat yield was about 2 per cent lower, the barley yield about 8 per cent lower and the yield of oats about 6 per cent lower. The national average yield of more than 1 ½ tons of barley and oats to the acre and slightly more than 2 tons of wheat per acre is high, even so. In our heavily urbanised society it is easy to forget that British cereal yields are about double those of North America and that the value of British farm produce is greater than that of Australia and New Zealand combined. The maincrop potatoes were being harvested, too, and at about 13 tons to the acre were yielding about 6 per cent less than they yielded in 1978. Other crops were developing well and even the winter keep looked sufficient, provided the winter was not unusually long. This was slightly surprising because of the bad weather early in the year that set back the production of grass and the making of hay and silage. The average protein content of the hay was about one per cent higher than in hay made in 1978, and, although it varied quite widely from place to place, the quality of the silage seemed satisfactory. For farmers seeking alternative feed for their stock, it looked as though hay would be selling at about £71 per ton, barley straw at £40 per ton and suger beet pulp at £91 per ton. For most of the month the grass continued to grow, though slowly, and there was pasture to be grazed.

The spiders were active and feeding early in the month. Most of those that I saw were common diadem spiders, but the tube webs were still occupied and there were some sheet webs as well. Perhaps some species were still mating. On the 8th I saw a pair of small spiders, the female on the web and the male nearby, apparently waiting for an opportune moment to approach. There were some lycosids as well, small ones running about in the grass at the bases of the hedges. The spiders were being restricted by the weather, as were the insects that fed them. On the warm, fairly still days they were active, but when the weather was wet or windy there were none to be seen. Little by little the weather was forcing them into inactivity, damaging webs, depriving them of food, and forcing even the new, young lycosids to seek shelter. The harvestmen were less restricted. There were many of them and they were very active.

The mammals had fewer problems. The moles were burrowing vigorously. I counted three sets of mole hills along the bottom hedge, far enough apart to suggest that they belonged to different individuals. In all there must have been ten or twelve moles around the edges of the field. The most adventurous—or desperate—of them lived about one-third of the way down the north-eastern hedge. It had tunnelled its way fully a quarter of the way into the field, making many hills. In places there were holes in the hills. I did not see any moles above ground, but moles do surface and some people believe they spend quite long periods above ground at night, when they will capture any earthworms they find taking the evening air and also any small birds or mammals that may come their way. There should be ample food for the moles below ground—it can be only boredom that brings them to the surface.

Arable land contains far fewer soil animals than old grassland, but to compensate for this it is much easier to tunnel through soil that has been cultivated. The size of the soil population is surprising. There are, for example, twenty-five species of British earthworms, and ten of them are common in fields. Many estimates have been made of the total weight of earthworms in different soils and a kind of scientific consensus has emerged to suggest that on average an acre of orchard land may support about a ton of earthworms. Cross Park will support less than this, but after it had been under grass for the best part of a year the worm population may well have risen to around half a ton an acre. The size of the individual worms varies widely. One of the smallest, *Eisenia rosea*, weighs less than fifty milligrammes when fully grown. A full-sized *Lumbricus terrestris*, on the other hand, weighs more than five grammes. *L. terrestris* burrows very deep into the ground: it is when it climbs up its own tunnels that the alert mole grabs it.

In addition to the worms there are all the small arthropods—the millipedes, centipedes, beetles and other insects, and their larvae. An acre of farm land contains hundreds or maybe thousands of them and although the mole really prefers a nice, soft earthworm to a hard-bodied beetle, it will eat almost any small animal it finds when the going is tough. Grubs are as easy to eat as worms, though moles with a weight problem should avoid them. Worms contain very little fat and a great deal of water; insect larvae contain little water and much fat.

It is likely that the mole hills thrown up so energetically were made by young moles born this year. As they grow older, moles live deeper beneath the surface. It may be that it was the heavy rain that caused the vigorous tunnelling that produced the hills. The weather may damage tunnels, especially those close to the surface, so they must be cleared and renovated. Then, as the weather becomes colder, the small invertebrates abandon the cold upper layers of the soil for more temperate climes below, and the moles must burrow more vigorously.

The other burrowers, the rabbits, had gone right through the hedges in several places, especially along the south-eastern boundary, giving them passage from one field to the next without the trouble of scrambling over the top of the bank. The lighter grasses streamed out in the draught caused by their holes.

There were more new burrows, or renovated burrows. Along the south-eastern hedge two had been excavated to produce huge piles of earth, like landslides, to lie bare as raw heaps of red soil against the complex textures of the muted green and brown hedge. One of them was dug on the morning of the 15th. I know it was dug then, because it rained fairly steadily on the 14th and through the night. When I arrived the sun was shining and the fresh soil was dry and there was no sign of it having been pounded by the rain. Another was dug on the 22nd, just a week later, and again I arrived soon after work was completed to find dry, fresh soil amid grass still wet from the heavy shower of rain a couple of hours earlier. In fact I may have interrupted that particular excavation for as I walked beside the hedge there was a scuffle and a scurrying rabbit bobbed its white tail at me as it ran for the cover of the corner of the field.

The other corner had been used, too, the one with the large slide. The slide itself was almost obscured by overhanging vegetation and although I searched hard I could see no tell-tale hairs caught on brambles. It was difficult to determine whether the slide had been used. Any animal that did use it would push away the vegetation, all of which hung from above or projected from the sides, and the vegetation would close behind it again as it passed. On the 31st, though, the long grass at the base of the slide had been trampled or pushed down to make a track that ran in towards the hedge and then along it for a few yards. There is a large rabbit burrow beside the slide and the track could have been made by rabbits, but in some of the fresh earth thrown from a new burrow there were footprints. Most had been made by sheep but among them, and rather indistinct, there were others that could have been made by a badger. The day was showery and there had been heavy rain during the night, so that none of the prints was clear or even complete, but these were the wrong shape for a fox and far too large for any member of the weasel family except the badger. Had the Cross Park badger escaped the gassing? It had not been proved, but at least it seemed possible.

The field voles *(Microtus agrestis)* prefer the grassland close to the foot of the hedge and along the field headlands to the hedge itself. They were still using their tunnels, made by eating their way through thick clumps of grass and in one or two places tunnel entrances were exposed. The bank voles, too, were probably active. They had not started to eat the rose hips, but both they and the field mice would start to do so as other food became more scarce. You can detect small mammal activity in winter by watching the fate of the rose hips, and it is possible even to estimate the mammal species that are around and the size of their populations using rose hips as a yardstick. The hips that are eaten are removed by a bite that cuts the stem cleanly and diagonally just below the hip, so you can see how many hips have gone. After that it is a matter of finding the remains of the hips and distinguishing between vole and mouse feeding. They feed differently, like Mr and Mrs Spratt. The mice prefer the seeds, which they remove and eat, discarding most of the flesh. The voles prefer the flesh and leave the seeds. As the vegetation thinned and it became easier to peer into the hedges, I found several small flat areas, about at head height.

The mice may use these as feeding platforms and if they do it is on them that the remains of the hips may appear.

It was a time for burning the rubbish. On the 15th there were about half a dozen small bonfires in the paddock to the north-west of Cross Park, burning thinnings from the other side of the hedge.

The larks still rose startled from their quarter of the field whenever I approached too close, but they were fewer and their cries more muted. Their alarm was for themselves, not for their young, and it did not turn into rage and panic.

On the 1st I saw a kestrel. Kestrels are common but I wonder whether they are becoming fewer? My impression is entirely subjective, but it seems that a year or two ago I could not walk anywhere without seeing them and it was not unusual to see several of them hunting within sight of one another, in a quite small area. While I still see them now and then, I have the feeling that I see fewer of them than before, and certainly this was the first kestrel I had seen at Cross Park. In fact it was working on the Moor above the field, hovering, swooping down, and then returning again to its station. I watched it for several minutes, mainly to see whether it caught anything. So far as I could see, it did not.

Buzzards, on the other hand, seem to be more common. Often they were very high, circling slowly and watching for the smallest movement that would bring them into their attacking dive, like avenging angels. There were three of them close together high over the Moor to the north on the 1st, and on the 15th there was another—or more probably one of the same trio—also working from a high altitude.

It was on the 1st that I saw a buzzard being mobbed by rooks again. The birds were to the south of the field, engaged in an old-fashioned dog fight over the valley. The buzzard wheeled and turned, climbed, dived and twisted as it tried to shake off the two rooks, but the smaller birds were too fast and too manoeuvrable for it. Eventually, and it seemed inevitably, it lost the encounter and left what they clearly regarded as their territory. It is not surprising that smaller birds may overwhelm larger and more heavily armed birds by force of numbers—after all, an army of ants can and will kill an animal many millions of times the size of an ant. What is surprising is that the larger birds of prey are so helpless against just one or two smaller birds (unless, of course, they happen to belong to those species that specialise in the hunting of smaller birds). This vulnerability is one of the main causes of breeding failure among birds of prey. Even the fearsome eagles can be driven from their eyries by small birds, leaving their eggs undefended and allowing them to cool. It seems not to occur to them to

173

Elder and oak, missed by the clippers, growing from the far side of the north-western hedge

counter-attack, or in the case of the buzzards even to climb out of reach. I imagine a buzzard could out-climb a rook, and certainly its operational ceiling is higher. Yet the fight never leads to an exchange of blows. Bills and talons are not used. The larger bird recognises that it is being out-flown and retires. It is a contest of aviation skills more than a battle.

As the autumn developed the field began to prepare itself for the spring of 1980. The oaks produced the first tiny buds that would open as soon as winter was done, and the sycamores did the same. The hazels went further and produced the first male catkins, the flowers that, strictly speaking, they are not supposed to produce until the end of winter is in sight. There is no clear point at which one year ends and the next begins. 1980 is implicit in 1979. Much of each year's activity reaches its fruition in the following year. It is in autumn that this is most evident, as plants and animals prepare to continue their lives after the brief, sometimes harsh and cruel, interruption of winter. Thus the principal task for the autumn of 1979 was the creation of the spring of 1980.

November

'We had horses when I was a boy. I used horses up to the end of 1942. Dad was using horses until then. That's when we had the first tractor. That was wartime. There was a lot of work to do then. You had to go for a tractor.'

We were sitting in the farmhouse kitchen on a bright November afternoon. It was a time for story-telling, for remembering the past. We were sitting round the large table, Geoff, Doreen and I. Geoff was leaning back, relaxed, his back to the window, talking slowly and quietly.

'You had to plough so much. We ploughed about a third of the farm, didn't we?' He turned to his wife for confirmation, then corrected himself. 'It was more than a third. We ploughed nearly half the farm. The committees used to tell us what we had to grow. We had to grow four acres of potatoes and so much corn. When they stopped it was all grass, but that was what you had to do. It was a good idea in some places, but they ploughed a lot of land that had never seen the plough. It didn't hurt us but it did hurt some smallholdings, where the land didn't want to be ploughed.

'The only help we had was Italian and German prisoners-of-war, except for potato pickers. There was Father and myself and we had one man, Mike. He used to help us with the horses down in the stable to start off with.'

I had asked Geoff about the changes he had seen. He was not born on the farm, not quite. His birthplace is Millpark, a mile or two away, but his parents moved to the farm when he was four or five months old and he has lived there ever since. His wife was born at Millpool, a mile or so away, and their two sons were born on the farm. 'They're the fifth generation that we know of,' Geoff said. He has watched, lived through, taken part in the great revolution in agriculture that has changed the face of much of the landscape of Britain in the second half

175

The farmhouse. The window taken from the old chapel is on the right

Geoff

of this century. Yet seen as Geoff sees them many of those changes appear superficial, even ephemeral. It was the hedges he remembered first.

'Things have changed, in the sense that the hedges are all trimmed down, the wood's all cut.'

They were cut this year, and every year, in mid-November. When I visited Cross Park on the 19th the hedge trimmers were at work in the field across the road. Everyone was trimming at once and all the Cross Park hedges were cut down to an inch or two above the bank. They looked bare, forlorn, and it was easy to see why birds did not nest in them. In summer, when they grew to their full height and were thick, the bank was hidden and you could believe the plants grew ten or twelve feet high. The bank was there, though, deep inside, and ten or twelve were, in truth, no more than four or six. That is high enough for some birds, but in spring, when the birds are nesting and the vegetation is only beginning its reach for the sky, it is not. As I looked along the hedges they were neat, square, geometrical, and in some places they had been cut back as well as down. The hedge at the top of the field was more difficult to reach and for part of its length it had been cut back and down at the front but at the back it still grew tall, so it assumed a stepped shape. The trimming of hedges has some effect on wildlife—though less than is commonly supposed—but to the farmer it is merely one seasonal activity and it does not affect the overall pattern of farming.

'The farming part of it's exactly the same. Mixed farming.'

Even some of the original permanent pasture is there, centuries old.

'The field beside the garden there, I always understood, when our people came here in the 1840s, that was natural seeding. It's been the same ever since. But the record tells us we were here in 1778.'

The record, of course, is the parish record. The farm records do not go back quite so far, but they are old enough. Geoff showed me the tithe record for the parish for 1839. 'Apportionment of the Rent charge in lieu of Tithes' it was called, and it reported that 150 years ago the freehold of three-quarters of the farm belonged to Lord Vivian, who leased it to John Davey, the man who owned the remaining quarter. Apart from Davey, three other families lived on the farm, which amounted then to just over 79 acres. Much of it was arable land, with a small orchard, gardens, and about two acres of permanent pasture. Little Cross Park and Great Cross Park were growing arable crops. The farm as a whole had to contribute £9 12s 6d (£9.62½) a year to the rector. In times of hardship the tithes became a burden impossible to bear, but they were collected quite ruthlessly until well into this

177

century. I used to live in a small Suffolk village where a monument stood opposite the entrance to the church recording raids made by the 'heavies' hired by the Church. In one of them a family was stripped of all its possessions, even the cot in which the baby slept. That was in the depressed 1930s and Suffolk was the place where the grip of the Church was broken by farmers and their workers lying in wait in ditches armed with loaded shotguns to prevent the bailiffs from entering threatened farms.

The farmer of the early nineteenth century would have had to pay the notorious window tax as well. A ready reckoner, dated 1823, included a table for calculating the amount of tax payable. 'In Houses under the value of £5 per annum, from 1 to 6 windows, 6s. In Houses of the value of £5 per annum or upwards . . .' There followed a table of taxes starting at 8s for 1 to 6 windows and rising to £83 for more than a thousand windows. 'And every House containing more than 180 Windows, is chargeable with 2s 6d for each Window above that number'. I worked out that my own house would have been charged £7 a year. That was no mean sum in those days. I expect I would have bricked up some windows and sat in the dark. Still, there is something to be said for a tax that is so predictable you can publish details of its charges in a ready reckoner!

There were accounts books, too, from those early days, books filled with neat copperplate handwriting, learned at school by boys and girls who spent hours with their slates and their steel nibs painstakingly forming loops all at precisely the same angle, alike as peas in pods. Whoever kept the books had a methodical mind. Each person for whom things were bought or to whom money was loaned had a separate page. Geoff believes the owner of the book augmented his farming income, or supplied a local service interest free, by functioning as the local moneylender. Did his little notebook come to be hated and feared? Probably not, for it has survived and the entries are mundane and for small sums. The most common item in the first book, filled between 1843 and 1846 by a direct ancestor of Geoff, was for boots and shoes. New ones cost from 4s 6d (22½p) to 10s 6d (52½p) a pair and when they were repaired the nails were always charged separately. Perhaps you could bring your own nails? The shoes sounded ludicrously cheap, but they were not. The second book begins in 1850 and by that time a pair of boots cost 14s (70p). On Midsummer Day, 1852, one William Taper was paid 7s 6d (37½p) for five days' work. If you reckon that today the average wage is, say, £80 a week and that a reasonable pair of shoes cost, say, £15, the modern worker can buy rather more than five pairs of shoes from one week's wages. In 1852 a week's wages were insufficient to buy even one pair.

Nor was food cheap, despite what seems to be its low price. If you work out the price of items as a proportion of Mr Taper's wages, and then calculate the same proportion of a modern wage, the result is startling. A half bushel of wheat (4 gallons volume, or about two bucketsful) cost 8s (40p, in today's money £85), a pound of butter from 8½d (about 4p, or today £8.50) to 11d (about 5½p, or today £11.70), a peck (2 gallons) of oats 1s 6d (7½p, or today £16). An umbrella, essential for walking out on Sunday in Cornwall, cost only 1s (5p, or today £10.60)—expensive enough.

'Father and Grandfather, they had oxen here but I don't think they ever used them. There were always oxen here. We've still got the yokes now.' Later he took me to a small summer house in the garden and showed them to me.

'When I came here I heard that Cross Park was partly furze. All that top side of the road was. It had been taken in but it was all neglected. There is a little terrace that used to be cultivated and there are two small fields the other side of the bungalow belonging to us and they were the same. In the 1800s they came into cultivation again.

'The horses were a lot more work. It was slower work. Longer hours, that's what it meant. I wouldn't go back to them. You couldn't, the economics wouldn't allow it, but even if I could I don't believe I should. When Father was here there were four boys, Grandpa and men besides, back in that day. They used to grow a tremendous amount of roots for cattle and horses, that was the big thing back then. They're turning back to it again now. On Sunday's programme they were talking about the value of roots. It's the same in New Zealand, our people are always talking about what turnips they grow there, for stock feed. We're going round in a big circle. We used to grow acres and acres of turnips and mangolds and feed them to the stock.'

'That's why all the men had a job then. I mean, today there's a machine to do it, probably not so good . . .' Doreen prompted.

'It was hard work,' she continued, 'hard work and poor pay and a lot of people were very poor. People were all one big family and they all had to chime in. In your Dad's family there was the girls as well. The girls all had to work outdoors as well as in the house. They had to do a certain amount round the yard, the milking, calf feeding and all that sort of thing. That was their job, the men didn't do that. And they made the men's clothes.'

Geoff's father used to drive animals to markets in Camelford and beyond, staying overnight at the Leathern Bottle. The men rode horses, of course. Grandfather had his horse right up to the time he died and Father, too, used his. He used to ride up on the Moor. That was how he met his first motor car, up by Jamaica Inn on what is now dual carriageway.

'He was up there early one morning taking some sheep to close to Ivy Plain, what we call Davidstow now. This car came popping and snorting along and he was thrown off his pony. The pony went away and left him stranded. He couldn't pull it down till close to Blisland somewhere. By the time he came back with his pony the sheep had gone. That must have been before the First War. He was in the First War.'

The sheep are highly mobile and once on the Moor they can travel for miles. On one occasion Geoff found some sheep that had come from Week St Mary, halfway between Camelford and Bude. They must have found their way over Rough Tor and after that it is open moorland all the way.

In the early 1800s many people emigrated from Cornwall. Those were hard times in the mines as well as on the farm. Part of Geoff's grandmother's family, called Clemoes, went to New Zealand, 'back in the sailing ship days'. Land there was a pound an acre then. They used to burn one year to cultivate the next, then burn again, starting to farm as farming has always started until very recent times when large machines became available to speed the process. They were slash-and-burn farmers, as many farmers in the tropics are to this day, but little by little their cultivation of the cleared ground became permanent. The New Zealand relatives have visited them three times, journeying half way round the world to visit what they still call 'home'. One of them comes from St Just-in-Roseland, where his grandparents are buried in the churchyard, miles away to the south, on the other side of Carrick Roads from Falmouth. What they were doing all the way down there remains a mystery. It is a place from which people move either to the opposite ends of the earth, or else no more than a mile or two.

The Moor was always a wild place and perhaps it is becoming wilder as people leave it. The changes in farming that have reduced the workforce have compelled many people to move to the towns. The daughter and son of one old farm worker still both come back to the farm once a week for cream. They used to live up on the Moor in a house with earth floors. After they left it the house became derelict, the roof collapsed, and eventually Geoff cleared away the rubble so there is nothing to see of it now. Many houses must have been removed in this way. The evidence for their existence, and for that of their occupants, remains for the archaeologists. When you plough, or clean out the bottom of a hedge, old fragments of coarse pottery, glass bottles and broken clay pipes are all that is left, the litter left by ghosts.

Some of this litter is very old indeed, although it is difficult to date accurately. Outside the house Geoff showed me three millstones that had been ploughed up, two of them making a complete pair so you can put the two halves together and make a quern that might work if anyone had the strength to try it. The third is an odd one, missing its fellow. They are made from granite—the local moor-stone—and no doubt they were humped out of the house with a sigh of relief when some mill was built to relieve families of an arduous chore that was far less romantic than it may have looked. He had found spindle whorls, too, the weights that fit on the bottom of the spindles used by handspinners, and small because they were made from granite, which is heavy. We can guess at their age, because hand spindles were replaced by the spinning wheel. The first spinning wheels were introduced to Europe in the fourteenth century and the more advanced wheels that are popular again today were invented in the sixteenth century. This means that the whorls found on the farm—they were lying quite deep in the soil—are probably either more than four hundred years old, or date from the revival of interest in handspinning that has taken place in the last ten years.

The garden is decorated with stone mushrooms. These are not the concrete variety sold at garden centres, but the original versions, made, like everything else, from granite. They used to find employment on the farm. A framework of wood was laid over them and the harvested corn stacked there, off the ground, to dry.

I reminded Geoff that Cross Park used to be a football field.

'Yes, it did. The boys that lived in the council houses used to play football. When we were youngsters we used to play cricket there. They had a football pitch there for years. The old ammunition store for the Home Guard was there, too. They had a Nissen hut there built on concrete in the corner down in the bottom end during the war.' Geoff was on the farm throughout the war.

They remembered the past with amusement and affection, but they would not return to it. Doreen was emphatic.

'I don't think anybody would ever want to go back to this business of taking out the manure from the farmyard in a horse and cart and putting it in little heaps all over the field and then throwing it about. The labour is too expensive to even think of that. Nobody would ever want to go back to that, I wouldn't think. We say to our boys very often, ''You don't really know what hard work it used to be when we were your age, what we used to have to do''. They'd hardly believe it.'

However: 'You never seem to have any more time now than you had

181

In the garden, millstones ploughed up on the farm. The one on the left has no companion, but the one on the right is complete. The upper stone could be made to grind corn against the lower if someone had the strength and energy to turn it

The stone mushrooms in the garden were once used in the farmyard to dry corn

all they years ago when you were just plodding along with the horse and cart. Now you're flying from one thing to another as fast as you can go and you never seem to catch up. Take the hay harvest, and all that. Now it's just nothing, is it? The seasons must have changed or something. We must have had better weather for longer.'

In fact the climate has changed a little. It is more prone to deliver extreme weather and it is not simply a matter of remembering the better summers of one's childhood. Doreen went on: 'Years ago you'd reckon that you'd have three weeks for a hay harvest. You used to cut the third week in June, then you'd reckon to be finished by the first week in July with good luck, or the end of the first week or the second week in July, but it's not like that now, you can't even start.'

The impression is a general one. A lot of hay and corn must have been lost by bad weather in the years we forget, even if there were fewer of them than there are now. Then again, as Doreen pointed out, 'I don't think probably they were quite so fussy then as we are now. I mean, you've got to get it to a certain state anyway, haven't you? And they didn't grow such big crops. It wasn't manured to the extent it is now, and sprayed, to get as much as ever you can out of it. A lot was lost to weed.'

Yields have increased, especially, Geoff suspects, on grass, and with silage crops.

'They used to grow it then. We call it "zero grazing" now, but we used to grow lucerne and carry it away green in the spring exactly the same as we do now. That was the sort of thing that took up labour, in the scythe days.'

There was discussion about wages.

'Nineteen shillings a week they would get then, if they were very lucky', said Doreen. Geoff remembered Sam, an old worker with a family of five or six who worked on the farm in the 'thirties.

'Thirty-two shilling a week he earned. Lamb was down to sixteen shillings and it was taking two fat lambs a week to pay him his wages.'

'Farming doesn't alter much, though. Grass grows every twelve months. Corn grows every twelve months and has to be harvested. Cattle are born every twelve months and so it goes on. There's a cycle all the time. It does change, but you can't alter the basics, as a lot of them have found out, I think. They've come in and changed the farming pattern, but you can't. Nature's nature and it ties up with the weather, the seasons.'

Machines have come in, but now you have a job being done by one man and a machine, and two or three men backing him up, a back room full of boys servicing the robots. Anyway, there are some things machines cannot do. They cannot handle hay bales, for example. Machines can cut it, bale it, lift it, but in the end someone has to put his hands to it. They have to be stacked.

Fashions change, too. A few years ago everyone was growing short-strawed varieties of corn. Today the short-strawed varieties have gone and the long-strawed varieties are coming in again. They stand up better. This is odd, because it was their ability to stand up, to resist 'lodging' that made the short-strawed cereals attractive. The principle is simple. If you apply water and fertiliser to a long-strawed cereal it will grow taller and its ear will grow heavier. This makes it unstable mechanically, so that strong wind or heavy rain can knock it down. The solution, it was argued, was to develop varieties with short straw that could support the weight of the heavier ears. But:

'If you've got short ones they fall down. If you've got long ones they tangle and it holds the heads up better. When the short ones fell over the grain was in the ground. If you've got a long one and he falls over he doesn't fall all the way. It keeps it off the ground. Once it touches the ground it grows again.'

The grain harvest was revolutionised by the combine harvester.

'The harvest is made so much easier with combines and all that', said Doreen. 'There's no comparison with what we used to do by hand before. They'd cut it and then you'd put it all in the shocks, carry the sheaves, it would take weeks. Ten days I think they used to say, from the time you cut before you'd taken it away. Now the combine comes in as soon as it's ripe and it's done the lot and baled it up and carried it away and by the next day they've ploughed the field ready for the next crop. All the family were involved in that lot, though.'

The sheep were taken down from Cross Park on the morning of the 12th, to be given a medical check-up, and they returned to the field on the third week of the month. I saw one of them lame on the 5th. It walked badly, staggering a little, and it spent much of its time alone, standing against the hedge away from the main body of the flock. Its feet hurt. Most sheep suffer on wet ground. There are some breeds that can tolerate perpetually wet feet but most cannot. Their hooves are soft and if they become soaked and cannot dry out they soften more, like the skin on our fingers when they have been too long in water. In the end they develop foot rot, which is very unpleasant indeed. The Cross Park lamb felt sorry for itself, but its condition was not bad. Foot rot was a long way off and it was cured before it happened. I thought Geoff might not have seen the animal so I went down to the farm to tell him. He had seen it and was not especially worried. He paints the hooves of the sheep with Stockholm tar, which helps. It is possible to spray a coating, almost like a boot, over the hooves. This keeps them dry enough, but if an infection should develop inside the 'boot' it is sealed in and can spread and grow worse.

I found Geoff and his son laying a hedge beside the farm drive, chopping out surplus growth, selecting the good, strong wood, splitting it, then bending it over and securing it with sticks cut out from the hedge so that upright plants were made to grow horizontally. The technique is ancient and to this day it is the best way to make a hedge that is proof against all stock. Do it well and even a charging bull cannot penetrate it or a goat climb over it. It is less common in Cornwall, with its stone and earth hedges, than it is in places where hedges are made from living plants. A few years ago they were saying that the craft of hedge-laying was dying, although hedge-laying competitions were a feature of many lowland agricultural shows. That was in the days when East Anglian farmers were getting rid of their livestock in favour of corn and grubbing out their hedges at the rate of thousands of miles a year.

'Tis some showery!' Geoff shouted, cheery in the sunshine. It was, too. There was a time, in the middle of the month, when winter seemed very close. There was rain, hail and even sleet for several days and then, on the night of the 12th, a hard frost. In the north of England and in Scotland there was snow, some of it quite deep. Milder weather returned and at the end of the month it was more typical of November. I went to the field on the 26th, past hedges from which the last of the leaves were being torn by winds that, now and then, brought thin, soaking rain. It was a bleak kind of day and I got very wet. Other days, though, were mild and often sunny, so you could walk about without a coat, at least in sheltered places. The official reports said that October had been warmer than usual and, at least for the first half of the month, fairly dry. It meant that work on the farms went well and everyone was cheerful. The grass continued to grow, if slowly, and the animals continued to graze it. Fodder crops also grew well, so that feed for the winter seemed adequate provided the winter was not too long. The roots that Geoff says are so fashionable again for winter keep were thickening satisfactorily. Land was being ploughed and, while this year's grain still lay in store, next year's winter cereals were sown before November began. The month began with about 70 per cent of the national potato crop harvested, and some of the sugar beet.

As the vegetation died back, earth and stone emerged again. The bracken was slow to go. It had turned brown and now it began, very slowly, to collapse as the rain soaked it and the cells whose rigidity had given it support began to soften. As it fell the boulders of moor-stone began to appear again to the north of the field, and along the lower hedge, formed of little but bracken, you began to be able to see into the road. You could see, too, that many of the rabbit burrows went right through the hedges. On a windy day the draughts blowing through them were strong enough to make them visible from several yards, betrayed by the fluttering grass. Indeed, the rabbits were very active. There was much fresh burrowing throughout the month and on the 19th I found earth that had been thrown out of a burrow that morning. The number of rabbit droppings had increased and I found them well out in the middle of the field, showing that the rabbits were having to move farther to feed as their own young, born during the year, grew in size and in appetite, and as the vegetation began to fail them. They seemed healthy enough, by their behaviour, and there was no sign of the myxomatosis that had been reported in the region a few months earlier.

In fact, we may see less and less myxomatosis in years to come. The disease has an interesting history. It is caused by the *Myxoma* virus, which originated in the Americas and was introduced to Britain in 1953, under mysterious circumstances. It might have been introduced deliberately in order to control rabbits—at least, this is the popular theory. There is a difficulty with it, however, in that it would have taken a skilled and almost visionary biologist to predict its devastating effect, because in America it does no harm at all. The cottontails are adapted to it and it to them, and like all efficient parasites it lives in and on its host without causing serious injury. If it did, it would reduce its own chance of survival. When disease organisms cause huge epidemics it is because something has gone wrong. They are not meant to have this effect and they do not profit from it. The idea of bacteria or viruses sweeping across the countryside like avenging angels, looking for creatures to kill, is quite wrong. All the bug seeks is a quiet life and the chance to pass unnoticed in the body of the host. Virulence gets you nowhere.

The European rabbits had never encountered *Myxoma* before; they were not adapted to it nor it to them, and so it caused serious illness in the course of which 99.8 per cent of all rabbits died. The hares were not affected seriously, because *Myxoma* had the greatest difficulty in establishing itself in them. Only two rabbits in every thousand survived the plague. They bred; the rabbit population increased; *Myxoma* infected it again, and there were more deaths. The cycle was repeated several times, but both the rabbits and the virus were changing. It was those rabbits that were resistant to the disease that bred most prolifically and their offspring inherited their parents' resistance. This was natural selection at work and after a number of generations its product was a population of rabbits able to live at peace with the *Myxoma* that lives in their bodies. On the other side of the equation, as it were, the virus was becoming less virulent, also as a result of natural selection. The more virulent the viral strain the greater the likelihood that its hosts will be killed, and their deaths spells the death of the parasite, so it is the less virulent strains that survive. So the rabbits and the *Myxoma* are learning to live together. In fact, the rabbit population as a whole, if not individual rabbits, are becoming dependent on the virus, for it can still act efficiently in killing off the weak and so helping to maintain a vigorous population that does not over-stretch its food supply. Healthy viruses mean strong rabbits!

The rabbit has been through all this before. It began life in the western Mediterranean region in warm, rather dry conditions. The Romans, among whom a rabbit pie was a tasty delicacy, domesticated it. They probably developed breeds that can resist diseases transmitted by humans. They may have modified rabbit behaviour, too, making the animal less likely to evade capture, and by selecting the most prolific strains they may have improved its breeding performance. When the Normans introduced the animal to Britain in the twelfth century, it did not escape immediately and proliferate in the wild to become the pest it is today. Life was very hard for it. The damp, cool forests were no place for a Latin beast that once hopped free through the vineyards. Nor did it get on well with some of the native animals it met. The foxes and weasels were as hungry then as they are now and for them a half-tame rabbit was, literally, easy meat. Nor were they alone. There were wolves in those dark, antique forests, and wild cats, and, possibly, lynx. It was a long time before the rabbits learned to survive the rigours of the British environment and the first totally self-reliant wild populations of them were not recorded until the seventeenth century, five hundred years after they entered the land. Even then they were confined to the drier parts of East Anglia. It was not until the late eighteenth century that they began to appear all over the country. It was the enclosure of open land by hedges that helped them to spread by providing them with the sites they needed for burrowing and with a virtually inexhaustible supply of food. Pests they may be, but it would be sad if, after more than half a millenium spent adapting to conditions in a country to which they were brought through no choice of their own, they were to be exterminated by a virus stolen from their American cousins. It seems very unlikely that this will happen. The long history of the British rabbit raises interesting questions about those other species that have been introduced more recently and that today survive in small pockets as isolated wild populations. The grey squirrel, coypu and mink have adapted to British conditions, but in years to come will we be plagued by wallabies, porcupines and budgerigars?

The most exuberant—or desperate—of all the Cross Park creatures was the mole. The individual who lived beside the hedge on the upper side of the field was burrowing busily later in the month, and so was the one living round the corner from it, a little way down the hedge on the south-eastern side of the field. On the 26th, though, I came across the manic tunneller. It was working like a demented and incompetent prisoner-of-war in one of those movies where whole camps seem in imminent danger of collapse into the mazes of tunnels that subvert them. Was this mole descended from one trained by Geoff's wartime workers? It was incompetent, for a captive, in appearing to lack any sense of direction, and in being so obvious that to miss it the guards would have had to be portrayed not merely as buffoons, which we might accept, but as blind, which would stretch credibility too far. It had worked its way out from the hedge on the north-western side of the field until it was about thirty-three feet into the field itself. There it raised a great colony of hills, all freshly dug as though it was determined to work night and day to realise some vast and obscure scheme. The hills were so large, so numerous, and appeared so suddenly that I wondered whether one animal could possibly have completed such an excavation. Perhaps there was a whole tribe of moles working away down there?

There may indeed have been more than one mole, and part of the intense activity may have resulted from their efforts to avoid one another. That may explain also the incoherence of the tunnelling system: each time a tunnel crossed another the tunneller, sensing the proximity of his or her rival, dug away in a new direction. On the whole, though, the vigorous tunnelling indicated a decline in the food supply as, despite the mild weather, the soil grew cooler and the invertebrates sought shelter at lower levels, or simply died.

The invertebrates were becomes fewer. There was a large, hairy, dark brown, plain caterpillar feeding on the wilting bracken on the 5th, and the dung flies continued to appear from nowhere as soon as returning sheep supplied them with hunting grounds. The dung flies were predominantly female and by the end of the month I suspect that only females were present. At all events, I saw no males. I saw a flesh fly on the 12th, and on the same day I found a seven-spot ladybird. It must have been a late developer, for most beetles, including the ladybirds so far as I know, spend the winter as larvae or pupae and produce only one generation a year.

There were a few late slugs. *Arion ater* was there, but sparsely, and by the end of the month it seemed to have gone. Most of the snails were in hiding, but I did see a pretty *Cernuella virgata*, the common snail that looks like a peppermint humbug.

The tube webs I had been watching for months were empty and starting to deteriorate early in the month and by the end of the month they had gone, possibly because of the damage inflicted by the hedge trimmer. There were other spiders. A few lycosids continued to scuttle about my feet as I stood close to the hedges, and on the 12th I saw three *Zygiella atrica*, one female with two males, behaving as though it were high summer and time to mate, their tryst set to take place on the large and delicate orb web built and owned by the female.

The larks were still there, tied now by habit to the place from which their young had been sent forth to seek their fortunes in the wide sky, and other birds, released from the bonds of family life and driven by a dwindling supply of food, were visiting. There was a great tit, an occasional magpie up from the valley and, just once, a pied wagtail patrolling the roof of one of the cottages over the road in search of insects.

On the 5th I saw what may have been a badger footprint and on the 26th, in the hedge on the south-eastern side of the field, I found three feeding platforms. Made from small, flattened areas at just below the height of my head, they were not easy to see but, once seen, they were easy to recognise by the droppings in them. One had been used by a mouse, for it contained the remains of a rose hip that had been opened and robbed of its seeds. On subsequent visits to the field I tried to find those platforms again, but I was unable to do so.

The bryony berries that had made a bright show only a few weeks earlier were rotting disgustingly by the beginning of November, but other plants were becoming visible. There was wood sage (*Teucrium scorodonia*) and what I took to be wild clary (*Salvia horminoides*). Nor was flowering quite finished. The Herb Robert flowered throughout the month and in sheltered places the red campion was still there.

The oaks, stripped of leaves almost completely, produced buds ready for next year, and some of the brambles continued to defy the season. The blackberries had gone, except for a few isolated ones that the birds had missed and those small, hard, shrivelled ones that were not worth the picking.

Then, on the 26th, I saw the first flower buds on the gorse in Cross Park. They did not open, but in the road beside the field, facing south and sheltered from the cruellest of the winds, there were a few blossoms, tiny specks of yellow that indicated not so much the onset of winter as the promise of spring, for the gorse is not the last of the plants to flower, but the first, and others will follow later.

I did not see any gorse fires. I would not expect to see any very close to Cross Park, for gorse creates no problem there these days, but in many places farmers set fire to the countryside in an attempt, usually futile, to rid themselves of it. November 1st marked the beginning of the 'open season' for the gorse. Fires are permitted before that date only if you have a licence from the Ministry. Burning does not kill the plants. The soil is not heated strongly by the fire and the roots descend deeply enough to be protected. The effect is to clear old wood and encourage new growth. In the days when they used to harvest the furze that may well have been the object of the exercise. The heath fires also favour those other plants whose stems lie below the ground, most especially the bracken, which has died back anyway by the time the fires are lit, so that the fires that succeed in checking the gorse usually allow it to be replaced by bracken, which is no easier to remove. Repeated each year, or every few years, for long enough, heath fires create deserts of thin, acid, eroded soil the colour and consistency of ashes.

As the lowland pastures deteriorated with the slowing in the growth of the grass, so they were claimed for the cattle and sheep, and the horses had to give way. Kept, often very profitably, for riding in the summer, in the winter they spend much of their time fending for themselves. I did not see them but I heard them, up on the Moor where they are turned out to make what they can of the grass and herbs that grow in those places that are not bare rock and that have not been taken over by bracken or gorse. One hard winter a few years back, when winter keep was exhausted and there was talk—somewhat exaggerated because people panicked—of stock dying from starvation on the high moors, I saw horses up there eating gorse. It is a hard life for the working horse.

It was ever so, for horses as for the men who worked them, and between the two species the symbiosis must have been reduced many times to a battle of wits and wills, with no assurance of victory to either. Offer the beast or the man too rude an insult and you may expect retaliation. For the horse this may take the form of ridding yourself of the encumbrance on your back and heading for liberty in the wide world. I turned for home thinking of that first motor car up by Jamaica Inn and the man, with bruised bottom and dignity, trying to decide whether to pursue his fleeing pony or to round up his scattering sheep.

December

The manic mole went beserk. If its labyrinthine excavations appeared ambitious in November, in December they appeared positively ostentatious and not far short of megalomanic. The beastie tunnelled frenetically throughout the month until, by the 31st, it had churned up an area about fourteen yards by sixteen yards, most of which was covered with hills of freshly turned earth. It became difficult to believe that all this was the work of a single animal, even of one with a ravenous appetite facing a seasonal decline in its food supply. Other moles were active along each of the hedges and there was usually a fresh hill to be seen, but none could compare with the fellow who began a little way out from the middle of the hedge on the north-western side of the field and proceeded to devastate so large an area. He may not have known it, but he was jeopardizing his own safety. A molehill or two may be tolerable close to a hedge on ground that is beyond the reach of the plough. Even in the open field an occasional hill does no great harm and, in any case, it is almost impossible to remove without causing more damage than the mole, but this was something else. The mole city was visible as soon as you crossed the brow of the gentle rise from the lower side of the field. It looked like a small battlefield, full of the heaps of rubble tossed out by tiny shells and bombs that mysteriously had left no craters. I do not know what Geoff could have done about it, but such blatant demolition of his pasture must have been enough to strain the patience of the most placid of farmers. Ploughing would persuade the mole to migrate, but it would complete the destruction the mole had begun and set the mole tunnelling again somewhere else. Gas might work. Even traps, placed here and there in the tunnels, might arrest the culprit. Moles are good at avoiding traps, usually by tunnelling beneath or around them, and the older they grow the more cunning they become. This young swashbuckler, though, might have been too reckless, too absorbed in his incessant industry, to

191

The manic mole was covering the field with its underground network in November and December

notice the danger. I do not know what Geoff could have done to get rid of the animal and if I had known I am not sure I would have told him. I begun to conceive an admiration for this Haussmann, this Corbusier among moles, who was so determined to rebuild the world to express his opinion of what it should be. I pictured him, a little mad with his obsession and probably quite without humour, shovelling away by day and by night, barely pausing even to devour such delectable morsels as fell his way. No gourmet he, his food was gulped unchewed and unsavoured with no more than the merest reduction in the speed of his whirling limbs as he bored his belching, dyspeptic way through the earth. He was a Stakhanovite hero of moledom.

Compared with the moles in general, and the Stakhanovite in particular, the other mammals were taking life at a more leisurely pace. I found one feeding platform in the top hedge on the 18th and there was some rabbit burrowing in the banks, but that was all. Rabbits were moving far into the field to feed, but as always they fed discreetly and with a keen eye, ear and nose alert to danger. The sheep, too, nibbled placidly enough until the very end of the month, when they were taken down from Cross Park. The grass was very short by then, its growth arrested temporarily, but the cover was good. Except where Sir Mole had subverted the system, it was difficult to see the soil beneath the herbage.

192

The sheep were well enough, although one of them was lame on the 18th. It spent much of its time standing against the hedge and moved at my approach only when its nerve finally broke and sent it hobbling after the rest of the flock as fast as it could go. Livestock was said to be in good condition throughout the country and by and large the stocks of winter keep seemed adequate. By the end of the month Geoff had begun to feed his beasts on the silage he made in summer in his new pit, and the countryside was filled with the sour-sweet, unmistakable smell of ripe, pickled grass. I like the smell, but I admit that some do not. Once you learn to like it, silage can seem positively appetizing. I heard of one farmer who liked it so well that he ate the stuff. I have not gone so far, but I wonder whether it might be good fried with bacon? I suggested this to Doreen, mainly to cheer her up, for she does not share my enthusiasm for the odour that wafts into her kitchen. Might it be a substitute for laver bread? She offered to cook some for me. Unhappily I remembered an urgent appointment elsewhere and could not wait. One day, though, I shall try it. Perhaps it will be next year, or the year after. At all events, the smell is almost as good in my nose as that of new-mown grass, and in mid-winter, when the very air is crisp and liable to shatter into a billion tiny splinters of ice, the rich smell of silage reminds me of the summer. For an instant I can hear again the background hum of distant tractors on still, warm air, the clatter of garden mowers on suburban July evenings, and the smell of the silage translates itself into the smell of fresh hay.

A few of the smaller creatures were still to be seen in the earlier part of December. On the 3rd I surprised a late bee collecting the last of the nectar from the few remaining flowers, and there were several hammock webs low down in the hedges, especially in the hedge on the south-eastern side of the field.

I say the bee was searching for the last of the nectar, but for the perceptive insect this was far from nothing. There were a few red campions tucked away in places sheltered from the chilling winds and battering rains, most of them low down in the hedges. The herb Robert was flowering and so was the speedwell, the dead nettle, betony, yarrow and smooth sow thistle, and as late as the 18th I found one solitary and slightly pale scabious flower. Most of the flowers were by the side of the road, on the outside of Cross Park, and it was there that the first gorse flowers appeared, flowers for 1980. My late bee should have been able to find a modest supply of food to tide it over for the rest of the winter.

It was not the only insect. Early in the month the dung flies, all of them female so far as I could see, were still flying. Perhaps they were laying the last of the eggs that will produce grubs to spend the winter sheltering in and feasting on the dung left in large amounts by the sheep. There were large numbers of dung flies on the 10th, but a week later, on the 18th, all of them had gone and I did not see them again. Their work completed, their lives were at an end. They are very functional creatures, slaves to the survival of their species, Stakhanovites like the mad mole, but much more mechanically so, and they cannot survive the loss of their relevance. They do not exist for themselves, but for their progeny, for the genes they carry, and their lives are spent mainly as larvae.

Frank Smith, the lepidopterist who had led my rather fruitless and damp nocturnal excursions in search of his fluttering fancies, sent me the names of some common microlepidoptera that we did find. One of them, *Argyresthia curvella*, he hatched at home. The larvae spin hawthorn leaves around themselves and if you find curiously curled up leaves it is worth removing them, and the bit of twig on which they grow, and keeping them in a jar until the adult insect emerges. Frank's collection had emerged on 2 and 6 July, from leaf spinnings collected on 21 May. They are pretty little moths with metallic, pale rust-coloured wings bearing a white streak crossed by a black stripe. *Glyphipteris fuscoviridella* is bronze in colour. Its caterpillars feed on the field woodrush *(Luzula campestris)*. Another spinner, this time of blackthorn, that emerged early in July was the plum tortrix *(Hedya pruniana)*, a small moth with forewings that are black at the base and white at the outer edge. The many tiny, pale, ochre-coloured moths we found flying near the bottom of the south-eastern hedge were *Elachista rufocinerea*. Their larvae are believed to mine inside blades of creeping softgrass *(Holcus mollis)*. That is a plant we did not find on my walks around the field with Barbara Garratt, but it is not especially conspicuous. In this case its presence was indicated by its effects rather than by its visible presence; it was inferred but not seen. It is common enough, and so are the few moth species we found, but the list of them, arriving as it did in the middle of December, took me back to the days of promise when my friendship with the field and its inhabitants was young and many of them still remained undiscovered.

My most elusive visitor, the badger, remained elusive, but tantalised me to the last. The large slide that may or may not have been used by a badger remained unused throughout the month, but on the 18th I found some long, coarse, grey-white hairs by the north-eastern hedge. They could have been pulled from the leg, belly or back of a sheep, but they were unlike wool and unlike the longer guard hairs sheep sometimes carry as a memento of their original, hairy coats. Were they badger hairs? I do not know, but I shall allow myself to imagine a stocky, heavy, muzzle-striped owner for them.

In the south-eastern hedge there was a solitary, pale, small limacid slug on the 18th and on the 31st in the north-western hedge I found another one, similar to the first, but at ¾ in long, even smaller. The snails that had crowded together in large crevices in the stone wall on the south-eastern side of the field did not move. They were sleeping soundly and will not awaken until the warm air of a new summer raises their temperature.

A large fly sat feeding on a leaf on the 31st, its long labium, or proboscis, extending and dabbing at the surface as it collected food with the sponge-like tip. It was lethargic and did not try to escape at my approach. It had the hedge, indeed the field, to itself.

The birds were active, though. Large flocks of starlings wheeled and turned together, sometimes landing for a few brief moments and then, as one bird, taking off again and sweeping low across the hedge and away, only to return a few moments later. How do they manage to co-ordinate their movements? What message passes, and by what means, that instructs the birds to move together? Or is there no message at all, but only a swift reaction to the movement of a leader?

The ordinary, common-or-garden starling *(Sturnus vulgaris)* is so common-or-garden that we take it for granted. In fact it is a fascinating creature, and one whose habits have been studied little, simply because it is so common as to be almost invisible. We always look past it to catch a glimpse of the exotic visitor or the more spectacular native. I watch starlings feeding and wonder why the whole tribe does not famish. They are far too quarrelsome to be able to settle down to a good, square meal. No sooner has one individual seized upon some morsel than another tries to steal it and so the feast proceeds amid screeching leaps into the air, howls of jealousy and protest, and brief escaping flights, with or without food. Eventually, and in fact very quickly, all the available food is taken, but most of it must pass through several bills before it reaches the comparative security of a crop.

They are pretty birds, especially in winter, when they are more distinctly speckled, and they have a wide range of songs that they deliver from any convenient high vantage point. They are mimics, so that their song can sound like that of other birds. They will nest almost anywhere, even in holes in the ground if they can find nothing better. At nesting time the search for sites can get them into trouble as they crawl through small openings into lofts, or into my garage, from which they cannot escape without help. That is when you discover that their long, delicate bills are more robust than they look, and while some birds will go still with fright when you hold them, the starling will bite or stab if it can.

It is in autumn and winter that they become truly gregarious and live in immense flocks. I lived in Birmingham as a boy and I remember the clouds of them that used to darken the evening sky as I was going home from work. They were still looking for food or, if I was late going home, returning to roost high on the Town Hall, from which the Corporation sought vainly to dislodge them. I have no idea why they flock in such large numbers at a time of year when food is scarce. Obviously it would be impractical for them to do so while they are nesting and rearing young, but in winter I would have thought that their chances of finding food would be enhanced if they were to search alone. Yet they thrive and prosper. It may be that the frequent quarrels benefit the species as a whole by ensuring that the larger, more aggressive birds obtain most of the food, though even that does not explain why the flocks must be so large. The race is to the fastest; the bully prospers and breeds new generations of bullies; the small and weak succumb, and the society of the starlings is all very fascist until times become really hard. Then, I suspect, they suffer the same fate as the mice. The large, dominant birds require more food to sustain them than the environment can supply and they starve, while the liberals, the smaller birds with more modest requirements, come into their own and inherit the Earth, such as it is. At all events, the tribes of starlings scoured the December countryside in surrealist, abstract clouds that changed shape constantly, twisting, turning, swooping, climbing, swelling, contracting and, now and then, alighting.

An occasional magpie passed overhead and rooks landed in ones and twos pausing barely long enough to fold their wings before some more urgent errand took them away again, over the hedge. A few great tits dodged in and out of the hedgerows and perched precariously to plan each new manoeuvre.

November had been mild on the whole. Crops looked healthy everywhere and the harvesting of potatoes and of sugar beet (mainly in East Anglia) went smoothly. Harvest yields of all crops were rather lower than those in 1978, but not seriously so, and by the end of the month the total area that had been sown to winter cereals was greater than the area sown at the same time last year. All looked peaceful, almost dull.

Then, in the middle of December, the south-west of Britain was hit by a hurricane. Cross Park and the area just around it seemed to suffer little damage, but elsewhere the tale was very different. At sea, winds blew steadily for hour after hour at more than 120mph, and at

Penzance the wind was rated as a whole gale, Force 10 on the Beaufort Scale, for 24 hours, followed by a further period of moderate gale, gusting to fresh gale, Force 7 to 8. The Beaufort Scale measures constant wind speed and relates it to effects on vegetation and property. A moderate gale—Force 7, for example—produces steady winds of up to 38mph. Trees sway and walking may be difficult. At Force 8, called a fresh gale, winds blow at up to 46mph and twigs are broken from trees. A strong gale, Force 9, blows at up to 54mph and tears chimney pots and slates from roofs. A Force 10, whole gale, blowing at up to 53mph, uproots trees and causes much structural damage. On the night of Friday, 14 December, an elm 50ft tall and 10ft wide was blown down in West Cornwall. At the RNAS station at Culdrose the roof was torn from a hangar and strewn as large sheets of jagged metal across a main road. Glasshouses were blown away, roofs were removed entirely, and caravans were picked up bodily and dropped again. A storm, Force 11, blows steadily at up to 75mph and causes damage on this scale, but at sea, where winds exceeded 75mph and so were rated officially as Force 12, or hurricane, ships unfortunate enough to be caught were in serious difficulty. Not far from Cross Park, at Port Quin, a Greek freighter developed a severe list when part of its cargo of drums of lubricating oil shifted. It broke in two on the rocks and the Padstow lifeboat, which was launched at dawn on the Saturday, stood by until midnight in seas worse than any that even the oldest seamen could remember. In Devonport Dockyard a crane 200ft high was blown from its rail track and crashed across the decks of two frigates.

Then, on Sunday, the storm ceased as suddenly as it had begun and the day was almost calm. A friend with a chainsaw helped me dispose of the rowan tree that had fallen in my garden. The next time I visited the field, on the Tuesday, the wind had increased again but only, I would guess, to about Force 6, a strong breeze that turns umbrellas inside out and shakes the branches on trees. It sent me scrambling over a gate into the next field to retrieve my hat that had risen suddenly and with great deliberation and then levitated over the hedge.

The weather had not finished with us. On the 27th it rained and rained and rained. We were driving back from Somerset and saw people standing helpless beside their front doors, watching the water as it streamed inside. We had water up to our hub caps in several places as new and improbable rivers coursed along or across roads and as storm drains turned into cold, brown gushers. What the gales did not blow away the rains washed away and the year ended with devastation, mud and large bills.

The abandoned quarry buildings on the Moor above Cross Park

Then it was finished. It was New Year's Eve and I was standing in the field for the last time. The Christmas holiday had not ended and the towns and villages were quiet. Below the field there was no movement in the farm yard or in the village, where thin streams of blue smoke rose from cottage chimneys into the pale sunshine. The air was mild and at peace.

I stood on grass. A year earlier I had stood on bare earth in which the recently sown mixture of perennial ryegrass and clover had only begun to emerge as isolated blades. Little else had changed. Little changes.

The hedge, over to my right, looked as it had looked then, trimmed and neat. Was it really more than a thousand years old? Was it already an old, well established hedge, looking much as it does now though perhaps a little more unkempt, when King William was crowned on Christmas Day, 1066? As King Harold fell mortally wounded so many miles away, were the red campion and foxgloves blooming up here? Were there still one or two late flowers in bloom when Thomas à Becket met his violent end on 29 December 1170? Did the people here know of the disagreement between Henry Plantagenet and the primate he had created and who obstructed his reforms? It all took place far away in strange, alien, Norman Canterbury. Could I have stood here even earlier and watched while the old hermit down in the valley passed his dedicated life founding the first of the churches that stood where the village church stands today? Could I have waited and watched while it passed into Norman hands and then, over the succeeding few centuries, fell into disrepair and ruin? Could I have watched the medieval craftsmen build a fine, new church from the remains of the old?

Those craftsmen, and their fathers and grandfathers, would not have understood my speech, nor I theirs. They were Cornishmen and spoke Cornish, the Brythonic Celtic language, closely related to Welsh, that was introduced by the Iron Age invaders and settlers and that endured as a spoken language, and as the first language of some, until the eighteenth century. What would they have known or cared about the political schemings of their foreign rulers, the Romans, Saxons, Normans or English? It has been said that the drama of the Reformation was lost on the Celtic peoples, since the translation of the scriptures into English presented them with one difficult, foreign tongue in exchange for another, and that when it came to it they may have been more familiar with the Church Latin spoken by their priests than with English. The Church of England was no closer to them, in any sense, than the Church of Rome. In Wales and Cornwall they created their own, Nonconformist churches as soon as the English law weakened sufficiently to allow them to survive and to this day, though I do not know whether it is for that reason, the Anglican Church in Cornwall is what they used to call 'Anglo-Catholic'.

It was the first Iron Age Celtic peoples who introduced the wheeled plough and the characteristic field system that it produced. There are many such fields on Bodmin Moor and those ancient farmers left behind them the names they gave to their settlements, most of which were defensive, for the Celts were a quarrelsome lot. There are more than 200 place names in Cornwall that include the words *castel*, *din*, or *caer*, all of which mean 'fortress' or something rather like it. Yes, Cross Park could be very old indeed.

The farming has changed over the centuries, and yet it has not changed. As Geoff said, the grass grows, the corn ripens, ewes lamb in the spring and cows must be milked twice a day. The rain falls, the sun shines, and nothing can alter the natural cycle of the seasons. The changes are very superficial. Farmers drive tractors now. Not long ago they drove horses and before that, oxen. In the eleventh century, when the farm was listed in Domesday, it kept a few serfs. Today workers are paid wages and can change jobs as they please, provided, of course, that there are alternative jobs to which they can move. Have the people changed? I doubt whether the changes in them are much more

By the time it was ready for cutting the grass grew tall and dense, forming a stand that was penetrable only to creatures able to move about at ground level

profound than those in their farming system. They speak English now, but if those of them who have learned the old language—and their number is growing—could sit by the fire for an evening with a few flagons of ale in the company of some of those old farmers whose speech they understand, I suspect the conversation would be free and not complicated by the differences in values and experiences that separate and divide the centuries. The modern farmers could tell of wonders, of new and powerful machines, of chemical aids to farming, of new breeds of livestock and new ways of performing traditional tasks, but the old farmers, too, might be able to tell of skills that have been forgotten and should not have been.

Today, men are free. Slavery has been abolished. Land can be bought by anyone, regardless of social status, and the worker expects a decent standard of living. Yet even this amounts to a less dramatic reform that it appears to do. In November, 1979, farm land in England was selling at an average price of £4,002 per hectare or, for the benefit of our pre-metric visitors, for £1,620 per acre. Farms can be bought only by the rich. Nothing has changed there. Nor is life much easier for tenant farmers. In October, 1979, they were paying an average of £47.66 per hectare (£19.29 per acre) annual rent. In Cornwall, where rents are a little lower than the national average, they were paying £40.80 per hectare (£16.51 per acre). A tenant, renting a modest 50 acres in Cornwall and producing milk from it, would have to sell 1,200 gallons of milk a year, at current prices, just to pay the rent. Probably he would have to sell more because many rents are higher than the average, and milk prices fall in the summer. There is no fortune to be made as a tenant farmer. Nor is the life of the farm worker particularly comfortable. True, he is a free man, but his wages are far lower than those paid in other industries. The new, improved wage rates, announced in November, 1979 amid howls of anguish from employers for fear of imminent bankruptcy, and to be paid from the third week in January, 1980, will give a full grown man a basic wage of £58 for a 40-hour week, rising to £78.30 a week for the most highly skilled of agricultural craftsmen. When the average industrial wage is more than £80 a week, when trained craftsmen in other industries can earn well over £100 a week, and when a family of four needs an income of more than £55 a week to escape from poverty, it is clear that the lot of the agricultural worker has not improved sufficiently to provide him with any real advance in his social status. The appalling poverty and hardship of earlier times has gone, but it may not have gone so far as we sometimes imagine.

My eye was caught by the line of trees standing bare and starkly wintry against the sky in the small copse to the north-west of the field, and my ear was caught by the song of a bird. The larks were still in Cross Park and around it, returning to that part of the field in which they had built their nests. For all I could tell the birds I saw on the ground—always in the middle distance for they did not trust me—and above my head may have been the offspring of those that had nested in summer. The sheep had obliged me by cropping down the grass, but I never did find the nests. Perhaps I did not search with sufficient diligence. Perhaps I enjoyed too well the sight and sound of the larks fluttering noisily on the air and did not wish to cause them more distress than I could help. My gloomy thoughts of rural hardship past and present evaporated and I found myself thinking of the countless small creatures whose Cross Park lives go on regardless of what humans may think or do. True, the building of the hedges all those years ago provided them with nesting sites, but after thousands of generations the hedges are taken for granted. Down in the eastern corner where summer bracken and brambles turn the pile of disordered stones into an impenetrable thicket with no sure foothold below it, the field mice were sheltering, huddled together for warmth and waiting for the evening and the time to forage. Their corner may have been provided by the demolition of the wartime Nissen hut that housed the ammunition the Home Guard never used in anger. Even that was a long time ago in the history of the mice. It was odd that this particular corner was occupied mainly by mice, while the ancient hedge housed mainly voles. The mice are almost completely nocturnal. Even bright moonlight will deter them.

The voles, curled up snug in their nests on the other side of the field, were experiencing their first winter. At least, most of them were; their parents had been born in spring and had died long before winter began. Voles breed even more rapidly than mice, producing four or five litters between April and September, from parents born at the beginning of the season. Most of the overwintering voles are young and sexually immature. They are growing very slowly. When spring arrives their rate of growth will increase, they will produce the first generation of the new year, and then they will die. The new generation grows very fast and four or five weeks from birth its members are reproducing. The second generation grows more slowly and it is these litters that survive the winter. So it proceeds, year in, year out, and each generation lives through half a year, and so in an environment different from that known by its parents. Most winter voles never know the summer and most summer voles do not live long enough to experience the winter.

The tiny shrews, eating about three-quarters of their own weight in beetles, earthworms, carrion and insects every day, grew more slowly. They too were nesting in protected corners and below ground. They do not hibernate, of course. Their minute bodies lose heat so rapidly that they cannot afford to stop eating. When she is nursing her diminutive babies, a female shrew must eat one-and-a-half times her own weight daily just to keep going and to provide milk. The shrews alive now were born in the spring. They become sexually mature when they are about a year old, then breed, raise their litters, and die. By late summer almost all of them will be dead and the new generation will be scurrying through the long grass in an incessant search for food that must be eaten where it is found so that the search can continue. They are solitary creatures, except when they are mating, and when two shrews meet they quarrel, screaming abuse at one another and sometimes coming to blows. Injuries are rarely serious, and the victor is satisfied when his vanquished opponent retires from the scene. A conquered shrew is never pursued and the fights, which are desperate bids to obtain or retain feeding ranges, are not in the least malicious. The shrew does not deserve its reputation for 'shrewishness'. It is not at all shrewish. In fact, shrews can be kept in captivity, where they will live quite contentedly on a diet of tinned dog meat.

There were no small mammals to be seen now, by which I mean that, whether they were alive and active or not, I did not see them, and apart from the one fly that fed in the north-eastern hedge, there were no insects. What a year it had been for insects! I remember the bright scarlet cardinal beetle and the lousy watchman. the red *Apion miniatum* weevil, the grasshoppers, ants, crane flies and the dung flies that had been among the last to depart. I remember the bees and wasps, the butterflies and moths. These were not abundant, and none of them was rare, but they were gay and the memory of their cheerful hedgerow flutterings was a memory of summer, like that of the huge hawker dragonflies that once patrolled their beats, archaic hunters that had emerged from the dark quarry pool.

I thought the insects had gone but at the top of the field, by the gate that opens on to the Moor, there were two of three clouds of midges. They, too, are more characteristic of summer than of winter, but these were winter gnats, insects belonging to the family Trichoceridae. There are ten British species of them. They are flies about 5mm long, with long legs and narrow abdomens that betray their close relationship to the crane flies. Their larvae live in decaying matter and although they swarm throughout the year they do so most in winter, which gives them their common name.

The clouds of midges and gnats that float on the air in damp places consist almost entirely of males and they are looking for mates, just like gangs of youths loitering on street corners to watch the girls go by, but with the single difference that they are much more decisive. To them one female is as good as another. Fortunately the females enjoy a similarly robust, practical view of the matter. When a female passes, one male—the nearest—seizes her and the two of them depart together into the golden sunset. Clearly there is an advantage to be gained by flying on the outside of the cloud. Once a certain proportion of the young blades has been matched and the cloud has diminished in size, I wonder whether the females cease to take much notice of it, knowing that it consists of the old, the weak, the neurotic and the gnats with a mother fixation?

I turned back from the gate, into the field again, and continued my slow nostalgic walk around the edge. I passed close to where I had found a solitary crock egg in May. There is nothing odd about a crock egg, of course, but the one on which I almost stepped as I was walking up the field to the Longworth traps I had set in the top hedge had no business to be there, and it has not been there since. I had looked for it several times, casually—one does not wish to devote too much time and effort to a search for a crock egg!—as I passed. It was there on one day of the year, and on that day only. I made one last check to see if it had returned; it had not.

Behind me, horses I could not see whinnied on the Moor. There were great tits, three or four of them, busying themselves around a telegraph pole. I stopped again and looked down over the valley, slowly, from east to west, from left to right. The fields were green and the coniferous trees that form a wood in the valley bottom were also green, so that they looked little different from the way they had looked all year. Away to the right, on the higher ground just this side of the main road that brings the summer visitors streaming across Bodmin Moor on their way to and from the holiday resorts, tiny high-wing monoplanes moved on the airfield as amateur aviators took advantage of the weather for a little Yuletide practice. Some keen spirit had been flying circuits earlier in the morning, but now he had landed.

I walked on, past the corner through which a badger may or may not have entered, and down the slope, past some half-hearted rabbit excavations, and towards the gate by which the first mole of the year had entered the field. It was still there somewhere. The smell of Geoff's silage drifted faintly across from where the sheep were being fed. I paused to check that the hibernating snails were secure in their crevice. A final lark landed some distance from me and then vanished, and a robin skipped from plant to plant, always a safe distance from me, unlike the garden robins that allow humans to approach them.

The thin cloud thickened and the promise of sunshine faded. I began to realise that I had grown cold, that it was high time I headed for the car and for home. It was New Year's Eve. The old year was gone at last, according to the arbitrary measure we use to mark the passing of the years. I must go, my visit but an instant, an event of no significance whatever in the life of the field. Already its preparations for the New Year were well advanced. Some of the stinging nettles had fresh new leaves, some of the flowers were new, rather than fading blooms the autumn and winter winds had overlooked and on New Year's Eve itself, towards the top of the north-western, most antique hedge, where the gorse bushes were covered in pale grey buds, the first bright yellow flower had opened. Soon all the gorse would be covered with patches of yellow and, one by one, the other plants would begin to grow again. That was no longer any concern of mine. I felt as though Cross Park had dismissed me. Slowly, regretfully, and yet not too slowly, for I was growing colder by the minute and my nostalgia was turning to thoughts of the heater in the car, I dropped the chain over the gate post, looked back once, crossed the road, and left.

Bibliography

Balchin, W. G. V., *British Landscapes Through Maps—Cornwall*, Geographical Association, London, 1967

Barton, D. B., *Essays in Cornish Mining History* (vol. 2), Barton, Truro, 1970

Barton, R. M. (ed.), *Life in Cornwall in the Mid-Nineteenth Century* (edited extracts from *The West Briton*), D. Bradford Barton, Truro

Beedham, Gordon E., *Identification of the British Molluscs*, Hulton Educational Publications, Amersham, Bucks, 1972

Chinery, Michael, *A Field Guide to the Insects of Britain*, Collins, London, 1972

Ciba Foundation, 'The mole: its adaptation to an underground environment', proceedings of a Ciba Foundation guest meeting, 5–6 January 1966, *J. Zool. Soc.*, vol. 149, pp. 31–114, London

Clapham, A. R., Tutin, T. G. and Warburg, E. F., *Flora of the British Isles*, Cambridge University Press, 1962

Coate, Mary, *Cornwall in the Great Civil War and Interregnum 1642–1660*, Oxford University Press, 1933

Darby, H. C. and Finn, R. W. (eds.), *The Domesday Geography of South-West England*, Cambridge University Press, 1967

Fitter, R. S. R., *Finding Wild Flowers*, Collins, London, 1971

Flowerdew, J. R., 'Field and laboratory experiments on the social behaviour and population dynamics of the wood mouse *(Apodemus sylvaticus)*', *Journal of Animal Ecology*, vol. 43, pp. 499–511, June 1974, London

Flowerdew. J. R.. 'Residents and transients in wood mouse populations' (1977), in Ebling, F. J. G. and Stoddart, (eds.), *Population Control by Social Behaviour*, Institute of Biology, London, 1978

Godfrey, Gillian K. (Mrs Crowcroft), 'A field study of the activity of the mole *(Talpa europaea)*', *Ecology*, vol. 36, pp. 678–85, Zool. Soc. of London, 1955

Grieve, Mrs M. and Leyel, Mrs C. F., *A Modern Herbal*, Penguin Books, Harmondsworth, Middlesex, 1976

Henderson, Rev C., *The Cornish Church Guide*, Diocese of Truro, 1925

Higgins, L. G. and Riley, N. D., *A Field Guide to the Butterflies of Britain and Europe*, Collins, London, 1977

Hudson, Kenneth, *Patriotism with Profit*, Hugh Evelyn, London, 1972

Jefferies, D. J., Stainsby, B. and French, M. C., 'The ecology of small mammals in arable fields drilled with winter wheat and the increase in their dieldrin and mercury residues', *J. Zool. Soc. London*, vol. 171, pp. 513–39, London, 1973

Kerney, M. P. and Cameron, R. A. D., *A Field Guide to the Land Snails of Britain and North-west Europe*, Collins, London, 1979

King, Carolyn M., 'The home range of the weasel *(Mustela nivalis)* in an English woodland', *J. Animal Ecology*, vol. 44, pp. 639–68, London, 1975

Kruuk, Hans, 'Spatial organization and territorial behaviour of the European badger *Meles meles*', *J. Zool. Soc. London*, vol. 184, p. 119, London, 1978

Lane-Davies, Rev A., *Holy Wells of Cornwall*, Federation of Old Cornwall Societies, Truro, 1970

Mabey, Richard, *Food For Free*, Collins, London, 1972

Mabey, Richard, *Plants With A Purpose*, Collins, London, 1977

Mammal Society, *Mammal Review*, vol. 5, no. 3, September 1975, Blackwell Scientific Publications, Oxford

Mead-Briggs, A. R. and Woods, J. A., 'An index of activity to assess the reduction in mole numbers caused by control measures', *J. App. Ecology*, vol. 10, pp. 837–45, December 1973, London

Norden, John, *A Topographical and Historical description of Cornwall, Speculi Britanniae, 1728*

Partridge, M., *Farm Tools Through the Ages*, Osprey, Reading, Berks, 1973

Peterson, Roger, Mountford, Guy and Hollom, P. A. D., *A Field Guide to the Birds of Britain and Europe*, Collins, London, 1954

Pollard, E. and Relton, Judy, 'A study of small mammals in hedges and cultivated fields', *J. App. Ecology*, vol. 7, pp. 744–57, London, 1970

Pollard, E., Hooper, M. D. and Moore, N. W., *Hedges*, Collins, London, 1974

Quiller-Couch, M. and L., *Ancient Holy Wells of Cornwall*, Charles J. Clark, 1894

Ravenhills, W. L. D., 'Cornwall', Chapter V in Darby, H. C. and Finn, R. Welldon (eds.), *The Domesday Geography of South-West England*, Cambridge University Press, Cambridge, 1967

Savory, Theodore H., *The Spider's Web*, Warne & Co Ltd, London, 1952

Smyth, Michael, 'Winter breeding in woodland mice, *Apodemus sylvaticus*, and voles, *Clethrionomys glareolus* and *Microtus agrestis*, near Oxford', *J. Animal Ecology*, vol. 35, pp. 471–85, London, 1966

South, Richard, *The Moths of the British Isles*, 2 vols., Frederick Warne & Co Ltd, London, 1961

Southern, H. N. (ed.), *The Handbook of British Mammals*, Blackwell Scientific Publications, Oxford, 1964, 1978

Speeding, C. R. W., and Diekmahns, E. C. (eds.),*Grasses and Legumes in British Agriculture*, Commonwealth Agricultural Bureaux, Farnham Royal, Bucks, 1972

Taylor, Christopher, *Fields in the English Landscape*, J. M. Dent & Sons Ltd, London, 1975

Taylor, J. C., 'The introduction of exotic plant and animal species into Britain', *Biologist*, vol. 26, no. 5, p. 229, London, 1979

Van den Brink, F. H., *A Field Guide to the Mammals of Britain and Europe*, Collins, London, 1967

Watts, C. H. S., 'The regulation of wood mouse *(Apodemus sylvaticus)* numbers in Wytham Woods, Berkshire', *J. Animal Ecology*, vol. 38, pp. 285–304, London, 1969

Index

208